'A stimulating new study of Margaret Atwood's fiction which also offers a substantial authoritative overview of recent trends and key debates in Atwood criticism. This is something no other book on the market has attempted. This book will be worth its weight in gold to students and researchers.' — **Coral Ann Howells**, *University of Reading, UK*

Margaret Atwood is an internationally renowned, highly versatile author whose work creatively explores what it means to be human, through genres ranging from feminist fable to science fiction and Gothic romance.

In this timely new study, Gina Wisker reassesses Atwood's entire fictional output to date, providing both original analysis and a lively overview of the criticism surrounding her work. *Margaret Atwood: An Introduction to Critical Views of Her Fiction*:

- covers all of Atwood's novels as well as her short stories
- surveys the critical reception of her fiction and the fascinating debates developed by key Atwood critics
- explores the main approaches to reading Atwood's work and examines issues such as her interventions in genre writing and ecology, as well as her feminism, post-feminism and narrative usage, both conventional and experimental.

Concise and approachable, this is an ideal volume for anyone studying the fiction of this major contemporary writer.

Gina Wisker is Professor of Higher Education and Contemporary Literature, and Head of the Centre for Learning and Teaching, at the University of Brighton, UK. She is the author of *Margaret Atwood's 'Alias Grace': A Reader's Guide* (2002) and has written a number of books for Palgrave Macmillan, including *Postcolonial American Women's Writing* (2000).

D0303623

Margaret Atwood: An Introduction to Critical Views of Her Fiction

Gina Wisker

palgrave
macmillan

First published 2012 by
PALGRAVE MACMILLAN

Palgrave Macmillan in the UK is an imprint of Macmillan Publishers Limited,
registered in England, company number 785998, of Houndmills, Basingstoke,
Hampshire RG21 6XS.

Palgrave Macmillan in the US is a division of St Martin's Press LLC,
175 Fifth Avenue, New York, NY 10010.

Palgrave Macmillan is the global academic imprint of the above companies
and has companies and representatives throughout the world.

Palgrave® and Macmillan® are registered trademarks in the United States,
the United Kingdom, Europe and other countries.

ISBN 978–1–4039–8711–2   hardback
ISBN 978–1–4039–8712–9   paperback

This book is printed on paper suitable for recycling and made from fully
managed and sustained forest sources. Logging, pulping and manufacturing
processes are expected to conform to the environmental regulations of the
country of origin.

A catalogue record for this book is available from the British Library.

A catalog record for this book is available from the Library of Congress.

10 9 8 7 6 5 4 3 2 1
21 20 19 18 17 16 15 14 13 12

Printed and bound in China

For my students - we have enjoyed reading and talking about
Margaret Atwood's books together

Contents

Acknowledgements

Before embarking on this book, I spent many years enjoying discussing and teaching the work of Margaret Atwood with numerous Women's Studies, and English Literature students at Anglia Ruskin University, and with a particularly regular, lively-minded group at Cambridge Board of Continuing Education at Madingley Hall, so my first acknowledgement is a thank you for their insights.

Atwood knows how important libraries and those who work in them are and I would like to thank colleagues at the Thomas Fisher rare book library of the University of Toronto, particularly Jennifer Toews and Dr Philip Oldfield, who have uncovered acres of the treasures of her archived materials, notes, reviews, cuttings and letters which provided context even where they did not directly feed into comments. I can never produce a book without the support of local, tireless editorial help from friends and colleagues, mainly from Michelle Bernard, also Tracey Kellock, Samantha Cochrane, Charlotte Morris, Emily Thompson, Zoe Lee, Rebecca Wells and Tim Johnson.

Colleagues at Palgrave Macmillan, particularly Sonya Barker, have been very patient and supportive throughout. I should also like to thank both the Higher Education Academy for giving me a National Teaching Fellowship, which has enabled me to travel to locate those archives, and the University of Brighton, most importantly the Dean of Education and Sport, Paul Griffiths, and Deputy Vice-Chancellor Stuart Laing for supporting my need to take the trips to do the work. Final thanks to my family, Alistair, Liam and Kitt, and Roxy the dog, who variously put up with my endless reading of Margaret Atwood over the years.

Cambridge, Brighton and Toronto

A List of Abbreviations

The following abbreviations are used in this guide to refer to Margaret Atwood's works.

AG   *Alias Grace*
BA   *The Blind Assassin*
BE   *Bluebeard's Egg*
BH   *Bodily Harm*
B&M   *Bones and Murder*
CE   *Cat's Eye*
DG   *Dancing Girls*
ESS   *Early Short Stories*
EW   *The Edible Woman*
GB   *Good Bones*
HT   *The Handmaid's Tale*
LBM   *Life Before Man*
LO   *Lady Oracle*
MD   *Moral Disorder*
MiD   *Murder in the Dark*
O&C   *Oryx and Crake*
RB   *The Robber Bride*
Sg   *Surfacing*
Sl   *Survival: A Thematic Guide to Canadian Literature*
ST   *Strange Things: The Malevolent North in Canadian Literature*
TS   *True Stories*
TT   *The Tent*
YF   *The Year of the Flood*
WT   *Wilderness Tips*

A Note on the Text

Where possible, dates have been given for key authors and other significant figures, and for titles when they are first mentioned. In some cases, however, dates were unavailable.

Introduction

Margaret Atwood's exploration of what it means to be female, Canadian and a writer in a period when all of these identities and terms have been problematised has accompanied me throughout my own development as an academic, writer and mother, as it has done also for many of my students, friends and colleagues. Her explorations and discussions of how women writers can deal with life, performance, and women's roles have offered and still do offer an intellectually and emotionally engaged response which twists and turns as the expectations and constructions also twist and turn, in time. It is a real privilege to be able to have the opportunity to write about the different developments in her lengthy career and critical response to that career, as that response has most recently suddenly burgeoned into a huge industry. Margaret Atwood's work is as popular as ever, or even more so, and scrutinising it again now reminds us that *The Handmaid's Tale* (1985), for example, still speaks to a modern Iraq and Iran where women's reproductive rights are controlled and 'honour killings' are prevalent, while *The Year of the Flood* (2009), her most recent novel, engages others of her consistent themes, survival, ecology and sustainability, which are at the forefront of everyone's concerns today in the second decade of the twenty-first century.

Margaret Atwood (born 1939) is an internationally renowned, highly versatile writer, whose work, comprising poetry, novels, short stories, literary criticism and essays, has been translated into more than 20 languages and published in over 25 countries. Recognised as a feminist author and the greatest living Canadian writer, engaged with issues of gendered and national identity, she also problematises these labels and trends in her work.

Atwood began writing when very young, producing poems and an unfinished novel about an ant. She was initially known primarily for her poetry, and at 19 finished a privately printed collection of poems, *Double Persephone* (1961), which won the E.J. Pratt medal, followed by *The Circle Game* (1964), which won the Canadian Governor General's Award for poetry in 1966.

The wide variety of critics who have exhaustively commented on Atwood's works take various approaches and concerns, from the feminist to the ecological, and the postcolonial to studies in humour,

1

Gothic, science fiction and other genres. As a feminist, Atwood deals with representations of women, women's perspectives and values, critiques, and myths and versions of what it means to be a woman. As an ecological writer, she is concerned with nature, people, the planet and its possible destruction. As a postcolonial writer, she criticises the aggressive, invasive ways of some cultures (most specifically North America, the US), which overtake and erase the ways and values of other cultures, and instead she emphasises the importance of cultural differences and diversity. This emerges mainly in assertion of the rights of others, Canadians in particular, but also in pointing out, for example, in *Bodily Harm* (1981), that much damage is done through ignorance, stereotyping and misreading cultural differences. As a Gothic writer, she uses strategies such as irony, horror and myth to upset and undercut social complacency and highlight how people, values and events can be vulnerable and threatened. Atwood also suggests how they could be different, as a positive alternative to what is taken for granted. In using both fantasy and elements of science fiction, she can project current or possible situations into other worlds, ways and futures, so we might speculate about avoiding disaster, and see how life could be otherwise (for better or for worse). All of these are contested terms, and critics debate their use in her work.

As she became more established with the huge US success of *The Handmaid's Tale* (1985), so Atwood was seen also as one who could reinterpret and rewrite the genres, as an ethically engaged writer whose play with the forms and concerns of representation, metafiction and storytelling accompany and articulate her concern for humanity and ecology and her critique of sexism. Like Angela Carter and Suniti Namjoshi, Margaret Atwood rewrites myths and fairytales to excise the constraining visions and the ways in which they can constrict representations of self, relationships and power. Like Salman Rushdie, Toni Morrison, Jeanette Winterson and Sarah Waters, she is a magic realist, and a Gothic writer who intermixes the fantastic, speculative and mythic with the everyday. Although Atwood has said: 'when in college, my generation felt that "Canadian" and "writer" were mutually exclusive terms', [1] she has literally put literary Canada on the map. Her constant output of critical, as well as creative and conversational work, enables readers to see her as part of lively debates about issues that matter, whether they are local to Toronto, or broad and crucial global issues such as survival and sustainability in the face of ecological destruction and the brutality, ignorance or ethical disengagement of humanity. Atwood engages with experience, existence and what matters through her writing. Her output is marvellously varied yet consistent in its richness.

She is, above all, a creative explorer of what it means to be human and how this can be expressed through the strategies and genres of fictions, language and narrative. Her interventions into literary and popular fictional genres, such as Gothic romance, spy thriller, science fiction, feminist fable, comedy and crime fiction have enabled those genres to be scrutinised once more. She is also a major industry. She is known to her readers as a commentator on a variety of local and global issues over time, and an expert in the management of her own presentation, reception and representation in the press, in the many interviews, taped or videoed, over the span of her writing career to date, in her published conversations, and as represented in the snippets and guided directions from her own website. Although Atwood's secretary manages her communication with her many fans, she is still a local everyday presence. There is a sense of someone you might bump into in the vegetable shop on Bloor Street or in a restaurant in downtown Toronto. She is around, commenting, writing, making appearances, and the massive critical engagement with her work continues to stun those who enter these dialogues because, at a comfortably managed distance, she is such a notable contemporary literary presence.

Biography

Margaret Atwood was born in Ottawa, Canada, the second of three children. Her father was a forest entomologist and so regular parts of her early years were spent either living in the bush of northern Quebec, where he undertook research, or, in the winter, in the suburbs, where she and her scientific brother Harold Leslie, and younger sister Ruth went to school. Later, Atwood's childhood experiences of the bush provided material for her realistic and metaphorical use of the wilderness and its animals in *Wilderness Tips* (1991), her focus on rediscovering identity in the wild in *Surfacing* (1972), and various locations and short stories, including sections of the much later *Moral Disorder* (2006). In this latter, a fictionalised character, Nan, returns readers to what seems like a retrospective on Atwood's own life, revisiting the bush locations of her childhood.

Atwood's family moved to Toronto in 1946, and she was 11 before she attended school full-time. She graduated from Leaside High School in 1959 and studied at the University of Toronto, in Victoria College, where she was deeply influenced by the great literary analyst and critic Northrop Frye, notable for his Jungian theories and myth criticism. Her college became the site for the origins of two of her female characters, Tony, the military historian, and Roz, the businesswoman, in *The Robber Bride* (1993). Here, she wrote and reviewed for the college magazine and designed programmes for the drama society. Atwood won a Woodrow Wilson Fellowship, and became a graduate student at Radcliffe College, Harvard, in Cambridge, Massachusetts, receiving her MA in 1962. She continued her studies of Victorian literature at Harvard (1962–63, 1965–67), then in 1967, interrupted her PhD on 'The English Metaphysical Romance', and instead went to work for a market research company in Toronto (the source for Marian's workplace in *The Edible Woman*, 1969). Atwood taught English at the University of British Columbia in Vancouver (1964–65), followed by other academic posts and roles as writer-in-residence at numerous Canadian and American universities. She has lived in Boston, Vancouver, Montreal, London, Provence, Berlin and Edinburgh, though her consistent home has always been Toronto, where she lives with novelist Graeme Gibson and their daughter Jess.

The Margaret Atwood website at http://margaretatwood.ca/ lists her speaking engagements in the United States, Canada, and worldwide, more recently, updates on her planned writing and sales for charitable (usually bird preservation) causes. She also has a Facebook page maintained by her publishers.

The US-based Margaret Atwood Society has as its main goal the intention to promote scholarly study of Atwood's work, publishing an annual and midyear newsletter with annotated bibliography, and meeting annually in conjunction with the Modern Language Association (MLA) convention as an official MLA Allied Organization.

While working as an editor at the Toronto publishing house Anansi in the early 1970s, Atwood published her controversial study *Survival: A Thematic Guide to Canadian Literature* (1972), which began to put Canadian literature on the literary map, although some criticised her text choices and comments. Atwood's irony was also criticised when she argued that Canadian literature has remained blighted by a subservient, colonial mentality. Later, she returned to the theme of the overwhelming fascination with certain narratives in *Strange Things: The Malevolent North in Canadian Literature* (1995).

Atwood's poetry is both accessible, yet carefully crafted. It deals with everyday life, expresses forms of perception and demystifies the stereotypes, the personal, national or gendered myths and representations through which we conceive and manage our lives. In her fictions, poetry, short stories and essays, she continues to engage with issues of human behaviour, the paradoxes and delights of living in the twentieth and twenty-first centuries, being female, postcolonial, Canadian, and also questioning limiting representations of gender, nationality and identity. She once remarked to an interviewer that her responsibility to deal with the political, cultural and social issues was: 'not as a writer, as a human being'.[2] If this sounds worthy and sanitised, then such a reading would be one ignoring her Gothic, critical and incisive vision, and her irreverent humour. Atwood has been described as giving: 'The impression of a quiet Mata Hari ... who pits herself against the ordered, too clean world like an arsonist.'[3] Matched by the many images of her public presence, diminutive in size (5ft 3in) and usually wearing a striking hat, she is a fierce interviewee who manages her time effectively and does not easily suffer those who patronise or underestimate her.

Jeremy Brooks establishes the tone and range of praise for Atwood's perception and imaginative expression, noting 'the balance between the narrator's interior vision and sharp observation of the real world'.[4] Her work engages with modernist and postmodernist philosophical concerns, with the nature of reality, history and identity, and she has tackled a whole range of conventions, social, personal and political issues, from sisterhood to reproductive technologies, eating disorders to identity theft, and in *Oryx and Crake* (2003), and *The Year of the Flood* (2009), the end of the world as we know it, a logical next step from current trends in anti-emotional, anti-artistic scientific rationalism and dehumanisation. Although she is seen as a feminist writer, starting as early as *Surfacing*, Margaret Atwood questions this limitation:

> Every woman who appeared in the early seventies was called a feminist writer. Suddenly we noticed women in a different way than they'd been noticed before – as neurotic, with their heads in the oven or strange spinsters. I am a writer who writes for people who read books.[5]

Canadian identity

Throughout her long, extraordinarily productive career Margaret Atwood has probably contributed more to put Canadian writing on the map internationally and in Canada than any other writer, living or dead. This springs from the original discovery that there was at home and abroad a real dearth of recognition for Canadian writers, and an inhospitable climate for those who did publish, so much so that Canadian writers were either unheard of or went into a kind of exile abroad to gain a readership, de-emphasising their Canadian origins in the process. Her work has helped identify characteristics of much 'Can lit' and established it as worthy of study. Since Atwood's *Survival*, criticism of Canadian writing has flourished. Faye Hammill's *Canadian Literature* provides a useful guide.[6]

Canadian culture is a 'settler-invader' culture, like the Australian culture with which it is often compared. Each produces tales of pioneering life, the inhospitable bush and a tendency to re-tell outdated stories from a now changed homeland. Canada is also somewhat culturally schizophrenic, split between French and English influences in its language and history, and very closely affected by the US, its near, grand, powerful and rather more brash neighbour.[7] In much Canadian writing, including Atwood's, the US is portrayed as an invasive entity, penetrating culture, language, values, violence, and merchandising. This is not merely commercially but also psychologically engulfing, since Canadians and Americans are often elided in international consciousness. Canada imported and adapted English and French institutions, cultural values and writing traditions, and is largely bilingual. It also has a wide variety of international settlers, including Irish, Scottish, Japanese, Vietnamese, Chinese and latterly Eastern Europeans.

Diana Brydon comments that in relation to other nations affected by imperialism and colonialism: 'Canada ... has tended to see herself as the undervalued orphan in the imperial family.'[8] It is a 'Cinderella' country awaiting its moment. Historically, Canada sought a national identity but underwent national land demarcation disputes beginning with the Free Trade Agreement with the US, and followed by problems generated by the failure of the Meech Lake and Charlottetown Accords. As I noted earlier:

> One of the intentions of those establishing a sense of the nation and identity of Canada was to construct a shared community rather than an oppositional identity. Canada still sees itself as a culturally harmonious, peaceable kingdom, and many outsiders perceive it as grey, its cultural tranquillity a little dull, if safe.[9]

Atwood talks sparingly about indigenous peoples in her fictions, although she does mention First Nations people in *Surfacing* and passes on their ecological wisdom in *Oryx and Crake*. In their own writing, indigenous people, including Inuits, Native Canadian American Indians, and First Nations writers represent Canada and their own lives, marginalisation, the loss of lands and identity, and reassert cultural difference within the single, nationally harmonious, homogenising representation of Canadian culture. More recent settlers deal with the racism, appropriation and settlement which have been their lived experience in Canada. Japanese settlers were interned during the Second World War.[10] Atwood talks of European-originated settlers in the *Journals of Susanna Moodie, Wilderness Tips,* and *Alias Grace.*

Cultural and literary contexts

Catherine Pepinster positions Atwood as a Canadian writer who shows a continuing determination to identify and place Canadian literature on the map and who deals with both the bush and the city. Pepinster's review also recognises and places Atwood in relation to other great Canadian writers who present versions of strong women:

> Canadians never developed the concept of women as mere brainless decoration. Canadian folklore is still full of tales of our grandmothers' generation when women ran farms, chased off bears, delivered their own babies in remote locations and bit off the umbilical cords.[11]

And Carol Ann Howells adds: 'Whatever the reason, if you're looking at writing in Canada, you can't just footnote the women.'[12] Canadian women, Atwood argues, are tough and resilient. This echoes the kind of 'battler' motif we find in other settler tales from Carol Shields, another great Canadian woman writer, and from Australian writers.

Coral Ann Howells has been a notable critic of Atwood's work for many years. There are now two editions of her book on Atwood, published by Palgrave Macmillan, and an edited Cambridge Companion (2006). These are an excellent source from which to gain a deeper understanding of Atwood's works over time. Howells' *Margaret Atwood* (2005) traces the development of various themes through her novels and discusses the placing of Atwood within a cultural and literary context as a: 'token feminist, poet and Canadian'.[13]

Howells suggests that because Atwood is first of all a poet, she emphasises the power of language and representation, and opens up narrative space. Atwood's writing is both grounded in a strong sense of her own Canadian, female and white identity, and engages with the bigger picture, the international stage. She remains involved with cultural politics and human rights, although the political implications of her work, Howells argues, are less important than psychological themes. Howells tentatively describes her as a feminist writer, one who is aware of the changing trends within feminism and who also attends to questions beyond those trends.

Both Coral Ann Howells and Barbara Hill Rigney, established critics of Atwood's work, see her as dealing with issues of women's roles and feminist critique, and using a mixture of realism and the literary Gothic to do so. In her comments on *The Edible Woman* and *The Handmaid's Tale*, Howells traces Atwood's exploration of sexual power politics through social myths and representations of the female body and looks at how her work has shifted. She compares and contrasts the novels to the essays of Betty Friedan in *The Feminine Mystique* (1963), which in turn introduces criticism on *Male and Female* by Margaret Mead (1955), and Sheila MacLeod's (1981) *The Art of Starvation*, each of which are connected with body image and identity.

Rigney sees the Canadian literary tradition as victim-oriented and suggests that Canada's political status as a colony lends itself to the use of the Gothic to express a sense of being both exploited and isolated. Atwood takes this bigger picture of the country into her characters and depicts Canadians and women as an oppressed minority. However, 'Although defined by several critics as pessimist and negative – Atwood herself sees herself as a realist.'[14]

Nathalie Cooke's full-length critical biography *Margaret Atwood: A Critical Companion*[15] offers a concise introduction to Atwood's published novels and her central themes and, like Rigney, Howells and others emphasise a Canadian focus showing how readings of work can be enriched by attention to the Canadian literary and cultural context. However, because Atwood is internationally renowned, many commentaries ignore the Canadian roots of her work. Cooke summarises feminist, Canadian and postmodern influences on Atwood and illustrates how her work is shaped by, and has shaped, the Canadian literary scene. She argues that all of Atwood's novels can be read as satires which expose society's double standards and she provides close scrutiny of three of the novels: *Cat's Eye*, as an artist's novel; *The Handmaid's Tale* as a dystopian novel; and *The Blind Assassin* as a 'villainess' novel.

In her role as a postcolonial, post-feminist, eco, Gothic writer, Atwood critiques common-sense constructions of identity and power, explores how people seem to see their lives as scripted and constrained, and reveals the power structures which control language, sexuality and identity. Atwood's extensive use of the Gothic and her version of postcolonial writing enable an undercutting of controls and constructs, the 'grand narratives' which maintain constrained versions of identity, power and culture. As an ecological writer, her work links land, speech and self-preservation. She revisits a number of constructions and themes to critique identity, myth and deadly investments in life-denying behaviours, and in so doing she provides opportunities to revise and re-imagine the self, to celebrate personal and cultural difference and, more broadly, to explore and expose the potential for damage limitation and sustainable development. Her inquisitiveness makes her seek the unusual: 'I have been looking under logs most of my life', she says, 'I learned early on that when you look under a log that has been lying on the ground for a long time, you will more than likely find something.'[16]

Language and identity

Hilde Staels' *Margaret Atwood's Novels: A Study of Narrative Discourse* (1995)[17] draws on Julia Kristeva's (psycho) linguistic theory as a conceptual framework which links identity, thought processes and articulation in language. We construct and project a version of self and identity through the language we use and, Staels notes, Atwood's first-person narrators are presenting constructions to us rather than directly articulating the author's own pessimistic or optimistic views:

> Readers who neglect to investigate the form of Atwood's novels are often inclined to passively accept the discursive statements of Atwood's first-person narrators, instead of questioning them. The narrators might be ironic, or the text might, placing their misreading of events and people at odds with what we read and see more widely in the novel.[18]

Staels explores the mindsets of Atwood's protagonists, which reflect their culture in complex ways and warns that certain feminist readings are reductive in their interpretation because they mistakenly affirm '[a] fatal and inescapable coincidence of the protagonist with cultural norms'.[19] In such negative readings, Atwood's protagonists are victims. They seem to achieve no personal freedom or authentic self-expression.

For Staels, critical discussions about split selves and questions of identity, within a feminist, psychoanalytical critical frame, can be enlightened and informed by Julia Kristeva's theories. Kristeva discusses the textual subject as split, fragmented, with two types of operations, conscious and unconscious, characterising its signification process. Kristeva's theory of language and her view of the modern subject seem to suggest a subject in crisis and multiple selves in dialogue. In readings of Atwood this focus on ambivalence, split selves, lack of wholeness identifies her work as 'polyphonic', offering many voices and versions at once. Kristeva's psychoanalytic concepts can also help us to critically explore the mental operations of Atwood's protagonists. We can see debate and diversity, and 'carnivalesque' moments.

Sherrill Grace takes such a view in *Violent Duality: A Study of Margaret Atwood* (1980).[20] Grace sees polarities as structuring devices, motifs, and ways of exploring and identifying representations of the self in Atwood's work. Split selves and variation appear formally and thematically, and are noticeable, for example, in the split structure of her poetry and her doubled/split characters. Grace sees 'the central dialectic and tension in Atwood's work, the pull towards art on one hand and towards life on the other'.[21] Duality is a vital part of Atwood's creativity: 'For Atwood the dynamic of violent duality is a function of the creative act ... To create, Atwood chooses violent dualities, and her art re-works, probes, and dramatizes the ability to see double.'[22] Grace emphasises the need for affirming experience through an acceptance of duality as opposed to polarity, identifying duplicity as a central theme in Atwood's work, in which freedom emerges from accepting such duality rather than a rigid single version or view. Atwood's explorations of and challenges to notions of fixed or duplicitous selves, and to single-voiced versions of reality and values are often enabled by her widespread use and reuse of fairytale and myth, including modern and urban myth.

Myths, fairytales and the Gothic

In *Margaret Atwood's Fairy-Tale Sexual Politics* (1993),[23] Sharon Rose Wilson explores the role of mythology and fairytales in Atwood's works, tracing her rewriting of familiar and less familiar tales from the French author Jacques Perrault (1628–1703), and the German philologists and scholar brothers, Jacob Ludwig Grimm (1785–1863) and William Karl Grimm (1786–1859). Both brothers collected fairytales, usually from women oral storytellers, and wrote them down, inflecting them with historical and cultural context, then circulating them widely. Atwood's plots and themes draw heavily on fairytales and their biblical and mythical associations and she also uses other European and Canadian sources.

Wilson meticulously classifies Atwood's sources. Wilson's is an essential guide for anyone exploring the various intertwined fairytales and myths in any Atwood text, however ostensibly realistic. In her later essay, 'Mythological interests in Margaret Atwood's works' (2000) Wilson argues that these operate as intertexts, i.e. they offer stories and arguments which refer to and remind us of others in other texts, myths and media. 'Atwood intertwines these and other cultural master narratives with radio, television and film stories, not only to provide mythic resonance and polyphonic melody, but to parody or undercut narrative authority in a postmodern way.'[24] Wilson suggests that in foregrounding fairytales and folklore intertexts, Atwood reminds us of our own entrapment in patterns of reading and belief. Atwood's interest in rewriting fairytales and myths intersects with her engagement with politics and feminism.

For Howells, the Gothic as used by Atwood is both about being afraid[25] and, sinister, self-aware and also highlights the *game* of being afraid. Identity, recognition of mis-identity, 'other', doubles, split selves, conscious and unconscious self are all characteristics which Atwood uses and which force the reader to confront her or his own desires and fears. *Lady Oracle* (1976) is described as a comic novel colliding with Gothic conventions.[26] Howells compares her earlier novels and notes the changes in her use of the traditional Gothic motifs, seeing *The Robber Bride* as a 'mutant form of female gothic':[27]

> The Gothic takes many routes in Atwood's fictions, from Joan Foster, Gothic writer suffocating and trapped in her own labyrinths of Gothic romance plots, through to the Gothic vampire Zenia in *The Robber Bride,* and the consistent forms of duplicity offered by Atwood's lying or storytelling narrators, such as Iris Chase in *The Blind Assassin* and Grace Marks in *Alias Grace.*[28]

Such subterranean threats and horrors belong to the literary Gothic, most familiar to the twentieth-century audience in films such as *The Exorcist, Jaws, Poltergeist,* and *Rosemary's Baby,* a genre in which a threat comes variously from primitive, underground, underwater, or subconscious sources and brings to view hidden histories, experiences and versions.

Other significant critical views

As we have seen, there are a number of lifetime critics who follow the development of Atwood's work and comment on it as it emerges, in both journal articles and books. *Margaret Atwood: Writing and Subjectivity: New Critical Essays* (1994), edited by Colin Nicholson,[29] was the first collection of essays published in the United Kingdom to focus on Atwood. Nicholson argues that her unique achievement is that she manages to sustain her popularity with reading publics around the world while bringing feminist perspectives to bear upon personal and private experience and upon the public structures of power shaping individual lives. The essays derive from a variety of theoretical perspectives, and include European and North American contributions. They take a woman-oriented view to explore how Atwood articulates the pressures and determinations which condition 'the feminine' before allowing it to speak for itself. They also consider how she writes as a Canadian, exploring complicated relationships between representation and self-representation amidst uneven distributions of power and responsibility. The book is a unique combination of feminist and postcolonial perspectives, and examines Atwood's poetry and short fiction as well as her novels.

Brutal Choreographies (1999) by Jane Brooks Bouson[30] investigates the psychological and political concerns in Atwood's novels. Drawing on recent feminist and psychoanalytic theory, Brooks Bouson examines Atwood's recurring self, family and romantic dramas, her novelistic subversion of romance ideology, and her critique of gender and power politics. She considers the oppositional strategies used in Atwood's novels, their plotting and retaliation rhetoric, their enactments of female revenge fantasies, and their self-conscious manipulation and sabotage of romance and other traditional plot lines and conventions. Moving from the proto-feminism of *The Edible Woman,* the cultural feminism of *Surfacing,* and the examination of the perils of Gothic thinking in *Lady Oracle*, to the domestic and sexual warfare of *Life Before Man*, the antifeminist backlash terrors of *Bodily Harm* and *The Handmaid's Tale*, and the power politics of female relationships in *Cat's Eye*, Brooks Bouson argues that Atwood's women-centred fiction has strong oppositional appeal. Because Atwood does not shun what she calls the 'story of the disaster which is the world', her tales are often brutal, portraying female victimisation at the hands of the husband or male lover, the mother, or the female friend. But if Atwood's novels have the power to disturb, compel and at times brutalise readers, they are also carefully choreographed, using form and design to contain and control female fears, anxieties and the anger that drive the narrative.

My own studies on *Alias Grace* (Continuum, 2002), and *Atwood's Handmaid's Tale* (Continuum, 2010) and Pilar Cuder's *Beginners' Guide* (Hodder, 2003) provide readers and students with a range of critical comments on Atwood's œuvre, information on her life and times, and some comment on her place within both Canadian fiction and contemporary women's writing.[31]

Atwood has made full use of the variety of genre fiction in her work and an example of attendant issues emerges in the labelling of both *The Handmaid's Tale* and *Oryx and Crake* as science fiction. *Oryx and Crake* invoked a rash of online responses from, for example, the 'Fantastic in the Arts' discussion list (www.iafa.org), over whether it was or was not science fiction. Atwood denied that was its main definition, in line with her comments on *The Handmaid's Tale*, that: 'there's nothing in it that we as a species have not done, aren't doing now, or don't have the technological ability to do'.[32] Other debates continue in relation to her feminism and post-feminism and narrative usage, both conventional and experimental.

This current study scrutinises Atwood's work throughout her career to date and traces continuities of theme and argument, critical interpretation, and the increasingly fascinating debates about genres. *Margaret Atwood: An Introduction to Critical Response* covers her entire fictional œuvre up to 2010 and engages with the debates developed by the various key critics of her work, interweaving these with sustained critical comment, and providing guidance on critical issues and approaches to reading Atwood's work. It provides both an original contribution and an overview of the criticism on her work. This Introduction should be useful for undergraduates, postgraduates, lecturers in higher and further education, sixth form teachers and other students and readers interested in Margaret Atwood's writing and the critical reception of that writing. The book is concerned with charting, coordinating and contributing to the critical discussions on Margaret Atwood mainly as a writer of fiction. Comments on her poetry and essays are included where they enhance these discussions.

1

The Quest for Identity: *Survival: A Thematic Guide to Canadian Literature* (1972), *Surfacing* (1972)

Margaret Atwood's work began to receive international critical attention in 1972, with the publication of the novel *Surfacing* and her influential, if not always locally popular, critical analysis of Canada's literary tradition up until that time, *Survival: A Thematic Guide to Canadian Literature*. While the critical work put Canadian literature firmly on a map, where previously it had been lacking, both books considered similar themes, in particular, the victim's response to inhospitable cultural contexts and values, which Atwood identified as common to both postcolonials and women. She argued, it was 'not only the Canadian stance towards the world, but the usual female one'.[1]

In *Survival*, she recuperates Canadian literature and charts its main themes. In *Surfacing*, she explores the life of a woman who returns to nature while on a quest for her lost father, thus rejecting the encroaching American colonisation and destructive tendencies of the period.

Survival (1972)

Survival explores and charts a range of Canadian writing, focusing on themes popular in Canadian literature, and the importance of writers' national identity and commitment. In her essay, 'Atwood's Fictive Portraits of the Artist' (1986), Judith McCombs explores the development of a portrait of the artist which encompasses being a Canadian, a paralysed victim, a creative Trickster, a visionary and mystic, and a sell-out and a manipulator. In this range of descriptions,

Survival is an evocation of the artist as mystic, and *Surfacing* is a criticism of the artist as a sell-out and manipulator. McCombs recognises the importance of the establishment of a Canadian literary presence in *Survival* and its impact on an American readership, who previously had largely ignored Canadian writing. She revisits the history which began to put Canada on the international literary map: a challenge and an achievement much credited to Atwood. *Survival*'s 'quest for national identity via literature'[2] was successful because:

> [I]n the then-emerging Canadian cultural renaissance, *Survival* became the first and basic handbook for the literature whose existence Canadians now take for granted: Canadian literature. It is a bit of a shock now, in 1985, to go back to the grim and wintry barren landscape of the Canadian literary scene which *Survival* explored, where living Canadian writers had been choosing between live burial in the provinces versus perpetual self-exile abroad – i.e. between being Canadian but invisible, versus being a writer but without a country.[3]

Not all the themes and concerns Atwood chose pleased every Canadian writer. She is described as using 'shock tactics' to define the isolation of the 'last heroes', a familiar Canadian theme. Atwood comments: 'We speak of isolated people as being "cut off", but in fact something has been cut off from them; as artists, deprived of an audience and cultural tradition, they are mutilated.'[4]

Artists, Atwood argues, need to reject their roles as victims:

> [H]e is paralyzed, frozen, the equivalent of the stiff corpses that litter the winter landscape in [Canadian] stories about Nature and the monster. The corpses have suffered physical death at the hands of an indifferent or hostile Nature; the artists have suffered emotional and artistic death at the hands of an indifferent or hostile audience.[5]

Survival is not Atwood's personal critical response to the texts she introduces; rather, it collates, clarifies and focuses the variety of themes in Canadian literature. In producing the book, she provides a unique introduction to Canadian writing, both 'audacious and ruthless'.[6] She sees Canadian writing as sombre, bleak, the viewpoint of the victim rather than the victor. It is a 'literature of losers, the trapped and the lonely'.[7]

If journeying and expeditions (many fraught and fruitless) are one main Canadian motif, then enclosure and entrapment are

another. Much of each results from the climate or the social structure in which people live. Atwood defines British families as a
mansion, American families as a skin you shed, and Canadian families as a trap in which you are caught. Nonetheless, the literature
of entrapment and failures shows a real empathy for threatened,
endangered societies.

Survival received mixed critical responses. Enthusiasm from both
genders was followed by criticism of what Atwood had omitted
and her emphasis on a rather negative view of Canadian literature.
George Woodcock and Gloria Onley (1974) found its Canadian victim themes troubling, as did Robin Matthews (1973).[8] In considering
their reviews, Judith McCombs finds: 'a language of bitchiness'.[9]
These reviewers felt Atwood had shamed Canadian writers, had
'clamped down hard on the wriggling body of Canadian writing;
leaving much mangled or headless or untouched'. [10] Frank Davey
saw Atwood as concerned with power and politics, playing the
'castrating bitch'. He argued that *Survival* generally subordinated
and distorted writers who did not fit its thesis. For him, it was an
example of: 'culture fixing: An untouchable canon of Canadian Lit
according to Atwood.'[11] The whole *Survival* controversy is widely
discussed in Jerome K. Rosenberg's chapter 'Margaret Atwood'.[12]
However, not everyone supported these rather damning views of
this crucial work.

Colin Nicholson sees *Survival* as a key text establishing Canadian
literary themes and presence, thus putting Atwood as cultural
critic centre stage and raising issues of the silencing and mimicry inherent in earlier postcolonial writing. He suggests that the
'academic sneer' which Atwood identifies among her critics could
be a response to the 'now notorious "basic victim positions"' she
saw 'encoded in a significant proportion of Canadian writing'.
Nicholson emphasises that Atwood's work shows that 'the major
profit from a colony is made in the centre of the empire', and that
there are 'cultural side-effects which are often identified as "the
colonial mentality"'.[13]

In this, Atwood's position is postcolonial. She exposes a worldview which figures some as in power, others as secondary, sometimes victims. The cultural issue of subordination is matched by the
personal, so that the victim position is seen as one experienced by
individuals and by Canada as a nation. Colin Nicholson takes the
discussion a little further and sees Atwood dealing with the traditional stages of moving from victim to survivor in her treatment of

what it means either to be Canadian, or a woman. These stages of movement are:

Position One: To deny the fact that you are a victim.

Position Two: To acknowledge the fact that you are a victim, but to explain this as an act of Fate, the will of God, the dictates of Biology (in the case of women, for instance), the necessity decreed by History, or Economics, or the Unconscious, or any other large general powerful idea.

Position Three: To acknowledge the fact that you are a victim but to refuse to accept the assumption that the role is inevitable.

Position Four: To be a creative non-victim.[14]

He argues that *Survival* was meant to provide some points of departure rather than a prescriptive list of texts. Nicholson considers ways in which *Survival* engages with subjectivity, the nature of the self, and says, '[it] makes a contribution to much of the recent theorising of postcolonial representations of literary subjectivity',[15] whether Indian, African, Caribbean or Australian. Sherrill Grace argues that, in *Survival*, duality is present in the contrast between domestic settings and wilderness. Atwood is 're-working, in comic form, a serious dilemma – the over-lapping of a "cozy safe domestic" world with "the world of dangers"',[16] a characteristic of Canadian fiction, particularly that for children.

The collection of Atwood's papers and critical responses in the Thomas Fisher rare book library of the University of Toronto includes popular connections with and use of her work. There is evidence of Atwood gradually becoming the first major critical voice on Canadian literature that affects the ways in which Canadian literature is read, seen and taught in schools. Some of the information, flyers and cuttings find Atwood exploring the development and teaching of Canadian literature in, for instance, an address to a secondary school in Ontario in 1972, where she questions the lack of teaching of Canadian literature. In the Preface to *Survival* she talks of literature 'teaching' as a political act.[17] Exploring her processes is fascinating. She quotes, cuts and staples comments onto sheets. The texts she has selected deal with survival, pioneering, brutality, and the death of animals, and her own work develops a sense of humour at the unknown. In *Survival*, she includes frightening tales – such as Fraser Sullivan's 'capsule myth' 'The Predator': 'You don't hear it but you see it. The silent slayer does its work. What has lived is now gone, what lives on are those small, implacable, predatory eyes.'[18] There are texts with wild imagery, brutality and loss, such as Duncan Campbell Scott's 'At the Cedars', which undermines with tragic events the natural beauty of the setting with its logs, snow, jolly gangs of girls, and natural, wild imagery. Isaac, caught in the logs, is jammed, bloodied and drowns. His small daughter, launching her canoe to save him, also drowns. There are many stories of snow, loss, madness, dreams of the flint entering the heart, animals approaching, food running out, and in the terrible poem 'Wild Horses', the shooting of wild horses.

Although Atwood's own writing rarely mentions First Nations people, she includes work in *Survival* which sees them shunned, shot and removed, such as Al Purdy's 'Lament for the Dorsets' and 'Remains of an Ida Village', both of which tell of dead Inuit and Indian villages, the culling of the seals and removal of food. Atwood also discusses Gwendolyn MacEwen's verse drama, *Terror and Erebus* (1965) of Franklin and Rasmussen, in the snow when Sir John Franklin's ships became trapped in the ice and 129 men died. The men are sent back to ships but die in blizzards. Most of those who were involved in the doomed 1845–48 Franklin expedition which sought the North-West Passage died.

Atwood's reading, collating, selection and critical analysis bring a range of Canadian literature to a wide readership. Themes found in selected texts in *Survival* reappear in her developing work and include journeying, false hopes and problematic expeditions. Some of these offer a place in life rather than just the 'malevolent north'. There is a fascination with storytelling, and versions of entrapment: in the body, place, in relationships, in images of what it is possible to be as oneself. In Atwood's own creative work, these themes are explored along with and through international myths, fairytales, storytelling motifs and the fascination with performance, narrative, construction and representation of the powers of the imagination.

Surfacing (1972)

Surfacing has been read as an ecological, feminist, Canadian work and concerned with exploring a quest for identity. Like the critical work, *Survival*, it emphasises essential interactions between people and their habitat. *Surfacing* established Atwood as a feminist writer because of its exploration of gendered identity and power relations.

Other reviewers saw it as concerned with ecology and survival, issues which continue to influence her later work.

In the novel, a young woman journeys into the remote Canadian wilderness where her parents once lived, in search of both her dead, presumed drowned, father, and her own sense of identity and self-worth. She takes three friends: Joe, her boyfriend, Anna, and David, who are far less used to the bush and who engage with and play out various scenarios concerned with capitalism and natural values, authenticity and representation in terms of advertising, consumer culture, and gender and power relations. Encounters with the artifice of merchandising and marketing and with wider American influence contrast with her search for authenticity and truth.

Coral Ann Howells defines *Surfacing* as a new version of a woman's, Canadian, national-oriented survival myth – a spiritual and political polemic. Roberta Rubenstein (1976) and Carol Christ (1980) see it as a journey into the self and Marie-Françoise Guedon (1981) and Kathryn Van Spanckeren (1988) develop an appreciation of Atwood's treatment of shamanism and the spiritual, and the wilderness.[19] Colonial and postcolonial concerns arise with Diana Brydon's (1984) recognition that the novel deals with silencing by America as a colonial power and the identification of intertextual connections with Conrad's *Heart of Darkness* (1902).[20]

There are many significant moments in this book: the death of the father, the young woman's re-establishment of her own sense of identity, the story of her parents and her own past and present, and her surfacing to something new, tortuous, potentially fraught, but a necessary new start.

Several critics equate the concerns of the novel with its Canadian origin, qualities and worldview. In this respect, Peter Martin sees in the protagonist's quest a kind of horror:

> Underneath, in the heroine's mind, the search goes on relentlessly, compellingly, terrifyingly. She is seeking not just her father, but herself and a set of meanings, answers to the questions that neither she, nor most of the rest of us know how to answer.[21]

The quest is horrific and cathartic:

> The horror begins within, moves southward, becomes an inevitable, predestined, manic frenzy, a rite of purification (of a nature I cannot conceive of anyone but a Canadian writer imagining), and then breaks, shatters in a climax of overwhelming power, and a new kind of peace emerges.[22]

Also taking a particularly Canadian view, Frank Davey's (1984) and George Woodcock's (1990) critiques of the novel focus on its narrowness, as compared with Paul Goetsch's (2002) celebration of Atwood's Canadian themes.[23] Alice Palumbo (2000) equates the trajectory of the novel with that of the protagonist and identifies the novel as Canadian literature, about Canadian experience, and about concerns of being Canadian, so the search, development and rise of the young woman can be compared to that of Canada finding its literary identity and expression.[24]

> *Surfacing* presents an archaeology of both a time and a person on the point of serious rupture. Early 1970s Anglophone Canada and its relationships with the United States and francophone Canada are presented in parallel to the story of the nameless narrator, a woman on the verge of complete breakdown due to an unvoiced, but real, grief.[25]

In an early conversation with the author Graeme Gibson, her partner, Atwood extends Palumbo's thoughts and suggests that the novel should be read as a refusal of the kind of victimhood adopted by both Canadians and women, where the realisation of one's freedom from being a victim can release new energy, new life. The protagonist needs to rise above the victim position – her own, and that of being Canadian:

> This above all, to refuse to be a victim. Unless I can do that I can do nothing, I have to recant, give up the old belief that I am powerless and because of it nothing I can do will ever hurt anyone. A lie which was always more disastrous than the truth would have been.[26]

Feminist readings

Most Canadian reviewers considered that *Surfacing* focused on nationalism, while Americans treated the book as feminist or ecological in its interests (partly, perhaps, because it indicts America as capitalist, materialist and imperialist). More explicitly, its concentration on a woman's search for her own identity aligns with a period concerned with beginning to get in touch with nature and the self through sloughing off materialistic constructions. Judith McCombs also directly relates the development of Atwood's work to a rise in awareness of Canadian identity and nationalism, and a new popular focus on feminism as the 'dissident and counter cultural revelations' in which Atwood and others are interested: 'the personal as the political and the literary as the national'.[27]

Critical essays from the US and Canada continued to see Atwood's writing as concerned with the suppressed realities of both Canadian's and women's lives. These are ongoing and intertwined issues for Atwood: women's roles, their lives, the ways in which stories are told, myths constructed about, and fictions perpetuated about and by women. McCombs wonders why Atwood does not pursue the female artist figure, even referring to herself in *Survival* among other authors as 'he', and suggests that: 'Canadian literature shows women as icy, stony Rapunzels *who are their own tower*.'[28] Atwood's female commercial illustrator protagonist in *Surfacing* (1972) begins to identify ways of overcoming problems of isolation. She claims: 'I choose not to be a victim, I therefore must create some way to live that is neither victim nor killer.'[29] For McCombs, she is a failed artist paralysed in the barren, grim landscape, facing her own guilt. She has sold out on her art, and on herself, each represented in the figure of the (possibly invented) child she lost. Through visionary experience and the numinous, she crosses over, as do Native American Indians, moving from human to sacred, tackling alone the sources of her dead father's animal photographs, trying to locate both his body and indigenous paintings, and plunging into the lake to recover her identity and survive.

McCombs first discovered Atwood's interest in the mystic in *The Journals of Susanna Moodie* and *Diaries of Underground* (both 1970). She argues that through engagement with this mystic self, the survivor moves into another way of existing – neither victim nor killer.

In 1974, Susan Wood Glicksohn agreed with what she defines as Atwood's 'alien vision truth telling' in 'The Martian point of view'.[30] Susan Fromberg Schaeffer[31] found a healing quest for the lost mother rather than feminist anger, and both Karen F. Stein[32] and Catherine N. Davidson[33] recognise *Surfacing* as aligned with the newly developing strain of women's work on madness and identity.

Milestone years for Atwood in 1976–78 produced a remarkable upsurge of feminist critical work on her writing, which was seen as spiritual, feminist, Canadian, and making a huge contribution to the definitions of each of these. Rubenstein's 1976[34] analysis of the multilevel quest in *Surfacing* was followed in 1978 by Campbell's[35] acclaimed reading of the protagonist's role as 'heroine of a thousand faces'.

Marge Piercy explores gendered relationships, and sees the protagonist's gradual self-discovery as moving from a specifically divided victim position to one of wholeness.[36] Margaret Laurence sees that women, like the land, are objectified, especially in the 'spontaneous film'[37] that Joe and David are making, in which Anna is photographed in demeaning, objectifying ways. The 'happy couple' David and Anna seem caught in a sadomasochistic relationship, in which Anna resents but nonetheless puts up with David's constant put-downs. This is an example of the way women and men are caught in destructive narratives which constrain their relationships.

For Gloria Onley in 'Power politics in Bluebeard's castle' (1974), the novel portrays Anna as an artifice, a sexual plaything. Her conformity defines her as a sexualised victim, 'locked into her Playboy centrefold stereotype, her soul trapped in a gold compact, her capacity for love locked into a sadomasochistic pattern',[38] Anna is:

> upon a packsack, harem cushion, pink in the cheeks and black discreetly around the eyes, as red as blood, as black as ebony, a seamed and folded imitation of a magazine picture that is itself an imitation of a woman who is also an imitation, the original nowhere, hairless lobed angel in the same heaven where God is a circle, captive princess in someone's head.[39]

Unable to eat, give birth, act as a normal creature, she is no more than a performing doll.

Sexual relations are represented as artificial, pornographic spectacle. Onley argues that the narrative sees this sexual activity as depersonalised, alien, like the 'screening Americanism' moving into Canada. This, she believes, can be interpreted throughout *Surfacing* as sex linked with mechanisation, coercion and death. Anna's need to conform to this dehumanised position makes it impossible for her to view other women as friends. The men in the novel are also deeply flawed. In David, Atwood creates a parody of the narcissistic, mighty hunter. Josie Campbell points out the effectiveness of Atwood's exposé of these beliefs and locked-in behaviours, a trajectory built on the Bluebeard story, a tale collected by Charles Perrault, in which an older, rich man marries a series of women whom he murders as soon as they fall for his trick and investigate a locked room, found to contain the bodies of previous wives. This tale exposes relationships in which men first trap women who collude with their fantasies, then destroy them. Atwood offers 'frighten-ingly precise image structures, iconoclastic keys to getting mentally outside of Bluebeard's castle'.[40] Hilde Staels continues the discussion of gender and power and sees the novel as a critique of normative gender roles, using stereotypical images of femininity that she knows from reading 'True Romance magazines'. She attacks the way in which the female is supposed to conform to a specular image in the eyes of the male. Society wants cultural images of 'normal' femi-ninity and masculinity to become a woman's and a man's desired images. These generic terms, which the sexist David imposes time and again on his female companions, give expression to his reduc-tion of the female to a (consumer) object in his eyes.[41]

David turns all women into fashion models or dolls. Popular fictional versions of romance and true love have proved illusionary for the protagonist previously, and part of her journeying aims to rid herself of both myth and a sense of failure in achieving it. These rejections are all part of her growth.

Brooks Bouson critiques masculinist worldviews, and the result-ing linearity and dualism, each seen as a restrictive limitation. She views *Surfacing* as emerging from an essentialist, romantic, cultural feminist tradition, and offering a psychological and aesthetic, rather than a political conception of liberation. *Surfacing* constructs a new feminist reading position; it undermines both masculinist and romantic ideology and any idealising of femininity through its exploration of female madness and rage: '*Surfacing* reverses the hierarchical binary oppositions undergirding patriarchal ideology by valorising femininity, nature, and the irrational and by devalu-ing masculinity, culture and the rational. It evokes 'a world of myth and mysticism'.[42]

The novel refuses rationalist, linear discourse and quest and offers a wordless, body-identified knowledge as salvation. It is possible to both follow the disjointed quest of the narrator/protagonist and to see how Atwood critiques this, by being aware of the authorial voice which Brooks Bouson sees maintaining cohesion, despite the troubling experiences of the narrator: 'although *Surfacing* is poten-tially anxiety-provoking as it invites readers to enter the narrator's delusional world and involves them emotionally in her madness, it also promotes the processes of sense-making, pattern-finding, and consistency building.[43]

Interpreting the world, history and events in binary terms is exposed as far too simple. Breakdown leads to breakthrough and a new order and interpretation, which is recognised as no more than that, a way of making sense of, and interpreting what is happening. The engaged reader is asked to read against a 'grid' of 'binary opposites – male/female, mind/body, and so on in order to 'schematize and thereby stabilize what is a potentially destabilizing, anxiety-provoking experience': the psychotic breakdown.[44]

We as readers, like the protagonist, move from repressive order, through a breakdown, to order and new ways of seeing and interpreting.

Religious and spiritual quest

Several critics discuss *Surfacing* as a spiritual or religious novel, identifying the resurrection myth embedded in it – that of the central, nameless character and the crucifixion of a heron, first seen flying free, then dead. Carol Christ, in 'Margaret Atwood: The Surfacing of Matriarchal Religion' (1980) develops comparisons between *Surfacing*, Marge Piercy's work and Doris Lessing's (born 1919) *'The Summer Before the Dark'*, arguing it is a 'proto feminist or transitional feminist novel'.[45] Lessing explored breakdown as a form of spiritual breakthrough and Piercy criticised internalised narratives which constrained women's lives. All three novelists comment on the psychological, confronting socially acceptable but limiting versions of being human, and especially of being female. Citing critics and theologians, Christ argues that women's quest is religious: 'Modern women's spiritual quest almost always involves an explicit conversion from the andocentric world to a different, more potent, order of consciousness, power.'[46] In the US, Carol Christ[47] responded to Marge Piercy's (1973)[48] political feminist critique of Atwood's earthly and spiritual, personal solutions by arguing that she uses a bodily and spiritual theme to define a spiritual, rather than a social, question. In so doing, Christ argues, Atwood connects the woman who surfaces to the transforming powers of the universe. Francine Du Plessix Gray[49] also sees the novel's quest as in a visionary female tradition.

These essays were followed by Barbara Hill Rigney's full-length study of related issues of identity, feminism, madness, breakdown and breakthrough,[50] and other works which debate the life-affirming, feminist, religious elements of the novel (or criticise these elements as a political sell-out).

There were a number of resisting voices, such as Frank Davey, who saw Atwood as cold, having a 'Gorgon view',[51] which focuses on death. Through the 1970s and 1980s, her work began to be more established and critics began to see *Surfacing* and *Survival* as significant in the development of Canadian literary expression. Reviews and essays led to Sherrill Grace's full-length study *Violent Duality*,[52] which found struggles for affirmation in both books.

The first collection of critical essays on Atwood's work, *The Art of Margaret Atwood*, appeared in 1981, edited by Arnold E. Davidson and Cathy Davidson.[53] This countered critics by discovering national, literary, mythic and factual sources of Atwood's more negative-seeming elements. At the same time, Annis Pratt's feminist Jungian analyses in *Archetypal Patterns in Women's Fiction*[54] celebrated the journey in *Surfacing*.

The quest for identity

The protagonist's quest for her own identity is both physical, involving travel, and personal. It takes her back to the island where her father has died, and leads to an inner quest for a sense of values which differ from the materialistic ones of the city. The protagonist questions what she has become, and the novel problematises versions of roles on offer to women. She rejects American men, offspring of popular culture, and precursors of tourists seeking a 'modified wilderness experience': 'It wasn't the men I hated, it was the Americans, the human beings, men and women both. They'd had their chance but they had turned against the gods and it was time for me to choose sides.'[55]

In Atwood's writing, the term 'American' is a criticism of a homogenising imperialism that cannot tolerate difference. The protagonist shifts from the Americans' technologically adept invasiveness, towards the native gods of the island. By doing so she aligns herself with a 'myth of Canadian identity as an alternative way of being North American'.[56]

As she searches for clues of her father, she also revisits memories and photographs of her childhood, tracking down who she might have been, what really happened, in order to work out who she might be now. In denying her name: 'I no longer have a name. I tried for all these years to be civilised but I'm not and I'm through pretending',[57] she also rejects the need to name wild creatures and places: a link between naming, language and the limitations imposed by civilisation.

Narrative voice, subjectivity and the role of the father and mother are issues for Hilde Staels, who notices how the narrator conceals traumatic experience, rationalises her father's death and 'ices over' irrational feelings. There is a tension between the influences of her mother and her father on the identity which she tries to determine for herself. In contrast with the 'benevolent order' of her father, she associates her more enigmatic mother with a voice that is foreign to her. Her mother, as memory, cannot be fixed in accordance with her father's rules. She is a problem unsolvable through logic, associated with the dangerous, alien wilderness, a disordered, incomprehensible, irretrievable time and space. 'The only place left for me is that of my mother; a problem.' It is 'Impossible to be like my mother, it would need a time warp; she was either ten thousand years behind the rest or fifty years ahead of them.'[58]

Her parents respect different ways of relating to nature and life, with which the protagonist needs to deal in order to develop her own identity. First, it is important for her to get back in touch with her own feelings and bodily self, and then move on in relationships. For most of the novel these are strained, artificial and distant. She rejects her boyfriend Joe, until the end when, more in touch with her own self and body, she develops a new relationship with him. Feminist readings are divided here and see her reconciliation with Joe as variably a success, failure or somewhere in-between. It could be a route to self-discovery. As Staels suggests, her re-engagement with dialogue and relationship with others, and her love for Joe, can be seen as an indication of her future survival, a restoration of her humanity: 'The final position of the protagonist is on the edge between being and becoming. In re-establishing the connection with the site of vitality and creative energy, the protagonist creates an opening towards ethical responsible action.'[59]

Christina Newman sees the novel as unusual; moving from 'plain perceptions' to 'the knife edge of madness and fantasy'. It is a 'journey, backward in time, northward in space'[60] as the numb protagonist searches for the father and questions her own identity and humanity.

She discovers what happened to her father, but not why it happened, and this leads her to consider both her own potential position as a victim, or alternatively, appreciate the 'knowledge of her own power', which had frightened her previously, 'and which she had therefore denied'. Realising she had been a willing victim, she becomes aware that this 'had of course victimised others'.[61] Others will consider that she has had a breakdown.

Joan Larkin in 'Soul Survivor' (1973) sees the events on the island as holding 'a number of epiphanies, unforgettable images that momentarily arrest and illuminate the story'.[62] Some images come from the inner stream, the inner memory: a semi-drowned child, a crude drawing of female genitals, and an aborted foetus. Others occur in the present action: a frog used as bait, a caught fish, a killed heron, a terrifying underwater shape of something dead (her father's corpse?). There are the things left behind by her parents which she talks of as spiritual guides: maps of the sites of paintings by vanished Indian cultures, places where powerful or protective spirits lived, and her own childhood drawing of herself as an unborn baby gazing out of the womb at a god with horns and a tail, 'a god that has attributes of the Devil'.[63] Death and evil are not just the properties of Hitler, the protagonist decides, but of all humans, so she chooses to become inhuman.

Reviewing *Surfacing, Survival, The Edible Woman* and five books of poetry, Marge Piercy continues the debate about being a victim or moving beyond this into new wholeness, which she sees concerns free will, trying to determine which events could be explained as God's will, or choice, not inevitable.

There is a sparse, underlying use of Indian material and Atwood connects with respect for place and life, which is more often found in the behaviour and values of indigenous people:

> The procedures for getting in touch with the power in a place that can connect you with the power in yourself in Atwood include openness to knowledge received from living creatures, fasting, unusual physical experience and respect of the earth, a concern with taking only what you need, respect for dreams and vision as holy and instructive.[64]

Atwood uses the trip into the forest as a move onto natural ground, the past inside the deep collective unconscious: 'you experience the other which is yourself, your deeper nature, your animal and god half. The experience of transcendence is the gift of the totem animal and the god who is both human and animal and something else, energy perhaps'.[65]

David Ward sees *Surfacing* as engaging with both external and internal frontier crossing – transits which are powerful, involving ritual, magical expression. A version of madness exposes the normalised sickness of contemporary forms of society: 'internal frontiers'. Like other contemporary writers: 'This concern is at its strongest where the writers, for cultural, geographical, historical or gender reasons, have a consciously oppositional stance towards the structures and centres of social, economic, political, ideological and magical-religious power.' What follows, is 'winning of an internal freedom, the invasion of forbidden territories of the self may involve a kind of painful transit'.[66]

Ward explores frontiers and borders, landscape, language and versions of a more holistic relationship between man and animals, relating Atwood's interests to that of First Nations or Amerindian people.

Language, form and storytelling

Language is a central motif, as are communication, labelling and mapping, authentic and inauthentic communications. The protagonist learns to rewrite the story of her own history, her identity and her values. She also explores various ways in which language warps or enables expression and vision, for example, the hack writing on which she is employed and the directive, brash artifice of the messages on advertising hoardings. Surfaces act as a metaphor for the difference between consumer-oriented, superficial communications represented by billboards and ads for multinationals and more authentic communication. Initially, the narrator is unable to express feelings and values so. Her shaping voice is that of a bored travelogue soundtrack, the content relentlessly visual, devoid of analysis or comment.[67]

Communication seems void of meaning and even the sign which says 'Bienvenue' or 'Welcome to Canada', is shot through with bullet holes, obliterating the message. The narrator exposes society's surfaces, superficialities, artifices and illusions of control. Through diving in a lake, returning to the native, moving beyond words and everyday relations, she begins to be able to review her history and her life. Evasive about herself and her past she exposes others: 'Disjunctions surface as the plot unfolds.'[68]

She returns to the cabin where her father lived, and the lake where he must have swum to take photographs of Indian artwork, but rather than finding the photographs, she encounters the real and the imagined, her dead father and the foetus she might have aborted earlier. She senses that he was drowned here, his camera pulling him down. As parallel to and metaphor of her own gradual self-discovery, his body finally surfaces and then she must heal herself so retreats into a wilder space, the primitive, and hallucinates, entering another form of reality where she 'experiences her body as part of the landscape'.[69]

Ward suggests the narrator explores the making and perception of surfaces as a societal compulsion. The ways in which the protagonist retraces and tries to make sense of her own confused history are conveyed in fractured language, mirroring her sense of fragmentation. Staels notes that the protagonist narrator finds that her sense of subjectivity is far from linear: 'During the act of narrating, which is the narrator's act of retracing the constitution of her identity, the protagonist unknowingly retraces her repressed experience, namely the part of herself from which she is disconnected.'[70]

This search which throws up disjointed versions of the past is matched by breaks in expression: 'At certain moments in the narrative, the search for logical relationships in fixed semantic fields is disrupted by breaks in symbolic discourse that communicate the existence of repressed experience.'[71]

Joe, experimenting with pre-human language, and birdsong, edges into using the pre-linguistic forms, as do Native American and other indigenous peoples. According to Ward, this breaks down versions of language, space and self, suggesting the entry into a pre-linguistic state, prefiguring the wordless signing of a territory, and the identity which prowls within its frontiers, like the self of dream: 'They were here though, I trust that. I saw them and they spoke to me, in the other language.'[72]

Ward uses linguistic anthropologist Jenness, whose work suggests there had once been a golden age in which man freely communicated with animals. However, this numinous time of equality disappeared after violence and deception so that: 'Latterly, a rift between man and animals opened up and they no longer revealed themselves.'[73]

Several critics relate language and form to the arguments and concerns of the novel. Its critique of linear, logical scientific thinking and materialism is linked to tensions between linear language and more suggestive, imaginative, symbolic expression. Hilde Staels focuses on the protagonist's relationship with her father and the debate between spiritual elements and rationalist values, in which her father, the 'head' of the family, would be seen to encode human nature and morality. During her journey, the narrator appears to distance herself from the logic which her father and her brother shared. 'It was my brother who made up these moral distinctions ... There had to be a good kind and a bad kind of everything,' she says[74] or '[my father's] way. Everything had to be measured.'[75]

Atwood reveals ironic contradictions in the narrator's use of language, her value systems and her quest. Although she blames others for using systems of logic, nonetheless she follows them herself. She argues that language freezes and reduces by naming, turning everything living into consumer items, and rejects mapping and labelling. However, searching for clues to discover the events of her father's death, she dissects reality, acting logically as a natural scientist in her observations of external facts, and need for empirical verification of hypotheses. She uses 'deductive reasoning, his bipolar logic, his social and moral codes, his axioms and maxims. These maxims are univocal truths about human nature, immobile solid essences, a meaning that is whole, eternal and closed.'[76] Staels sees the protagonist on a spatio-temporal journey, 'her quest is primarily motivated by a nostalgia to restore the illusion of a lost wholeness, authenticity and therefore happiness that she associates with her childhood'.[77]

Larkin quotes R.D. Laing's *The Politics of Experience*[78] in relation to the journey back into primal being, animal, vegetable, as a journey going in, back, through and beyond, where the protagonist refuses to be a victim and to withdraw. In discovering more about her past and herself she also learns that life is not so black and white. Neither Americans nor men can be defined as simply controlling. Canadians can also be materialistic, destructive hunters, and there is no need to reject all relationships with men. Larkin notes a change in the protagonist's being which leads to changes in the language. 'A crystal clear language and an increased pace' mark the late chapters .[79]

Myths, ghost stories and popular fictional forms

Like other great contemporary writers, Atwood engages with popular fictional forms which most directly connect with and dramatise cultural constructions, representations and conflicts, portraying versions of ourselves and our lives. Her work is a dialogue between popular fictional forms and 'high art', that is, the more literary, postmodern work which uses other works intertextually, referring to them as they suggest ways of interpreting life. This mode of reusing elements of literary expression helps rewrite and reinterpret history, showing us the everyday and the textual constructedness of our versions of our lives. Nicholson argues:

> [Atwood] constructs her own utterance of person and place, foregrounding the intertexts she is herself negotiating, in her fiction. Atwood produces patterns of textual archaeology and exploration in self-reflexive ways that connect her work to forms of attention in post-colonial – and postmodernist – writing elsewhere.[80]

Surfacing is also an example of how second-wave feminist work recuperates and rewrites myths of women's identities which have constrained and misrepresented women as guilty for the world's ills, sexually dangerous, predatory and destructive (these include Pandora, who opened a box filled with the world's ills, and Eve, who was lured by Satan in the Garden of Eden). The protagonist goes through various stages of a quest similar to mythic female figures. She resembles Persephone, in the Greek and Roman myth, which aims to explain the difference between summer and winter. Stolen by Pluto, the God of the underworld, Persephone descends into a world of the dead. Similarly, the protagonist plunges into a glacial lake, the site of her childhood, where she finds the body of her father. She decides to atone for an earlier abortion, which was a sacrifice to technology and male invasion – and to conceive and bear a child in a totally natural, earth-linked and located manner, just as the child of *herself* starts to resurface:

> This time I will do it by myself, squatting, on old newspapers in a corner alone; or on leaves, dry leaves, a heap of them, that's cleaner. The baby will slip out easily as an egg, a kitten, and I'll lick it off and bite the cord, the blood returning to the ground where it belongs, the moon will be full, pulling. In the morning I would be able to see it: it will be covered with shining fur, a god, I will never teach it any words.[81]

She feels totally at one with the natural world, but in so doing blurs her identity with that of trees, a frog, anything natural, 'I lean against a tree, I am a tree leaning ... I am not an animal or a tree,

I am the thing, in which the trees and animals move and grow.'[82] When she comes out of her trance state, she views with interest her matted hair and wild appearance, deciding to take this newfound sense of self as survivor, never more a victim, and live differently back in the civilised city world.

Defined as 'a remarkable and remarkably misunderstood book' by Fromberg Schaeffer in 'Is it time that separates us?',[83] and seen as a novel about death and survival by Rosemary Sweetapple,[84] *Surfacing* is a ghost story for several writers, including Keith Garebian, in '*Surfacing*: Apocalyptic Ghost Story' (1976),[85] a reading with which Atwood concurs, although she says hers is more of a Jamesian ghost story, 'in which the ghost that one sees is in fact a fragment of one's own self which has split off and that to me is the most interesting kind and that is obviously the tradition I'm working in'.[86] Ward argues:

> The climactic scene in *Surfacing*, in which the narrator dives beneath a cliff and is confronted by the deeply drifting body of her father, owes much to ghost-story techniques. It acquires fine tension from the controlled emotional confusion following this grotesque final confrontation of father and daughter.[87]

But it is a ghosting of her own history which is ever present on the island. Her father's haunting dominates her imagination, as she seeks a resolution to his disappearance and loss. In the end, she lays to rest not only his ghost but many of her own. Piercy celebrates this transitional moment and her subsequent return to the city but wonders what we can learn from such a very individualistic solution:

> To cease to be a victim, each of the protagonists fights an entirely solitary battle. Their only allies are the dead, the force in nature and the psyche, their own life energies. Yet they must live among others. Somehow the next step is missing.[88]

She suggests Atwood should move further from the joining of head and body to a more explicit relation with the women's movement and awareness of role playing and women's suffering, stating that 'she is part of that growing women's culture, a lead, a great quilt for which we are each stitching our own particular blocks'.[89]

Josie P. Campbell notes that the protagonist learns 'to accept loss and to confront [her] own mortality as conditions of life',[90] while Woodcock's mythic reading of the text sees a 'pattern of hope' etched with the lineaments of myths of surfacing to survive,[91] and Francine du Plessix Gray[92] considers the novel's mythic patterns and the archetypal heroine. Grace argues that the novel can be described as a ghost story, at a psychological quest level, due to the presence of doppelgangers:

> As the title implies, the novel is not about surfaces but about depths and the process of rising from those depths. *Surfacing* is not a realistic search for a missing person, but the multi-levelled quest of a contemporary Persephone for a particular type of freedom. On the psychological, ethical, spiritual, and perceptual levels, the narrator must discover a new way of being, a third way that transcends polarizations, thus enabling the individual to be free of crippling limitations.[93]

This quest for freedom is not viewed as an escape, instead, 'She will be free only when she can establish her relationship with her place, family, past, friends and self.'[94]

Surfacing is a powerful, sensitive, ecologically engaged novel, visionary and feminist, because of the woman's quest for an identity, which rejects the conventions of husband and child, the need for the partner, Joe, and enables a search for some kind of essential self. In this way, it is aligned to certain recurrent themes of feminist texts of the period, whether realist or fantasy. These, as Atwood's, reclaim rewritten myths and versions of woman as earth mother, at one with nature. Laurence ends on an ecological note:

> The themes are many, and the nature of reality is one of the most interesting. Some of the themes concern our most burning contemporary issues – the role of women, the facts of urban life, and most of all, the wounding and perhaps killing of our only home, Earth.[95]

Atwood interweaves themes and global concerns without propaganda.

Conclusion

Both the critical work (*Survival*) and the novel (*Surfacing*) helped establish Atwood as a Canadian literary figure and a woman writer. She returned to the theme of Canadian survival myths in her lectures at Oxford University, collected as *Strange Things: The Malevolent North in Canadian Literature* (1995), and to themes about women's roles, with *Lady Oracle* (1976) and *The Edible Woman* (1969), which are the focus of Chapter 2. Both these novels use humour to challenge popular romantic fiction versions of women's roles. As we shall see, the range of Atwood's writing shifts from the wilderness tale to the comic, science fiction, social realist and mythic/magical, exploring different representations and constructions of women, emphasising both fictionality and ways of constructing versions of self.

2

Constraining the Feminine: *The Edible Woman* (1969), *Lady Oracle* (1976)

Margaret Atwood's early novels and short stories use varieties of comedy and the Gothic to deal with issues of social constraints upon the development of women, and to replay, undercut or expose the myths and romantic fictions which offer seductive narratives leading (in particular) to women's disempowerment. This chapter builds on Coral Ann Howells' explorations of Atwood's engagement with Betty Friedan's *The Feminine Mystique* (1963) and the beginning of second-wave feminism. It explores Atwood's feminist re-visioning of representations of women's roles, and constructions of the self as woman, writer, victim, and survivor. In these two novels, Atwood's parody subverts both the marriage plot and women's 'feminine' destiny. She critiques and re-writes conventional romance plots using, while undercutting, the strategies of the popular literary Gothic. Both these novels deal with ways in which women can buy into, replay or reject various fictions about themselves in the world, in terms of relationships and gender as performance.

The Edible Woman (1969)

Feminism and romantic fictions

The Edible Woman, Atwood's first published novel, introduces themes and concerns popular throughout her work, of entrapping relationships and versions of self which constrain, diminish or subtly shape the way people, mostly women, see themselves, the world and their options. In both these early works, the target is romantic fictions and society's collusion in roles and narratives for women, which trap them in a male gaze – for Marian in *The Edible Woman*, caught in the camera view, like the sighting of the hunting rifle of her partner, Peter, or in *Lady Oracle*, the limitations of escapist fantasies for Joan Foster, romantic fiction writer, whose life overlaps with her tales.

The Edible Woman indicts relationships which figuratively devour women. Marian works in sales and marketing, as did Atwood.[1] She seems to be about to marry Peter but becomes aware of the engulfment entailed in conforming to marriage. She refuses his version of her as future wife, and serves up a representation of her head as a cake, breaking off their relationship. The book is comic, ironic, and satirical, with a serious message about self-worth and social relationships. Ironically, Margaret Atwood's signing of this body-oriented book took place in the men's sock and underwear department of Edmonton's Hudson Bay store. She sold two copies.[2] This lack of sales is unsurprising. Young men coming in for underwear met this young (feminist) novelist with a scarily titled novel, *The Edible Woman*, and probably felt threatened. The novel is controversial because of its exposé of conventional relationships as a form of devouring. Atwood defines it as a kind of anti-romance, basing her theories of a conventional romance upon the teachings of her professor, Northrop Frye, at Victoria College, University of Toronto. She was writing the novel prior to the widespread exploration and exposé of the damage done by romantic fictions to the lives of young women. Later books on this topic include critiques produced by Janice Radway (1991),[3] Lynne Pearce and Jackie Stacey (1995),[4] and Gina Wisker (1994).[5]

Drawing on feminist and psychological perspectives, Jane Brooks Bouson (1993)[6] argues that Atwood has a political and literary agenda, challenging conventional notions of romance and prescriptive roles for women as wives and mothers. She explores ways in which Atwood resists and disrupts conventional romantic plotlines, and how her heroines' internal lives are represented, highlighting the personally diminishing effects of accepting conventional, culturally inscribed feminine roles. Atwood contradicts the traditional trajectory of stories in which the growth of the heroine parallels courtship so that the denouement and the achievement of identity both rest upon getting married, instead:

> Enforcing the reader's discomfort with the romance scenario, Atwood's narrative elaborates on Marian's persecutory fears and disintegration anxiety as Peter assumes dominance over her. Instead of a marriage tale, *The Edible Woman* shows how female passivity and submersion in the traditional wife and mother roles can lead not to self-fulfilment but

to an intensifying sense of self-diminishment. She also stages female revenge fantasies.[7]

Brooks Bouson develops her argument around the psychological aspects of the novel and resistance to femininity, considering representations of the archaic mother, embodied in Marian's tyrannical landlady. She explores the implicit matrophobia, Marian's fear of being dominated by or becoming her mother, and the irony of how Marian's sense of self is eroded through her relationship with Peter. Marian hovers between two forms of devouring and engulfment, at first barely conscious of the choices ahead of her, then increasingly alarmed at the constricting roles as they come into view, seeing Peter as a barrier: 'against the amorphous world of femininity which she dreads'. But romantic love 'leads not to heightened self-definition but to a frightening sense of self-diminishment'.[8]

With its references to self-preservation, eating and cannibalism, in many ways this is a tale of 'writing the body', where society values part of the construction of the body as an item for consumption. Coral Ann Howells (1996) positions the novel historically, exploring how it critiques myths and social constructions of femininity which constrain women:

> *The Edible Woman* belongs to a specific moment in the history of North American post-war feminism, which registered the first signs of the contemporary women's movement in its resistance to social myths of femininity. This is the territory charted by Betty Friedan in *The Feminine Mystique* (1963), a study that Atwood herself read 'behind closed doors' like many other young women at the time.[9]

For Howells, the book is a significant second-wave feminist text, which explores and explodes the myths women internalise about being-in-the-world. She comments on Atwood's engagement with ideas influenced by de Beauvoir and Friedan. The novel 'goes beyond women's anger and bewilderment in its exploitation of the power of laughter to reveal the absurdities within social conventions'.[10]

Subversive and parodic, expressing the collision of the conventional comedy of manners with the marriage theme, it 'explores the relation between consumerism and the feminine mystique', in 'the language of the 1960s advertising and cookery books, adding a dash of popular Freudianism and a few of the Jungian archetypes'.[11] This novel is a satirical exposure of women's entrapment within their own bodies and within social myths.

The book is funny and topical. It equates eating with identity, and critiques the oppressive containment of stereotypical relationships. Woodcock recognises Atwood as a latter-day kind of Jane Austen, exposing the dull normality of everyday people, their wishes and constraints. Marge Piercy points out that although Peter is a Canadian lawyer, he is a type Atwood defines as American, i.e. a consumer:

> slick, ambitious, empty, laden with expensive gadgets that give him a sense of power (fancy camera, fancy guns, the accoutrements of the business playing sportsman), conscious of his image and locked into his head, alienated from his body, his sexuality, his emotions, whatever they may be, most happy when he is destroying something or consuming something.[12]

What disturbs Piercy is the 'hard wiring' in Marian's head that makes her comply so easily with the scenario of consumption – and the alternatives open to Atwood's characters to escape to other more fulfilling existences and jobs. Howells sees Marian lose her sense of being a unified subject: 'beginning to hallucinate her emotional conflict in images of bodily dissolution and haunted by hallucinations of fragmentation'.[13] As a novel of a particular moment in feminism, *The Edible Woman* divides critics over some of its arguably most effective (and parodic) moments. Marian's baking a cake to represent herself and reject Peter's consumption of her has been seen by critics as either evidence of a descent into self-destruction, or a comic turn. For Howells, it is 'a comedy of resistance and survival which subverts social definitions from within'.[14]

Not all critics are so positive, however. Some critics argue that Marian's dissolution of self and of those around her is a stage in a romance plot, a form of madness, or like the journey for many women in novels of this period, a breakdown which leads to a breakthrough. Others find the use of cake-making, a traditional female activity, as a challenge to Marian's sense of social engulfment, and see this and other cannibal metaphors as springing from enlightened feminist critiques of engulfing relationships.

Narration and form

The novel's expression and narrative voice have also received critical scrutiny. The split in narrative voice indicates a split within Marian's self, creating difficulties for both Marian and the reader. Sherrill

Grace gives an example of such a problem in Marian's escape from the bar, which she sees as indicating distorted thinking, paranoia and flight from reality. Grace argues that Atwood's fiction should not be seen solely in terms of realism but as symbolic, fantastic. She sees scenes in both *The Edible Woman* and *Lady Oracle* as: 'extravagant ... enmeshed in increasing improbability and comic absurdity',[15] Marian is an unreliable narrator who provides symbolic insights into her society and its consumer culture:

> Although Marian's perceptions of herself as hunted victim or tasty morsel about to be devoured are distortions of reality for which she is largely responsible, these perceptions carry a symbolic truth about the general nature of our society and personal relationships. Ours is a consumer society; we feed on each other economically and emotionally.[16]

The three-part structure subverts traditional romance for Catherine McLay.[17] In this reading, Marian sets out in a semi-satisfactory market research job, with a satisfactory enough relationship and room-mate, and begins Part 1 by saying, 'I knew I was all right on Friday when I got up. If anything I was feeling more solid than usual',[18] but her sense of security is threatened by signing a pension plan at work (leading her to think of the ominous days in the future alone, with a fire). Ainsley, her room-mate, announces she wants to have a baby and then Peter, who has: 'Carefully cultivated his Playboy image and seems to be averse to legal commitments, suddenly becomes domestic and proposes'. [19] Clara, her ever-pregnant university friend, looks like becoming a role model, and Marian begins to see this as a hellish move to captivity. As in the romantic fiction plot, she has other ordeals to go through before she realises she does not want this marriage and can actually move on with some new insight, even though she has to find a new job and at some point possibly a new love.

Marian becomes fragmented and removed from herself in the middle of the novel, Part 2, and McLay notes a sudden shift from first to third person narration, distancing her. It returns to first person in the final section. Peter's conversations equate the shooting of a rabbit and gutting it with taking girls home, which connects with Marian's nightmarish image of him taking photos of her, in which she feels trapped and isolated. The novel focuses on the hunt for partners and the escape from overwhelming relationships. It is not only the men who track and capture partners, however. Lucy, one of the 'office virgins', is described as fishing for a man with fish glue and various forms of hooks.

The Edible Woman critiques the contradictions or dualities where life is reduced to consumer artifice: Marian's market research job, and Peter's photography. Individuals are exposed in artificially constructed relationships. Sherrill Grace comments: 'The narrative text explores power relations established by a rationalist, individualist, profit-oriented society. The participants in the story form part of a capitalist-consumerist society with a market economy in which commodity satisfaction reigns supreme ...'[20]

Organic processes are opposed to artifice, while people treat each other as objects. As a social and romantic choice, Peter initially seems ideal: 'He's attractive and he's bound to be successful, and also he's neat, which is a major point when you're going to be living with someone.'[21] They need each other for social reasons, so 'Peter needs Marian as a future wife and mother, and Marian needs Peter as a "nice" man who will save her from the chaos of life.'[22]

Marian simultaneously resents, critiques and is seduced by the stereotypical idea of the sexually attractive female and future wife imposed on her by Peter. In return, she reduces him to a stereotype of masculinity, repeating the stale formulaic codes, functions, tropes, narrative sequences and so the underlying beliefs of popular romance. Marian both waits for Peter as the heroine does a rescuer/hero in a Gothic romance, then runs away when he pursues her. He seems to offer a vision of life, as if it were consumer goods. 'The version of reality with which Marian feels safe is the "myth" of love, protection and rescue guaranteed by the one right male.'[23] However, as the serving of a cake fashioned as her head suggests, Marian would be overwhelmed, ingested, and devoured by this oppressive, romantic myth and by Peter the hunter-photographer.

Feminist critics read the moment when Marian offers Peter the grotesque cake version of herself as cathartic. Sharon Wilson (1993)[24] relates cannibalism imagery to Atwood's fascination with food metaphors, deriving from her experience as a student of home economics and her production of *The CanLit Foodbook* (1987). Atwood's interest in edible art, we are told, was set off by seeing foodstuffs on sale or at weddings, which became 'part of the impetus for the cake in *The Edible Woman*, an anthropomorphic *object* made of foodstuffs, such as candy brides and grooms and Donald Duck cakes in Woolworths'.[25] Once she no longer feels she will be consumed by someone else's version of her, Marian eats normally. Such imagery lends itself to feminist readings of the body.

The body

Catherine McLay (1981) argues that Marian's rejection of eating is a form of bodily disgust, as she descends to a point where she identifies with the lowest forms of life and cannot eat meat, vegetables or even move mould. Marian, alienated from her body, sees eating as pointless and disgusting and her disgust is directed at the body which ingests food. She generates a list of words relating to digestion, burps and vomit, linking up domestic activity, natural intake and production alongside 'blood, sweat and tears'.[26]

This existential angst is excessive but a function of Marian's alienation from job, self and conformist roles – and her sense that Peter would be capturing and ingesting her should she commit to embracing the lifestyle he has in mind. Preparing for her engagement party, she has her hair ornamented, and wears a short, red, sequinned dress, make-up and gold jewellery. She sees herself in the mirror, as if a sacrificial victim or an Egyptian mummy, and her friend Duncan comments that she must be part of a masquerade. However, Peter and his friends commend this performative Marian, suggesting that dressing this way is part of her future. Not surprisingly, she finds this alienating. Peter's fascination with 'shots', both by camera and gun, suggest death and imprisonment to Marian, who feels Peter will trap her in this role, this performance. 'Once he pulled the trigger she would be stopped, fixed indissolubly in that gesture, that single stance, unable to move or change.'[27] She relates this to the poem 'Camera', as 'The protagonist sees the very act of photographing as an act of violation, an indication of a desire to stop the clock and to capture the other in time.'[28]

Marian realises her role is so dependent upon Peter's version of her that his engulfing and devouring of her personality resembles a form of cannibalism. She can eat nothing, finds her throat closes against meat, and hears the carrots shrieking as they are ripped up. As others gorge, she feels nauseated. Comedy modifies the disgust, and Marian uses this refusal of traditional body images and roles to escape from the versions of the feminine mystique which would engulf and deny her. A worker in commodity and consumerism, she refuses to be consumed and commodified.

The period in which the novel was written produced several books about breakdowns as breakthroughs, including Doris Lessing's *Briefing for a Descent into Hell* (1981), Susan Sontag's *Death Kit* (1967), several works by Samuel Beckett (1906–89) and Bessie Head's *A Question of Power* (1974). Like Sylva Plath in *The Bell Jar* (1966), Marian feels disgust at anything to do with the body or procreation, seen as messy, disturbing, and other, to be rejected. Hilde Staels characterises Marian's bodily repulsion as psychotic (and Canadian):

> Marian categorizes the visible crossing of, or the open play with the established boundaries of her outer body (the disciplined cultural shape) as an unacceptable exposure of underlying mess, horror or dirt. Her rationalizing mind further mortifies her inner life. She censors her disruptive extra-rational experience on the basis of society's norms, for open display of private feelings makes one an easy target for attack.[29]

Afraid of the revolt of her body, she prefers straight, linear paths to cycles, a contained identity to a terrifying crisis. Any act of self-probing or creative self-assertion is hindered by a sense of self-doubt, guilt and a fear of moving on.

The Gothic and fairytales

Several early novels and short stories by Atwood use the Gothic, humour and irony to critique constraining ways of life and women's representation and stereotyping. George Woodcock notes that *The Edible Woman* 'is about the distances and defences between human beings. The distances and defences are necessary – the suggestion is not even skin deep because human beings are predators. *The Edible Woman* is a novel about emotional cannibalism.'[30]

With her fascination for myths and fairytales as intertext, Atwood reminds us that so many of the great fairytales of wizards, witches, stepmothers and brutal or negligent husbands and wives actually use motifs and narratives of cannibalism (for example, 'Babes in the Wood', with the old woman in the gingerbread house, and 'The Robber Bridegroom', in which a robber marries a series of women and takes them home to be devoured).

She reverses the conventional Gothic romantic fiction plot in which the heroine from the perfect marriage overcomes any blockage and convenes a new society around the new couple. In *The Edible Woman*, both the hero and society are the blockage. There is no solution in marriage and: 'The comedy conclusion would be a tragic solution for Marian.'[31] Marriage would be a problem; rejecting it, however, lets Marian at least move forward and feel more comfortable in her own identity and body.

Duncan, a dark soul, reminds Marian of Dracula. He accompanies her on her journey through some kind of hellish perception of others and then back up to the light. During this journey, Marian is repulsed by the animal-like characteristics of those around her. Clara, becoming overwhelmed by her pregnancy, disappears inside her own flesh, 'a queen-ant bulging with the burden of an entire society',[32] while the women at the office are like 'a herd of armadillos at the zoo',[33] their eating habits disgusting, destructive, devouring, and her flatmate Ainsley's capturing of her partner reminds Marian of an early Christian sacrifice, although who is being sacrificed – the lions or Christians – is confusing.

Some critics were clearly either baffled by Marian's sense of engulfment and/or sympathetic to Peter, whom they viewed as unthreateningly normal. George Woodcock sees Marian's relationship with the men in her life, Peter and Duncan, as mutual cannibalism. He argues that her enticing of Peter is cannibalistic, and describes Peter as a 'highly normal young man'[34] and her latter relationship with Duncan as feeding his devouring self-pity while McLay sees Marian's attempt to make love with Duncan as some kind of union with death. Varma's interpretation is similar. He finds Gothic imagery in the representation of Duncan, haunter of laundrettes, who resembles Frankenstein's monster: 'His skin was even more unearthly ... eyes partly hidden by a crumpled mass of straight black hair that came down over the forehead'.[35] Duncan has a Gothic fascination for cannibal stories and appears emaciated, as though he eats the minute food offerings to those in dungeons. When he takes Marian into the Egyptian section of the museum, he prefers looking at the mummy cases. Wilson takes up the theme of evil and cannibalism, and recognises that Marian could be eaten up like the brides in 'The Robber Bridegroom'. In addition to the explicit fear of being chopped up and eaten, this fairytale has much in common with Atwood's novel, because in both the fiancé is untrustworthy, warnings are unheeded, and there is hiding, passivity, consumption of beverages, heartbreak, amputation, communal eating of precious food, and assistance from a 'godmother'.[36]

The ending: critical divisions

As we have seen when considering feminist responses, critics are divided over the ending in which Marian serves up her head as a cake, then settles down to eat it herself, sharing it with Duncan who Robert Lecke sees as embodying both life and death. Lecke fails to find Peter at all problematic. He is 'not the enemy after all, he was just an ordinary human being like most people'.[37] Alan Dane finds the ending 'ambiguous but somehow triumphant',[38] McLay sees it as a reprise from potential engulfment and death and Varma finally misreads the baking and presenting of the cake as Marian's affirmation that women are to be devoured. For Grace, *The Edible Woman* is circular, and Marian does not progress, although the use of the first-person narrator indicates a more unified perception of self at the novel's end.

It is a complex ending. Unlike the positive ending of *Surfacing*, where the protagonist develops and moves to another place, Marian recognises she is being constructed as something to be managed by others and devoured, but perhaps all she finally does is escape without moving on and growing. Atwood remarked to Linda Sandler that: 'The book does make a negative statement about society. The complications are resolved, but not in a way that affirms the social order.'[39]

Hilde Staels sees the novel's end as a defeat, a capitulation to life-denying forces, to Marian's repressed self, a feature of her origins in a Canadian consumer society:

> The desire for enclosed space runs parallel with the psychic desire to be closed and to exclude repellent alien forces that come from outside or that creep up from a dark, fluid, obscure space within. Marian's fear of too much unpredictable life that may invade her established identity makes her a suitable member of Toronto's living dead.[40]

On a more negative note, Lecke suggests that the ending erases identity, 'man (and woman) are seen only as faceless non-entities in a zombified crowd'.[41] Whether gloomy or celebratory, *The Edible Woman* satirises romantic fictions' constraining narratives, a satire taken a step further with *Lady Oracle* in the form of a protagonist who writes such fiction while her own life resembles, parodies and undercuts the message which such romantic fictions peddle.

Lady Oracle (1976)

Romantic fictions – and fictionalising the self

If *The Edible Woman* is a satirical take on consumer society, and consuming roles for women peddled by romantic fictions and marketing, *Lady Oracle* tackles storytelling, romantic fictions and Gothic
romances head on, with the figure of Joan Foster, writer of Gothic
romances and an influential book of poetry. Joan is ungainly in
childhood, and dominated by her slim mother. Escaping constraining versions of self, she escapes when young to England, and later
to Italy by way of a fake drowning, staging her own death to escape
her identity and her fame.

Increasingly, she escapes into fiction and poetry. She writes
visionary, mystic poetry as 'Lady Oracle', and adopts the name of
her novelist aunt, Louisa K. Delacourt, earning herself a reputation
as a writer of Gothic romances. Each one of her relationships con-
strains her, and, as the early reviewers comment, her life increasingly resembles and critiques her own romantic fictions. *Lady Oracle*
engages with the fictionalising processes of the artist as writer, and
Joan is described by Judith McCombs as a composite of Atwood's
previous artist characters, one who serves a number of purposes
and roles. She 'is everything mystic, Gothic, divided, multiple,
Canadian, female, victim, visual, satiric, visionary – everything to
exceptional excess'.[42]

McCombs compares Joan to Falstaff, Shakespeare's larger-than-
life historical figure from *Henry IV*, to the escape artist Houdini,
and a 'creative Trickster ducking in and out of Canadian and female
victimhoods'.[43] The novel parodies both *Surfacing* and *Survival*,
foregrounding issues of gender and sexuality. The woman and artist appear as mystic in *Survival* and 'sell-out and manipulator' in
Surfacing, and to a greater extent in *Lady Oracle*.

Storytelling

Atwood develops a favourite theme, focusing on how narrative
formulae, narrators and protagonists construct versions of reality
and self which can be entrapping, enlightening and revelatory.
This highlights the human tendency to try and make sense of life
through storytelling, engaging as self-aware fiction, reconstruction

and testimony. Throughout Atwood's works, testimony, lying and storytelling present versions of response to, and representations of, the human condition.

In *Surfacing*, the protagonist reconstructs her life through narrating her breakdown and breakthrough; narration in a taped diary keeps Offred in control of her own sense of self in *The Handmaid's Tale*; what is true and what is fabricated is increasingly questioned in Iris Chase's tale in *The Blind Assassin*; there are the various lies and versions of Grace Marks in *Alias Grace*; and the tales that Jimmy (Snowman) tells himself and the Crakers in *Oryx and Crake*. In *The Penelopiad*, the female weaver of tales tells a different version of *The Odyssey*. Each tries to reconstruct versions of their own past and explain self and life to themselves, while doing so to the reader. None of them are trustworthy, all of them fictionalise to make a kind of sense of themselves and their experiences.

Frank Davey comments on Atwood's suspicion of narrative art in 'Alternative Stories' (1984),[44] while Barbara Godard sees that storytelling is the way in which we make sense of our lives. For Godard, 'Atwood's fiction is self-reflexive',[45] and, as McFadden argues, it shows a deepening of 'human understanding' representing 'writer's block' as a version of life in a nuclear age: 'the book is a big breakthrough for Atwood both artistically and in terms of basic human understanding'.[46] As in the earlier *Surfacing*, there are embedded folktales, *Märchen*, and classical European fairytales, mixed with Quebecois oral tales. Godard locates several of these and finds the Bluebeard tale at the core of *Lady Oracle*.[47] Joan moves from Canada to the UK and, like Cinderella, turns from nothing to something, a mothball to a writer. Atwood uses refraction, mirrors, both convex and concave, foregrounding the central issue of the novel: that all reflections are distortions, all mimetic representations, lies. Embedded tales in *Lady Oracle* offer a subversive strategy, one of refraction, as Atwood plays with notions of distorting mirrors. But the refractions and travesties of mirrors furnish the material for the novel which contains them. Joan's is a metamorphosis narrative, although she expects that she will meet death rather than be carried away by romance. Several fairytales are intertexts here, including Snow White, with the revisiting, spectral, damning mother; in the references to Cinderella, Joan herself acts as the ugly sister; and the intertext with Hans Christian Andersen's 'The Little Mermaid' is a romantic tale with an unhappy ending, in which love is the problem. Andersen's mermaid dies when she comes on land for love, and

Joan repeatedly changes her location for love, faking her death in water when pretending to drown in Lake Ontario.

This is a postmodern novel which plays with traditional narrative structures and interpretations in order to challenge them. It revisits the past and rewrites ironically, presenting different fictionalised versions, much as Atwood also does in *Murder in the Dark, Alias Grace* and *The Edible Woman.* Joan falsifies versions of possible lives through her fictions. In this it resembles and references Jane Austen's *Northanger Abbey* (1817). Joan, like Catherine Morland, follows lies and lives which fragment her, leaving her stranded in transit between fiction and reality. Sherrill Grace sees the novel as an 'amusing yet serious treatment of popular literary forms and stereotypes'[48] and as 'a sustained double parody of the realist novel on the one hand and of the Gothic romance on the other'.[49] Grace argues that in *Lady Oracle* we learn to live with multiplicity.

Performing the self

Sharon Wilson identifies the main intertext in this novel from Hans Christian Andersen's story 'The Red Shoes', particularly the 1948 film version starring Moira Shearer (1926–2006), and directed by Michael Powell (1905–90) and Eneric Pressburger (1902–88). In this tale, characters can choose either to 'dance' (be artists, be 'themselves', be 'free') or marry (be conventional, be-for-others, conform to societal rules), but they cannot do both: 'Wishing to be a butterfly, *Lady Oracle's* Joan is forced to become an escape-artist. Like a slave pretending to dance so that she will be untied.'[50] Wilson suggests:

> Joan tries to be what her society wants her to be, a performer. She first dances as a brownie with red hair, also at another ball as a voluptuous circus fat lady and later as a triple goddess and a celestial nymph.[51]

Continuing the theme of presentation and the performative self, Brooks Bouson explores the significance of Joan's weight and her experience of obesity: 'The obese female body, then, is a complex psychocultural symbol used by the narrative not only to register protest against the social construction of femininity, but also to express anxiety about the uncontained femininity that becomes subject to social control'.[52] Transformation of Joan into some kind of a beauty also undercuts the romantic fiction plot, however, since

'Attractive to men after she loses weight, Joan discovers that she is the "right shape" but has "the wrong past"'; thus begins her life-long habit of compulsive lying as she creates 'a different' and 'more agreeable' personal history for herself.[53]

Undercutting romantic fiction

Joan writes Gothic romantic fiction, but in her own life a series of relationships consistently mimics Gothic romance plots and under-mines their promise. Brooks Bouson sees *Lady Oracle* as a complex, oppositional text, in dialogue with the promises of romance and marriage made by popular culture so, 'dialogically contesting the official voices of culture, Joan insists that the basis of heterosexual romance is not openness and honesty but secrecy and lies'.[54]

McCombs defines the poetry Joan produces as: 'a high-brow upside-down spirit-dictated mythic Gothic'.[55] One of the main influences on Joan's fascination with women's roles, entrapment and escape, is Alfred Lord Tennyson, whose poem 'The Lady of Shalott' is about a beautiful woman in a tower trapped by a deadly curse. If and when she seeks love and leaves the tower, the lady dies. This resembles another fairytale favourite of Atwood, that of Rapunzel, in which a beautiful woman is imprisoned in a tower by a witch, then rescued by a lover who climbs up her hair. Atwood uses this tale in several places in her work to suggest that Canadian women in particular, and all women in general, are constrained in their choices and freedom in seeing themselves as beauties pining in isolation and awaiting rescue by a prince, knight or some brave man. They are trapped in their fantasies and lack the energy and imagination to make their own choices and move on. Joan's life is governed by living the story, while also critiquing, reproduc-ing and trying to escape it. The men in Joan's life, her dreams and romances, are all ambiguous and untrustworthy. She is not quite sure who is good for her, or who she should be. One man who haunts her thoughts, the Daffodil Man, once exposed himself to her when she was a teenager, but, she reflects, he might also have been an inspiration. Joan needs to come to terms with these ambi-guities. She does try to escape to England, changing her name, but she always vehicles such escapes into and through romances with men. Perhaps there is a new seizing of power when later in her life she stages her own drowning and escapes again, to Italy. Judith

McCombs recognises Joan's deliberate plunge into Lake Ontario as a satirical take off of *Surfacing*, in which Atwood is parodying her own mystic writing.[56] Alice Palumbo also sees it as cathartic: 'Joan's "death" forces her to confront her many "lives," and accept the possibility of synthesis.'[57] Joan sees her many selves: Joan Foster, 'Lady Oracle' the famous poet, Louisa K. Delacourt, the Gothic novelist, and the 'Fat Lady' as 'a group of women in the centre of a maze, the plot of the Gothic she is writing blurring into her own life. The inset Gothic narrative integrates Joan's multiple selves; while the framing narrative leaves the question open.[58] Art helps Joan to change and express herself. As an opera singer she can shriek loudly, and dancing seems to offer a way of rising above the pain of this world. As Catherine Sheldock-Ross comments, Joan desires both to turn the shifting world into art and yet also seeks metamorphosis for herself.[59]

The Gothic

The Gothic qualities of the novel are parodies of our own social mythologies. Rosowksi says: 'In *Lady Oracle*, Atwood turns this tradition back upon itself, confronting the Gothic dimensions that exist within our social mythology. To do so, she uses fantasy to extend thematic and technical possibilities of the modern Gothic novel.'[60] She makes an interesting point that, while in the Gothic normally horror increases in relation to the difference and gap between the Gothic world and the real world, here, instead, horror is produced when the two become close. Each of Joan's bizarre loves with different men seems normal at the time. She lives the fantasy: it leaks through into her life, taking it over. The novel uses the characteristics and formulae of popular Gothic, both film and novel, while critiquing the ways in which it conditions women's fantasies and versions of their lives. 'The whole story of *Lady Oracle* itself is narrated from a state Edmund Burke considered the source of the sublime experience: the contemplation of death itself.'[61]

> But the death is a sham, a feigned drowning in a prosaically polluted Lake Ontario. The novel is full of such ironic deflatings, the primary narrative deconstructing the assumptions of the Gothic romances Joan writes for a living while simultaneously constructing a new model of female Gothic terror based on more mundane, contemporary dangers.[62]

Lady Oracle unfolds as a series of doubled, contradictory narratives, and presents a social archaeology of life in suburban North America in the 1950s, narrated by someone obsessed with cultural minutiae. According to Palumbo, Joan Foster negotiates media-driven consumer culture, illustrated by Atwood's use of a series of intertextual allusions, particularly 1940s women's films, 1960s art films, Victorian sensational fiction, and mass-market Gothic romance. She turns childhood interests in reading the social meanings of furniture, housing, and film into a key to success as a Gothic romance writer, where the romantic fantasy is bolstered by the material wealth surrounding her heroines, her 'goddess[es] of quick money'.[63] So Joan's Gothics mirror her own concerns, while the intertextual references mirror Joan's narrative. However, Gothics also increasingly expose her fear of disclosure and rejection.

The Gothic is a familiar Canadian form and Atwood's later *The Robber Bride* (1993) and several short stories use Gothic tropes: doubling, mirroring, twins, vampires and hidden secrets revealing alternative readings. Varma identifies hauntings and the supernatural in many Canadian fictions,[64] suggesting these emanate from the darkness and cold, as do the context of their writing, and that 'Canadian literature, therefore, is kindred to the spirit of magic and the supernatural, a fertile ground for the exploration of the unknown and beyond.'[65] He considers the 'threatening malevolence'[66] of the web surrounding red-haired Joan, who has a constant awareness of invisible presences and 'sees' her mother prior to being informed of her death. She sees her stabbed: 'she was standing very upright on the clay-coloured rug, dressed in her navy-blue suit with the white collar' and 'Through her back I could see the dilapidated sofa; it looked as though the stuffing was coming out of her.'[67] This is both a comic and terrifying image. Her mother is in her everyday clothes, and a domestic setting, but bizarrely displaced, and aligned with the deteriorating sofa. She appears in Chapter 33 after footsteps and sounds, pressing her face against the glass like a child, an image recalling Emily Bronte's *Wuthering Heights* (1847). Joan comments that: 'I loved her but the glass was between us, I would have to go through it, I longed to console her. Together we would go down the road into the darkness, would do what she wanted.'[68] Joan's oppressive mother constantly undermined her but she cannot get rid of her haunting presence.

Joan's inset Gothic novel, *Stalked by Love*, set in a stately home, comprises the usual Gothic elements: pursuit, terror, power, and the potential of real rape. Charlotte, the vulnerable but intelligent protagonist, has jewels in a casket, and the walls are covered in ivy. Varma finds echoes of Ann Radcliffe's *Mysteries of Udolpho* (1794) in the stealthy footsteps on the gravel in Chapter 18, and in mysterious night visits when Joan is in the bathtub. He identifies the moment where Edmund, the hero, offers Charlotte eternal love and dancing as a scene from *Lenore* (1773), a German ballad in which the demon lover dissolves, screaming, into a skeleton.

Joan, the novelist, like Atwood, tries to find ways to end her book which are not merely romantic clichés. In the final scene of *Stalked by Love*, Edmund metamorphoses through versions of the men with whom Joan has had relationships. He ends up with 'burning eyes and icicle teeth'[69] in a turtle-necked sweater, mixing the ordinary and the deadly (the Daffodil Man and her husband Arthur). Joan's costume Gothics might have space for a fantasy demon lover, but her own life is more mundane, despite the leakages between fiction and lived everyday life. None of the men in her life are really heroes, villains or protectors. The text exposes the unreliability of fictional, romanticised versions of self and reality, and it refuses the conventions and comforts of women's Gothic fictions. Emphasising the limitations of sentimental novels, picturesque fairytales and Gothic romance, *Lady Oracle* splices all of these with forms of feminist fiction, and so explores equally diverse versions of self, identities and representation.

Lady Oracle and *The Edible Woman* both replay and question conventional romantic fictional versions of women's lives. *The Edible Woman* explores marriage and conformity, seen here as engulfing, while *Lady Oracle* is a Gothic tale with Gothic intertexts, questioning versions of ideal relationships and marriage, which are defined as artifice and dangerous fictions. Atwood returns to the themes of romance and marriage as myths in several of her short stories and uses the Gothic as a vehicle to critique these and other entrapping fictions in *The Robber Bride*, in particular, while her focus on constructing narrative recurs again most obviously in *Alias Grace* and *The Blind Assassin*.

3

Explorations, Bones and Murders: The Short Stories (1977–95)

Much of Atwood's most experimental and outspoken work appears in her short stories, which are also often the crucible for the later novels, a place to try out a character, event and theme, and then build on it. Indeed, much of the formal experimentation and the playfulness concerning human behaviour and literary form appear here. The stories map against the development of the novels, consistent themes of which are survival and the wilderness. In Atwood's more overtly feminist phase she produced *Dancing Girls* (1977), *True Stories* (1981), *Murder in the Dark* (1983) and *Bluebeard's Egg* (1983), collections of stories concerned with women's identities, roles, relationships, constraints on and constructions of femininity, and the downsides of the norms of women's expectations. What she latterly chose to call 'flash fiction', a term used for very short fictions, can be found in her most recent collection, *The Tent* (2006).

Many of Atwood's short stories appeared in magazines before being reprinted in her collections. She has also written children's fiction, not dealt with here. In the mid-1960s she wrote 'The Upside Down Fisherman', 'The Perilous Camera', 'The Best of These' and 'Up in the Tree'. 'The Interviewers' and 'Are You the Woman Who Washes?' are described by Atwood as material or prelims for *The Edible Woman*. These early short stories air many of her major concerns – identity, relationships, performance, fictionalising, gender, nationhood and ecology. While her major critics do comment on her stories, they have received much less critical attention than the novels, probably because of the general tendency to see a short story as a lesser form than a novel.

Dancing Girls (1977): critiquing romantic fictions

Arguably at her most feminist in outlook, Atwood here explores the constricting myths with which women deal to develop (or fail to develop) their own sense of individualism. *Dancing Girls* critiques a variety of romantic fictions in its 14 stories, undercutting 'happily ever after' endings and indicting a simplistic version of romance and women's life trajectories and domesticity. These stories define relationships with men as concerned with forms of investment, which are more likely to render the individual disempowered than fulfilled. But Atwood offers alternative plots to the conventional ones she decries, using Gothic strategies which undercut, undermine and break open the simple versions of what it means to be a woman in a relationship. The insight which informs *The Edible Woman*, where Marian feels trapped inside a limited construction of self as only the other half of a man, permeates the collection. Judith McCombs identifies representations of the artist in three stories in *Dancing Girls*: 'A Travel Piece', 'Lives of the Poets', and 'Giving Birth', as harking back to *Surfacing*. They just as easily lead towards Atwood's novel of the Caribbean, *Bodily Harm*, where a culpable misreading of cultural difference exposes ways in which North Americans can simplify and misunderstand other languages and cultures, which can lead to danger. In discussing 'A Travel Piece', McCombs exposes the superficialities of tourism and travel writing, which take a surface, slick view of events and people. In this story, Annette, a travel writer, is involved in a plane crash in the Caribbean, and it seems that although she can both fit in and criticise the survivors in the dinghy, Annette might not survive the event herself. She is stunned after the crash and has increasingly bizarre images of the surrounding detritus and her possible fate. In her role as photographer, she is the artist, positioned to avoid engagement with challenges, and rather report at a distance. The constructedness of a journalist's work is juxtaposed with the immediacy of Annette's real situation, her possible death. Victim positions change in the next two stories, culminating in 'Giving Birth', which McCombs recognises as influenced by the work of Erica Jong.[1]

Roles for women

The collection explores a range of roles for women, including that of the essentialist mother figure. In 'The Artist as Housewife' (1972)

Jeannie gives birth and takes a maternal role, presiding as an earth mother over baby and earth. She moves on from the flux seen in *Surfacing* through her developing child, 'the place where these splits are healed, in maternal descents'.[2] This is a synthesising moment for the artist, who recognises that she can also be a mother, and contrasts with contradictions between roles of mother and artist painted by much second-wave feminism.

According to Lee Biscoe Thompson, Atwood continues her exploration of women's roles by using examples of the alien or other, and of alienation. *Dancing Girls* itself has alien encounters at its centre. The Gothic exposes a web of contradictory responses concerning aliens and alienation. Thompson finds in these stories: 'polarities of vulnerability and insensitivity, control and chaos, humour and age'.[3] Alienation and death appear in 'The Grave of the Famous Poet', and in 'Hair Jewellery', where strange jewellery is made from the hair of the dead beloved. Romance deteriorates in all these tales, as it does in *The Edible Woman*. In the short story 'Rape Fantasies', there are several mundane and manic monologues which recount fantasies in which potential rapists are all reduced to people you can talk to and win round. According to Thompson, 'A Travel Piece' and 'Tanning' concern human emotional paralysis, as does 'Giving Birth', which is also concerned with 'the relationship between language and the body'.[4] 'Polarities under Glass' and 'When It Happens' are apocalyptic tales of madness. In the latter, facing the apocalypse or some terrible human disaster, a woman looks ahead to the moments at which she must leave behind everything she knows and finds familiar. She slips even further away from the everyday as she identifies with the plant world, finding it difficult to make distinctions between the human and the non-human.[5]

Atwood's short fiction is compared to *Surfacing* by Charlotte Sturgess, who suggests that Atwood deals with both gendered and Canadian/American power relations:

> Atwood has constantly drawn attention to Canada's status as a victim of American domination, just as she has repeatedly examined power relations between men and women, and woman's marginalization in culture and society. This, however, is not a defeatist stance on her part, but a concern with 'the pointlessness of splitting the world into discriminatory categories and opposites'.[6]

Atwood does not merely criticise but uses the speculative to suggest alternative ways of seeing. Her artistic vision and committed political position led her to both deal with those oppositions, and to suggest revisions and modifications.

Sturgess sees the early stories in *Dancing Girls* as presenting female characters who fail to escape problems of identity, whatever their social and professional status. *Dancing Girls* considers ways in which men and women play social games and construct social identities with each other, emphasising Atwood's exploration and critique of post-1960s consciousness and the deepening divide between the sexes, as women's increasing emancipation brought a fresh set of conflicts to the fore, challenging former roles. The problem of roles, self-definition and complementary gender roles is taken up in 'Polarities' in which Estelle is both safe and entrapped as if in an Iron Maiden, within the control of the Wicked Witch of the West. She can take part in hippy parties as a result but is likely to critique the myths which they perpetuate about femininity, and a kind of caring earthiness aligned with some kind of religious fervour. Ted – 'hippy hippy husband, fisheyes her quickly; she has been uncool'.[7] The short stories offer opportunities to explore vignettes and extremes.

'The War in the Bathroom' is a tale of lodging houses and displacement. Focusing on the noises which emerge from the bathroom near her room, the protagonist narrator speculates on events, characters and meanings which they suggest and to the issue of possession of space. Thompson sees this tale as taking a somewhat typical, introspective, self-absorbed Atwood character and focusing on determined hostilities against the other person, in the bathroom. The narrator, 'self-analytic, keeping madness at bay only by a series of rituals and inventories',[8] catalogues things to keep them under control, but cannot control the other main user of the bathroom, an old man who is as meticulous as the protagonist and evolves into an alter ego, while the two other voices heard in the bathroom also seem to be two sides of one person. The story concludes on the same terms as almost all of Atwood's poetry and fiction: the view of life as a series of small, uncertain battles on the fringes of madness: 'For the time being I have won.'[9]

'The Man from Mars' is a kind of romance which exposes some of the expectations and constraints of relationships in a social context. Christine, a large woman: 'She was an exception, she fitted none of the categories they commonly used when talking about the girls ... she was an honorary person'[10] is, to her surprise, courted by an alien other, who is here defined as a Martian alien to Christine's lifestyle and cultural references. Sturgess considers ways in which Atwood deals with difference and victims, commenting on how each story has clear victims. In 'The Man from Mars', Atwood focuses on discrimination and strangeness more generally, showing readers that discrimination is a matter of many issues, including ethnicity and gender:

> Paradoxically, whereas there seems to be no such thing as a feminist subject here, for such a concept is presented as a contradiction in terms, it is the immigrant as the ethnic 'other' who reinstates Christine as feminine in the eyes of the males around her. His obsessive tracking of her on the university campus 'rendered her equally mysterious'.[11]

Although strange to Christine, this alien male makes her seem more interesting to others, as if he has brought her into focus by his focus on her, so making the otherwise unnoticeable, overweight young woman herself seem less Other or alien. When he does drift back home and war begins with his country 'Christine's aura of mystery soon faded; anyway, she herself no longer believed in it' and she hopes he is nondescript enough to fade into the background himself.

In many of these tales Atwood deals with the strangeness of the everyday, not least in 'Rape Fantasies', which was removed from the US edition. In this tale, young women discuss imagined interactions with potential rapists, and they seem to believe they could meet and handle potential rapists through everyday interactions. What this and other tales highlight and expose, however, is a kind of collusion between the mundane, the homely and the bizarre. One of the women imagines that she might turn her purse/handbag out onto the lap of a potential rapist, who would help sort out the lemon squeezer to squirt in his eyes. It is ironic, funny and offbeat. The everyday intrudes on the strange to expose various myths about romance and to dramatise the polarities which operate in popular constructions of gender roles and relationships.

Ontological insecurity (insecurity about your identity and self) is a dominant theme in this collection. Some characters find it hard to feel real, to feel comfortable, in the constructed identities which they present to the world. In 'The Grave of the Famous Poet', a couple who visit a space where a famous poet lived end up feeling insubstantial and apart.

The collection develops themes about identity, gender, representation, performance, constraint and victimisation. It often takes a feminist stance and shows how traditional gender roles and behaviours are just as artificial as the constructions of journalists. Many of these themes continue in the next collection, although in the later stories they are structured and infused by fairytales and myths, critiquing the beliefs and behaviours upon which they are built.

Bluebeard's Egg (1983): feminist rewriting of fairytale and myth

The stories in *Bluebeard's Egg* put forward an argument that we mythologise and invest in narratives about our potential selves which we try to fulfil. The collection continues Atwood's earlier work of exploring the fairytales and myths which both constrict and construct women. Contemporary theorists and writers such as Marina Warner, Angela Carter and Suniti Namjoshi, among others, have also exposed cultural myths which construct versions of gendered roles and lock women into a subordinate role. In such roles, women tend to be portrayed either as vulnerable victims, lacking verve or imagination, or hags, stepmothers and rivals. Atwood deconstructs versions of myths and fairytales as they play themselves out in the everyday lives of ordinary people. Her favourite is that of the entrapped Canadian woman from 'Rapunzel', a fairytale in which a maiden is incarcerated in a high tower by a witch, then lets her hair down so a prince can climb up it to rescue her. If you do not believe in princes, or if you prefer to be an individual, Atwood suggests, you would not be so keen to let your hair down.

Some of the relationships are quite bizarre. 'Encounter with the Element Man' uses fantasy shape-shifting to identify ways in which people are constructed and constrained. It works through a series of small, half-imagined, half-remembered snapshots of encounters with a man who shape-shifts into different elemental forms and chaos. The couple in the tale are employed in census-taking but they only meet the lonely, confused and dispossessed – versions of themselves. Asserting commitment, he says he always loved her but she nonetheless senses this is a construction, a lie. His reactions are extreme, and in form, elemental. Forlorn, he leaves a trail of carbon tetrachloride. The woman's assertion that she loves him is undercut by reappearances, change, sometimes violent exchanges, and an overriding sense of their lack of connection.

In her essay 'Tales within Tales', Barbara Godard examines *Bluebeard's Egg* in relation to Atwood's œuvre, recognising it as growing from an intersection with Canadian folklore and encapsulating tales within tales.[12] She uses the work of Carole H. Carpenter,[13] which identifies rifts between literary cultures and sees that high literary culture is imposed, while folk culture is that of the 'other' indigenous people on which cultural studies have traditionally focused. Cultural studies of Canadian folk culture consider not the here and now and Anglophone expressions but the lives of First Nations people. In such work, there is a tradition of dialogue, the development of which was in part an attempt to create a national literature based on oral roots:

> [A]ttempts to create a national literature in Canada have developed on this interface of metropolis and hinterland, of written and oral literary models, a most frequent literary device being the 'battle of the books' which pits high European cultural models against the real narrative of North American experience.[14]

Carpenter suggests that high art in Canada somewhat ignores folklore traditions, the culture of the 'other', while according to Godard, Atwood, in *Bluebeard's Egg*: 'promotes to high culture some of the forms of oral narrative – anecdotes, local legends and natural narratives – currently alive in Toronto',[15] and also undertakes a serious analysis of indigenous folklore. Atwood is among several Canadian novelists who discuss the forms of cultural imperialism which codify languages and stories through writing them down and fixing them and engage with issues of: 'oral and written communication, social power and ideological manipulation'.[16] Godard comments on Atwood's talk at Harvard University entitled 'Canadian monsters: Some aspects of the supernatural in Canadian fiction', which considers the function of the Wendigo (a mythical Canadian forest animal). Carpenter suggests that the oral traditions of indigenous people function for Atwood as 'the Other', which she both experiences and appropriates. While Atwood establishes links with the writers who use oral and folktale references, she also distances herself from them by using both the Wendigo and Coyote as metaphors for landscapes, rather than seeing them as they are more often seen, as Tricksters. Many of her tales double back and expose their origins, using spatial techniques. Carpenter argues that folklore engagement with the past is evident in short stories by many Canadian writers. Some, including Margaret Laurence, also use oral traditions, including Celtic tales, from their own background.

Sharon Wilson's essay on *Bluebeard's Egg*[17] links Atwood's lesser-known work with her other writing, arguing that almost all her work makes extensive, often unnoticed references to a variety of fairytales. Atwood's watercolour 'Death as Bride', which depicts a skull-faced bride carrying red flowers spilling down her gown (I would argue they look like entrails as well as roses) indicates the handmaid's red and white clothing in *The Handmaid's Tale*. The watercolour, according to Atwood, is based on 'Fitches Bird', a Bluebeard folktale collected by the Brothers Grimm, which has a motif of a secret chamber which it is forbidden to enter. Wilson also mentions Bartok's opera 'Duke Bluebeard's Castle', Grimm's 'The Robber Bridegroom', and 'Tales of the Arabian Nights', each referred to on a tape Atwood made for her in August 1985. In Atwood's version, clever women deny male power, refuse laws, and face death in seeking after knowledge. In 'Fitches Bird', this involves the woman carrying an egg which must not be harmed. The bride is taken by her sisters into the forbidden room, whereupon the egg transfers bloodstains, indicating to the bridegroom that they have gone against his wishes, and giving him an excuse to kill them. The clever third sister preserves the egg outside the room and fools him. She manages the bodies of her sisters and eventually both restores them and saves her own life. In 'Fitches Bird', the brides overcome and survive sexual power games. Here are recognitions of the dark other of the protagonist, twin selves, the murderer in the dark, an embodied enemy who might creep up. In this tale, her male stalker is a Frankenstein's monster alter ego. Atwood also plays with gender and genre limits and with forms of popular culture in 'Loulou or the Domestic Life of the Language', which Sturgess argues 'explicitly takes up the challenge of women's place in discourse'.[18] Loulou is a maternal figure to a group of poets whom she both literally and metaphorically nurtures. She is solid, on the side of nature, while the poets, professional manipulators of words, are positioned on the side of culture:

> Their favourite sport, while eating her meals, is defining and redefining her in terms she cannot understand: '*Marmoreal*,' one of them said … causing Loulou to make one of her frequent sorties into the dictionary to find out whether or not she'd been insulted.[19]

Just as she is a mother to them all, she is also their Muse, their sexual fantasy, their sexual object. The group around her kitchen table includes 'first husband and numerous other partners'.[20]

However, Atwood plays with the stereotyping of Loulou as Mother Earth and makes her more interesting than the men. The originality of the story is that Loulou escapes their definitions:

> as the focalizer, Loulou has singular definition and contours for the reader, whereas the poets are designated collectively and are seemingly interchangeable. What is more, the poets never find a fitting definition for Loulou; their poems are about her, but addressed to 'my lady,' 'my friend's lady,' 'my woman,' 'my wife,' 'my friend's wife'.[21]

Bluebeard's Egg replays a range of myths and fairytales exploring the damage people do to each other in relationships, the psychology and the pain. In 'Uglypuss', Joel and Becka suffer a dwindling relationship. She is seen as an irritating dependant. In response, she attacks Joel's front door with an egg, then takes out her anger on his beloved cat, Uglypuss. Hardly knowing what she does, she sprays the cat with boot spray and shoves it in a bin liner in a bin. This act of violent retribution against a pet illustrates how unbalanced the relationship has been. Joel picks up a predictable substitute, and Becka realises her losses. Life and energy leak away in the rain as Becka cannot even remember in which bin she left the cat. Relationships are unkind, apathetic, following lines set down in romances and fairytales but revealing the dullness and psychological cruelty beneath their structures and moves.

A claustrophobic, rather excessively stereotypical relationship unravels in 'Betty', whose life revolves around her husband Fred: 'Betty had almost nothing else to talk about' and: 'He unrolled from Betty's mouth like a long ribbon of soggy newspaper printed from end to end with nothing but the weather',[22] a most appropriate image for Fred's mundane life, which Betty, whose life is even more mundane, must rerun. It is a parody of coupledom. But Fred leaves Betty, despite her oatmeal cookies and wifely devotion, and eventually, after years of being the extra person at meals with friends, she suddenly changes her personality and becomes more assertive, but then dies. Fred is predictable, and Betty more mysterious, and together they enable the narrator to make different choices, since neither is the model she wishes to follow, preferring to be called intelligent, rather than good. Artifice and performance dominate relationships.

Yvonne, the painter of men's bodies in 'The Sunrise', tries on a variety of age-defying clothes and arranges herself in relationships like poses in paintings, occasionally appearing and disappearing, enjoying the sunrise as if each is her last, and always keeping control, like the sheathed razorblade in her paint box. These Atwood characters are guarded, vulnerable. They believe they control their representation but are actually victims of relationships. Each vignette explores potential and constraints, performances, poses, and endings.

Wilderness Tips (1991): moral wilderness and challenge

Wilderness Tips revisits some of the locations of *Surfacing*, particularly the bush and the city's outskirts. It focuses on relationships, their power, pain, lies and deceptions. In the opening story 'True Trash', a summer camp of young, romance-reading waitresses and wealthier schoolboys comes clumsily together, leaving one girl, Ronette (who always takes the romance stories seriously) pregnant and out of the picture, and another, Joanne, intrigued to tie up the loose knots of Ronette's story. Joanne re-meets Don, once 14-year-old Donny, and discovers he remembers a single sexual experience with Ronette, which must have led to Ronette's child. Joanne decides not to reopen their tale, instead treating it as a victim of bygone times and outdated moves.

This is effectively a moral wilderness in which individuals and couples find themselves, and which offers a challenge to constructions of selves in a literal and figurative wilderness. The 'wilderness tips' of the title tale is an ironic comment on the possibilities offered by survival guides, exposing the beliefs that tips might help someone to survive and interpret such a strange environment. Like many of Atwood's other stories, this first appeared in *The New Yorker*, along with 'Hairball', a story of twists and revenge in relationships, using a bizarre, women-oriented event and image. Kat, a professional woman involved in a long, fruitless relationship, enters the hospital for the removal of a benign tumour, an ovarian cyst which grows to represent versions of her own life, its choices and constraints. The cyst or 'hairball' containing hair, teeth and crushed bones is a substitute for the baby she will never bear in the work/power-based relationships she has had with the ever decreasingly named Gerald/Ger. It is also like an aborted child, a version of herself, preserved, shrunken, and sexless, now that, having fought her way to the top and the boss's bed, she is rejected and marginalised. Kat rejects her constrained life as mistress, and leaves Ger the hairball as a birthday gift. This both horrifies and exorcises him along with Kat's dependent version of self. As an act, it recalls the way Marian in *The Edible Woman* bakes a cake to represent a rejected version of herself as consumable.

Sturgess sees Atwood's *Wilderness Tips* as a critique of wilderness myths and agrees with Coral Ann Howells' interpretations of the treatments of identity and death within several of the stories. Atwood gives space to myths of wilderness and colonisation, national territory and appropriation, making up her revised nationalist ethos: 'wilderness is the major figure in Canadian iconography of landscape', according to Howells. In *'Surfacing* and *Survival* in the early 1970s wilderness is a sign of a distinctive national heritage, while in *Wilderness Tips* the myth of the wilderness collapses.'[23] Sturgess also makes comparisons with *Surfacing*, with: 'The linking of Canadian identity with landscape, which is expressed in the painting of the Canadian "Group of Seven" painters who align Canadian identity with its particular landscapes'.[24] *Wilderness Tips* focuses on accidents, losses, concerns about how we retell histories, the treachery of everyday life, and deceptions and doubts about the healing powers of nature.

Murder in the Dark (1983), *Good Bones* (1992): everyday myths and bizarre predictions

Atwood's next collections have been variously recoupled as *Murder in the Dark, Good Bones, Good Bones and Simple Murders,* and simply *Bones and Murders.* The tales develop an arch, ironic tone, in retelling fairytale and myth, speculating about constructions of the everyday, and the more bizarre. Her later collection, *The Tent* (2006), uses even shorter forms – flash fiction, drawing on and developing the interests and tone found in these surprising short fictions, and exploring similar themes about how we construct narratives, identities, versions of life, and how we are constrained by myths and cultural formations.

Nischik relates Atwood's form in these tales to the work of the poet Baudelaire because of the brevity and poetic qualities, the darkness and irony. In these two collections, Atwood introduces the Baudelairean prose poem, a hitherto unfamiliar genre in Anglo-Canadian literature, and makes a radical contribution to the

development of genre hybridisation. Looking closely at the texture
of the tales, Nischik sees:

> Atwood's 'poetics of inversion': her technique of undermining conven-
> tional thought patterns, attitudes, values, or textual norms by turning
> them on their heads. This leads to a multifaceted interplay between
> explicit and implicit meaning or, to put it another way, a prismatic mul-
> tiplication of sense.[25]

Representations are suggestive, intense and can be seen as satirical. Much of the wit and insight deployed in the scrutiny of other
people's work in her critical essays appears in her short fictions as
Atwood combines her skills to replay, invert, and use intertextual
references and inclusions, which depend on the reader knowing
original tales, and traditional constructions of versions of life, stories and narrative strategies. She uses feminist revisioning that can
be found in other second-wave feminist work, such as that by Suniti
Namjoshi and Angela Carter, particularly *The Bloody Chamber* collection (1979) and Jeanette Winterson's use of Renaissance texts and
fairytale in *Sexing the Cherry* (1989). Atwood and these other writers
seek to undercut the constraints of beliefs embedded in and taught
through traditional tales. Often they deliberately change the gender
or sexuality of the characters involved. Refusing traditional gender
role stereotyping, they expose undertones and sub-plots, and offer
alternative perspectives and endings.

Focusing on inversion, Nischik identifies 'Worship', 'Liking Men',
'Iconography' and 'Gertrude Talks Back' as key texts which allow
the past to be revisited with irony. 'Atwood's subversive poetics of
inversion defamiliarizes, irritates, disturbs, and amuses, opening up
explanatory chasms as soon as it closes them.'[26]

She is the 'murderer' of conventional stories, which are like
mirrors to that conventionality. Her use of prose poetry allows a
meticulous, controlled expression.

Sharon Wilson explores the fairytale and myth which infuse
Atwood's work, making comparisons between flash fiction or
sudden fiction (flash fiction is a 750-word story; sudden fiction =
1750 words). She notes that Atwood uses the prose poem earlier
in 'Marrying the Hangman' (*Two-Headed Poems II*, 1978, pp. 48–51)
and 'True Romances' (*True Stories*, 1981, pp. 40–4), and even in sections of 'Circe/Mud Poems' (*You Are Happy*, 1974). In flash fictions,
length and use of a minimum of short story characteristics are not

the only defining characteristics. Significance is understood in 'a flash'. Flash fiction offers at least the outline of story, plot (including temporal movement that may or may not be chronological), scene, and characterisation.[27]

The play with narrative structure, character, event and plotline is dependent on our knowing some sources, whether high art or popular culture, and on our awareness of the different ways such familiar narratives play out in different cultures. Wilson, a specialist in fairytale structures, reveals her own background in the work of the structuralists and formalists such as Propp and Lévi-Strauss (although she does not reference them here), in which the variety of versions of development of familiar plot lines and formulae are analysed. In Lévi-Strauss's case, this is partly in order to relate to a social and cultural inflection and context. Atwood's 'message', as such, in these fictions often critiques culturally produced values and belief systems. Some of this is discussed later with our consideration of *The Tent*, but what is visible in these earlier tales is the popular romance, the Hollywood formulae, belief in the American Dream, as well as those gender and power-related narratives and readings which infuse versions of the fairytales and folk tales 'Little Red Riding Hood' or 'The Little Red Hen'. Wilson considers the archetypal forms and formulae of Atwood's murder tales: the ways that John, Mary, and friends in 'Happy Endings' would eventually end up dying in every conceivable plot, no matter how faked.[28]

Prose poems emphasise language. Flash fiction can be lyrical. Wilson refutes critical versions of Atwood's play with gender stereotypes as 'male bashing', and instead points to subtleties which move beyond the victim position, to enable choices and agency. She sees as radical and enabling Atwood's use of a wide range of textual forms, genres and formulae, including the fairytale. Atwood's versions are able to undercut the cultural and social messages upon which such tales are built and which they reinforce:

> Through the interweaving, regendering, and parodying of varied genres and subgenres – including antifiction, metafiction, revisioned folk and fairy tales, myths, and other canonical texts; fables; parables; monologues; popular romance; biography; autobiography; theology; speculative, science or revenant fiction; recipes; advice; thriller, and adventure stories – Atwood's intertextual play in *Good Bones* undercuts cultural determinism.[29]

Plot, characters, point of view, motifs and themes all deploy intertextual references. Atwood uses parodic versions of familiar figures, including harpies, Rapunzel, the ugly stepsister, the witch
and the stepmother. All get to talk back, explain their roles and
challenge. The 'sometimes nameless, unlucky, and unloved'[30] come
into their own here. In 'Unpopular Gals', the ugly sister resents her
name, '"Life isn't fair," she says.' She loved the Prince more than
Cinderella, enough to cut off her foot to fit the shoe, and all she got
in the end was suffering and poor treatment at the hands of readers.
It is an anti-romance, since 'all my love ever came to was a bad end.
Red-hot shoes, barrels studded with nails. That's what it feels like,
unrequited love.'[31] Other tales directly indict cruelties meted out to
the female body, by parodying and taking to literal extremes some
familiar practices. In 'The Female Body', the writer, asked to write
on the 'topic' of the female body, deals with her own body as if it
were a version of the topic and discusses blow-ups, pornographic
examples, illustrative medical versions, Barbie and her wardrobes.
There is interesting slippage between the sense that objects such as
door knockers and nut crackers are shaped like parts of the female
body and that female bodies can be used as objects:

> The Female Body has many uses. It's been used as a door-knocker, a
> bottle-opener, as a clock with a ticking belly, as something to hold up
> lampshades, as a nutcracker, just squeeze the brass legs together and out
> comes your nut ...[32]

'It does not merely sell, it is sold.'[33] In such increasingly hard-hitting
comments, Atwood focuses on issues to do with fetishisation,
pornography, rape, and the brutalising of the female body, as does
feminist Andrea Dworkin. The polemic is interwoven in the parody,
and the intertextual referencing and humour carry the weight of the
argument. The text argues that the objective male brain finds it difficult to come to terms with the existence of female complexity, so the
final ironic advice is to incarcerate the female body as usable icon:

> Catch it. Put it in a pumpkin, in a high tower, in a compound, in a cham-
> ber, in a house, in a room. Quick, quick, stick a leash on it, a lock, a chain,
> some pain, settle it down so it can never get away from you again.[34]

Wilson identifies many of Atwood's characters as Tricksters,
who move beyond Jung's archetypes and offer instead reversals

of stereotypical characters,[35] while Sherrill Grace's 'Atwood's Postmodern Fairytale' (1994)[36] explores how she overturns traditional tales and exposes their subtexts. The human imagination is

> turning facts into fictions and friends into enemies, and projecting a violent inner world of turbulent anxieties and conflicting desires upon an external world and the people who inhabit it; *Good Bones* shifts to inherited stories, Gertrude's version of the killing of Hamlet's father, the long monologue of 'little hen'.[37]

The stories are arch and funny. In 'Making a Man', several domestic versions of construction are played out with the deft saving hand of the housewife at work, in the creation of a man who is 'an item that is both practical and decorative'.[38] Examples are the gingerbread man variety, who wants to be off on a motorbike at the first chance and needs tying down. The best part is that (literally) 'these guys are scrumptious!'[39] The final example is to make the best of what you have around already, which sounds like a piece of *Home and Garden* advice on domestic interiors: 'just coat your hubby with plaster of Paris and ...'[40] 'Hubby' domesticates and pokes fun at coupledom, and the objectification is a reversal of the usual popular cultural representations of women.

Conclusion

Perhaps surprisingly, there is much less critical comment on the stories than on the novels. Atwood's short stories deal variously with the role of the writer and forms of narrative as they affect ways in which we see the world. The earlier tales are overtly feminist, the later ones equally so but shorter, more parodic. She often chooses myths, legends and famous works on which to base her own stories, and focuses on rewriting fairytales and popular or traditional versions of narratives, many of which undermine, objectify or deny women. Atwood uses intertextuality throughout, but most particularly with the more recent stories, referencing directly sources we are likely to recognise in order to expose their subtexts. Many tales refuse the victim position, and offer critical alternatives. Short fictions provide opportunity for experiment and as we shall see, many of the ideas expressed and explored in the tales develop further in the novels.

The subjects of the next chapter, *Life Before Man* and *Bodily Harm*, have been considered realistic and politically engaged rather than Gothic and mythic. The first is concerned with mundane life in Toronto, relationships and their failings; the second is Atwood's only postcolonial novel, dealing with cultural misunderstandings and mistranslations.

4

Violence, Trauma and History: *Life Before Man* (1979), *Bodily Harm* (1981)

This chapter focuses on two novels which are considered examples of Atwood working in a realist mode. *Life Before Man* captures the daily detail of a particular moment in Toronto life, unfulfilling relationships, and the texture of the everyday mundane, and *Bodily Harm* focuses on Rennie, a journalist recovering from cancer, who gets caught up in the Caribbean in ways of life she sometimes dangerously misreads. Each novel deals with concerns about relationships and violence, including bodily violence and decay. Reviewers and critics consider debates about Atwood's use of realism and fantasy in both novels. Coral Ann Howells suggests that *Life Before Man* resembles George Eliot's *Middlemarch* (1874) because it supports a sense that life is controlled by fate, by determinism, set against individuals' views that they are in control of their own lives.[1]

Jane Brooks Bouson looks at issues of pornography,[2] and Molly Hite considers ways that *Bodily Harm* focuses on writing the female body, and on healing.[3] Atwood utilises the strategies of the female novelist and the Gothic, each element developed further in later texts, but usually seen as irrelevant to most readings of *Life Before Man* (except those of Sharon M. Wilson,[4] for example). Diana Brydon's postcolonial reading of *Bodily Harm*[5] and interpretations of Lesje's role as outsider and immigrant in *Life Before Man* show how Atwood scrutinises the dangers of Otherising, i.e. constructing those who are different as Other, foreign, and finding them both fascinating and dangerous.

Life Before Man (1979)

Praised for its perceptive realism in the US, *Life Before Man* was considered both a very Canadian novel and Margaret Atwood's first realist and therefore (according to some) best novel. Even its melancholy was judged powerful. However, not all the reviewers were positive. Its concerns with everyday relationships relate the personal to the political and highlight the tensions between survival and extinction, embodied in the dinosaur image central to the location, the Royal Ontario Museum, and to questions about what lasts of people and their relationships.

Early reviews

Life Before Man opens with the aftermath of a suicide. In Canada, almost half the reviewers found the novel banal, lacking compassion, hopeless, Atwood's coldest and bleakest novel, but nonetheless praised its perceptive realism.

Life Before Man focuses on the lives of ordinary Torontonians caught up in a series of largely disappointing but everyday relationships. It was Atwood's first book to be widely and positively reviewed in Britain, with twice as many English and Scottish reviews as *Surfacing* (1972), *Lady Oracle* (1976) and *The Edible Woman* (1969). Judith McCombs draws together a number of reviews, including Philip Howard, Peter Kemp and Herbert Michael, who praised Atwood's 'psychological and evolutional acute wit and symbols'.[6] This suggests that *Life Before Man* was closer to British than American traditions, as unlike the American reviewers, the British male reviewers did not seem to expect sympathetic characters, strong men or happy endings.

The most locally focused of Margaret Atwood's novels, it is possibly the most Canadian in outlook, and historically preserved in the 1970s. It is a tale of social mores and manners, of both emotion and lack of emotion, of people whose lives are intertwined yet for the most part lacking in passion. The novel deals with Elizabeth, who has an affair with Chris (Greek in origin), who commits suicide. Elizabeth is married to Nate, a failed artist, who is having an affair with Lesje, a Ukrainian/Russian immigrant, who has a lover, William. Elizabeth, Chris and Lesje all work in the Royal Ontario Museum. The focus is on life before man, but critics have felt the

novel is lifeless. Its concern with prehistoric layers, fossils, preservation and the banalities of relationships seems deadening, only
enlivened by the subtext of Lesje's imaginative life and the complex
manipulations of relationships. George Woodcock reacted against
the novel's version of life as not worth cherishing.[7] Sherrill Grace
saw a selfish view, a grey and empty book,[8] although in 1981–86
critics praised its moral realism and heroes' struggles.

Nate is seen by reviewers as sensitive, muddled, and by Marylou
Antonnelli as a realistic, 1970s Toronto figure.[9] Dave Billington's
'A novel of bleak brilliance' finds *Life Before Man* a carefully observed,
astute, serious but scarcely optimistic examination of Canadian and
American middle-class relationships, and gauges Elizabeth as a
carnivorous bitch; Nate, a dithering but well-intentioned lawyer;
Lesje is 'a willowy palaeontologist who believes in life, sees the
characters as specimens and Toronto, all well observed – so much so
that outsiders might be alienated'.[10] Carol Corbel in 'Surfacing from
a damaging decade' considers it fully realised, perceptively 'slicing'
through women, as women have historically through men.[11] It lacks
a moral centre, is clumsy, a study in shame but compassionate. Other
reviewers, however, see the characters as insignificant and unmoti-
vated. Several male Vancouver reviewers found it cold, dissecting
and selfish in its view of marriage. Paul Delaney, for example, notes
in 'Grim, nasty loves' that the leading characters include 'a wife who
does not know how to live, and husband who does not know how to
love ...'.[12] The only life comes from an offbeat, appealing and bless-
edly unmarried Lesje, but the reviewer sees her as becoming lost.
Robert Fulford finds the characters absorbing, the style readable
and the events a meticulously realistic portrayal of 1970s middle-
class relationships.[13] Some reviewers misunderstood or disliked the
dinosaur metaphor, and were clearly divided on their like or dislike
of the characters, possibly, one imagines, in relation to how far they
resembled themselves. For McCormick, marriage between Nate
and Elizabeth seems ramshackle, and the characters ageing; the
void affairs between Nate, Elizabeth, Lesje and Chris 'are more like
collisions than love affairs, accidental and motiveless'. McCormick
thinks perhaps the short episodes are to blame. It has a bland topic
with 'no real message, where the characters go through bumbling
rituals of life'.[14] Sam Solecki agrees, admires the novel but sees the
relationships deepening the pessimism and 'ultimately irrelevant
to most of our lives'.[15] The realism of this novel is acclaimed but
it is noted that no one gets any pleasure from life or death, while

feminism, nationalism and political activism are all discredited. One other reviewer actually calls it 'Dinosaurs in the wasteland',[16] finding the novel pointless and cynical, haphazard, with its dull days and its drifting characters who are dinosaurs unable to adapt. However, Adele Wiseman celebrates it as engrossing, mischievous and ingenious, the dated characters encapsulating each other's aims. She sees the Ontario museum setting as appropriate and notes that, as an erudite poet, Atwood has provided a title from Lévi-Strauss, i.e. 'humanism does not begin with oneself, but puts the world before life, life before man, and respect for others before self-interest'.[17] So here, life is revealed as a moral search for how to live. Even the cold, rather manipulative Elizabeth eventually accepts the need for putting the human into place when her oppressive, controlling aunt is dying. There is little transformation for the characters.

Politics

In an interview,[18] Atwood explains that there is a realistic political analysis in *Life Before Man*, and that her political commitment as a writer and her support of feminism are all part of human and bio-logical rights, in a context in which both nationalism and feminism are being widely discarded. She suggests that you can decide what is wrong in society by seeing what the characters do and what is missing and that through their debates about engagement the novel deals with the political in everyday Canadian life.

Elizabeth is strong, alone and sees politics as a boys' game, while Nate has lost faith in politics and Lesje rejects it for palaeontology. Brooks Bouson argues that the novel is founded on a deep-seated cultural pessimism set against a backdrop of disasters, environ-mental problems and political violence, 'more particularly it enu-merates the horrors human beings inflict upon each other in the name of politics'.[19] Bruce King in 'More than Novelists' finds it a 'fully social and evolutional novel with divided personalities, power plays, fantasies and sex, social roles and identity'. He says it shows how 'power, family, class and women shape … the main characters' sense of reality'.[20] King sees Elizabeth as growing away from her lovers and Lesje as a second-generation immigrant, a good worker. Valerie Miner praises its political and psychological accuracy, the way it creates multiple perspectives and emphasises the characters' isolation; for her it is about challenge.[21]

Canadian setting and themes

It is also very much a novel of Toronto and Canada, and of its time. Human likes the Canadian setting, audience and science,[22] while Janice Kulyk Keefer argues that it captures the dullness and the ordinary, representative of the limitations of 1970s Toronto, a city which North Americans identify with its dominant weather and empty lives concerned with:

> a very few lower-middle-class urbanites: deracinated, isolated, miserably pressured by the mundane. Her terrain of this novel's fictive world is irremediably flat, dun-coloured, harshly-lit; the weather foul, and tolerable accommodation near-impossible to find.[23]

It seems to appeal to readers who find 'a mirror of their own inert, constricted and bewildering lives'. They were '"sucked in" as surely as brontosauri into tar sands'.[24]

Life Before Man is a novel with a message, however, and not just one of anti-romanticism. In its concerns with fossils and everyday life it illustrates and critiques moral impoverishment. Rather worryingly, perhaps, in 1976, Atwood explained that, for her, writing was in part 'an exploration of where in reality I live',[25] so that *Life Before Man* can be seen as mapping much of that reality in downtown Toronto. Its main location, the Museum, functions as a collection of memories, a giant brain, unlike the earlier *Surfacing*, where the city is seen as an artifice. There are no lakes to be submerged in or reborn from in *Life Before Man*:

> the closed circle, or rather oval, of Queen's Park is the closest we come to wilderness, and even that Atwoodian *locus classicus*, the ravine, whose depth, darkness and solitude offer dramatic possibilities for destruction or salvation, appears only peripherally. No magical transformations take place in this novel.[26]

It is also specifically Canadian in other ways. Miner identifies Canadian survival themes, and that 'Elizabeth, Nate and Lesje all proceed through the darkness with intelligent and humorous resignation, aware that their survival has been a challenge since life before man'.[27] Blake Morrison notes that Lesje's 'sleeping beauty' love would suit D. H. Lawrence, but it is ambivalent in Atwood, as love is messy and complex.[28] He also sees it as a Canadian book, with its ecology-conscious central metaphor, and its typical Canadian nostalgia for an uncorrupted, pre-human nature. Atwood's insight prevents the heavy symbols from overwhelming the middle-class material. Peter Oecoott's review continues the theme of recognising its Canadian characteristics and suggests the work defines Canadian traditions of survival and failure, showing that being your own woman is not always satisfactory: 'with chilly compassion and even colder wit, Atwood exposes the interior lives of her specimens, the flies within a giant web, or perhaps trying to free their wings from amber'.[29] Oecoott continues the helpless insect theme, and judges Nate's livelihood and behaviour as a man as ineffective.

Romance and mundane relationships

Critics variously find the novel's focus on everyday realities and the mundaneness of relationships pessimistic or dully realistic. Jane Brooks Bouson sees Atwood taking up a familiar theme and 'deliberately interrogating bourgeois romantic illusions'.[30] There are domestic and sexual battles, women's sense of powerlessness and rage and 'a uniquely female pleasure of the text through its enactment of women's domestic and sexual revenge against men'.[31] In Brooks Bouson's view, it is very much a novel about the sick body politic as reflected in the harmed lives of the women characters. The narrative design is open to multiple, varied, conflicting interpretations, as Atwood 'positions her readers as privileged witnesses to the inner lives of her characters.'[32]

The novel revolts against the romance plot, and Elizabeth and Lesje, the two main female protagonists, are complementary figures. It 'presents a feminist-dialogic challenge to traditional novelistic discourse'[33] because it upsets the social order, flaunts myths of romantic attraction and love, and offers us strong women and a passive main male character. Nate is passive in the war for domestic and sexual mastery, divides his women up into persecutors and those who rescue him, and imagines them in terms of mass popular cultural fantasy. Rosellen Brown praises the novel and thinks the suffering Elizabeth 'challenges the reader to decide whether characters need to be liked' or understood. She sees the book as realistic, 'like a satisfying treatise for all lives that are far more true than what we wanted or expected'.[34] Although it is realist rather than Gothic, *Life Before Man* compares with Atwood's other novels and short stories, exposing the dangerous fictions of romance constraining women and men.

Survival and extinction

Survival and extinction emerge as central themes. In this respect, Marilyn French likes the novel because 'all of the characters are decimated.'[35] French finds Elizabeth powerful, cruel yet pitiable, suffering and surviving and Nate brilliantly depicted as liberal. Only Nate's mother sees beyond the self to know she must change the world, suggesting that they may either be becoming extinct or be part of some new beginning. Others hardly glimpse her vision.

The title might refer to Toronto man as not quite evolved. *The Kirkus Review* suggests that the novel is minutely designed and that Atwood writes 'poet's novels with controlling metaphors here of the extinction of the era',[36] while for Victoria Glendinning, the evolution affecting the main characters, traced though aunts, grandparents and children in the novel, is skilfully, precisely ordered and controlled.[37]

Form and language

Life Before Man is very particular in its accounts of frustrated relationships, joyless, paralysed communications, and dreary lives, which Kulyk Keefer finds perfectly caught in the mimetic quality of the prose, defined as having 'mimetic accuracy, its emphatic minimalism of tone and technique, and its masterly deployment of language – those "black, sluggish, lethal words"'. Although it is popular, it is one of 'her least typical texts, whose formula she has not repeated'.[38] Individuals are reduced to similarities, and language mimics this:

> [P]olyphony is subsumed into monotone: Lesje, Nate and Elizabeth may be quite different people, from a variety of backgrounds, and they may possess contrasting preoccupations and expectations, but they are hardly done 'in different voices'. What the reader hears, regardless of the occasional slip into first person narration by Elizabeth, is not the voice of individual characters, but that of their common predicament, as transcribed by a disinterested authorial observer.[39]

Instead of the distinctive storytelling voices of *The Blind Assassin* (2000), *The Robber Bride* (1993) and *Cat's Eye* (1988), the third-person narration distances us as readers from the lives of these bleak and dull, everyday people. The language catalogues them and goes little further, rather like Lesje's job and that of Chris, Elizabeth's lover, while all Elizabeth does is manage, and Nate whittle away. They are unsympathetic, Keefer argues, detached from ordinary life, and even Lesje, with her semi-fantasy work, seems very Otherised, since William distances her because of her foreignness.

The use of the present tense is seen by some critics as flat, rather than vital. There are no certainties or directions. It is a constrictive fictional world. Sherrill Grace argues that it offers no redemption since Atwood refuses her romance conventions and shows only 'the empty inconclusiveness of modern marriage and urban existence'.[40] It is also her darkest novel, because it makes life so very dull, although it can be argued that its fine attention to detail and restraint of the Gothic imagination are technically refined and appropriate.

Nate and Elizabeth are incapable of movement, paralysed; human actions and intentions are marginal, set against the museum's cataloguing of time past. For Atwood: 'far from representing some heroic mammalian advance upon dinosaurs, human beings are in fact a frighteningly inferior species' – Lesje even muses that man may have been invented by viruses 'to give them a convenient place to live'.[41]

Frank Davey sees the style and tone of *Life Before Man* as didactic, and that Atwood's choice of patterning and sequencing, her rationalist use of fiction, work against her.[42] However, Atwood argues that 'Story-telling at its most drastic is the story of the disaster which is the world.'[43]

Much of the critical response to the novel is contained in immediate reviews, as it is rarely a main focus for any full-length appraisal. The Gothic texts, and those more overtly challenging gender roles, are considered more popular subjects for major critical attention. Critics were very divided about *Life Before Man*, some preferring Atwood's more rational and realistic style, some finding it dull and prosaic. Some sensed that the very dullness was Atwood's main target and that the most mundane and catalogued museum exhibits are the relationships and characters.

Bodily Harm (1981)

Critics are also divided over *Bodily Harm*, Atwood's only novel to date which is set abroad, in the Caribbean. It engages fully with issues of postcolonialism and colonialism, the personal and the political expressed in the body of the protagonist and those to whom she relates. As with the earlier *Lady Oracle*, in *Bodily Harm* Atwood uses a protagonist who, as a writer herself, questions the fictionality and certainties of her own life and, in this instance, of her whole body. Rennie, a Toronto journalist from a very ordinary suburb, Griswold, escapes her life in Canada for a fictional Caribbean island where she attempts to cope with the after-effects of an operation for breast cancer. Her relationship with her partner, Jake, has often been problematic, as he needs to control her, but the life she meets in the Caribbean is far from that of a tourist or holidaymaker. The place is as riven, as cut up as her suffering body, and violent beneath its tourist façade. From being a self-absorbed tourist journalist coasting through, recording superficialities, she gradually learns to engage. Rennie has a relationship with a local man, Paul, and through various mistakes in interpreting the culturally charged behaviour of people in this troubled island, she ends up in jail. It is a significant moment, when her emotions and values are stirred and she learns to empathise with Lora, a woman friend met in prison, who has been beaten. The experience transforms Rennie. She stops merely reporting on superficialities, starts to develop a more authentic response to events and she moves towards bodily wholeness.

Early reviews

Early reviews were divided, introducing concerns about Canadian life and the Caribbean, the challenges of the political, colonial and postcolonial setting and events, and relating the riven body of Rennie to that of the island; all themes are developed in later responses. Helen Hoy finds *Bodily Harm*'s 'assaults on middle class self-absorption'[44] banal. Peter Kemp (in the *Times Literary Supplement* notes its mordant satire, its mature, accurate view of life, arguing that the cancer vocabulary applies both to the body and to politics, and sees Rennie as a two-ply person, her Canadian context concealing her anxieties.[45] John Mellor's 'Sweet Canadian' views it as a guide to Canadian life, the 'sweet Canadian, young, sexually active, vulnerability of small-town life',[46] speculating that the novel may end with release or distaste – and that its compelling story, like that of the ex-colonies, is still tainted with a history of subjugation. Several reviewers identify undertones of the ways in which the novelist Graham Greene (1904–91; author of thrillers and other novels, including *Our Man in Havana*, 1958) has portrayed life in the Caribbean, and Martin Seymour Smith, in 'Women often with Men',[47] argues that Atwood uses Graham Greene's intrigue and espionage as framework, creating a metaphorical thriller, an allegory of how the feminine becomes enmeshed in masculine ways. George Woodcock suggests that readers will like the artistry and the ways in which Atwood reveals different kinds of evil: 'not the drama but the banality, the negative innocence that is the most noticeable characteristic'[48] of real evil, which Rennie meets on the island.

Michael Dixon rejects *Bodily Harm* as a formulaic fiction of plots, power and victims, and criticises the novel's focus on sexism, because it suggests that 'all men are perverted thugs'. He argues that we are all stuck in the cell, and that Rennie only uses her ability to write to 'serve class-hatred based on sexual stereotypes.'[49] Margaret Dyment in *Quarry* enjoys the novel's entertaining humour,[50] but finds Rennie unconvincing, while Sal Enesin in 'Recent Fiction' finds it a sharp, profound, fun thriller, and that Rennie emerges 'ready to pay attention' to life.[51] Margaret Forster praises the novel as a brave and witty cancer survival tale which avoids the maudlin and faces up to how cancer affects the psyche.[52] Rennie knows the illness will affect her way of seeing and goes to the Caribbean to learn from it. Kate Fullbook's review also commends the book as morally serious, gripping and brilliant.[53]

While some critics concentrate on one element of the novel, others recognise the links between the personal female body of Rennie, which suffers and changes, and the body politic of the Caribbean in which there is such an immediate confrontation with corruption and violence that conventional forms of writing such as travel pieces cannot capture.

Feminist readings: fiction and the body politic

The novel is feminist, political and postcolonial, dealing with the female body recuperating after breast cancer and partial mastec-tomy and seeking wholeness of self and identity. Rennie's relation-ship with men is also in need of some revision. Rennie oscillates between Jake, her boyfriend, who treats her as a sex object in an eroticised controlling manner and her surgeon, Daniel, whom she sees as a father figure. As she starts to learn to understand her own freedoms with Paul, the man she relates to on the island, so she regains a sense of bodily wholeness.

Sharon Wilson compares Atwood's paintings to images in *Bodily Harm*. In 'A Note on Margaret Atwood's Visual Art in *Bodily Harm*',[54] she explores two images, including 'Untitled watercolour of microscope image', designed by Atwood as a possible cover for the novel, which features a scientific slide of a cut through a cell. This image suggests the invaded cells of the novel, Rennie's mastectomy and the revolutionary splitting up of the islands St Agatha from St Antoine at secession. Another image, 'Amanita Caesarea, egg, cross section on a cloud' was drawn in 1980 by Margaret Atwood and indicates cuts, imperialism, sexual violations, and wounds, whether personal, Roman, American or British. Rennie herself associates her cut open body with the picture of a cut melon on the wall of the Sunset Inn and feels her body will leak through stitches, with a decayed hidden past seeping out as worms.

Floating free, Rennie feels alienated but has a sense of the 'I' in the world and of what she could become. She also draws events into her own life and compares them with her existence back in Toronto so that they act as a kind of revelation of all she ignored or missed in her previously sheltered existence. She compares the shooting of Dr Minnow with the disruption and danger, death and battering of her friend Lora, as if it were a revelation of the hidden violence of her seemingly mundane existence in Griswold, Toronto, as a younger woman, and asks 'Did Toronto exist?'[55] Her self is divided but her operation, her experiences on the island and her reflections on what happens to Lora lead to her seeing things anew, including the difference between African American and Afro-Caribbean people, and the way in which Paul, in his lovemaking, can give her back a sense of her body by acting without either commitment or disgust.

Most critics of *Bodily Harm* affirmed its human compassion and moral responsibility as well as its feminist heroes, although, for example, Jennifer Waelti-Walters saw an 'unrelentingly vicious' political subtext of 'overt misogyny'.[56] Those celebrating the feminist voice include Roberta Rubenstein[57] and Lorna Irvine,[58] who praised *Bodily Harm*'s refusal of patriarchal femininity and its subversive life-affirming language. Mary K. Kirtz saw Atwood as didactic and morally humanist, celebrating her heroes' emotional and spiritual connection with humanity.[59]

Postfeminist readings and interventions on genre

Postfeminist readings tackle issues of authenticity and explore
both the ways in which Rennie learns to engage with events and
write something more than fashion or superficial travel pieces, and
simultaneously rejects being treated as a sex object in postfeminist
culture. *Bodily Harm* also engages with the ways in which genres
and forms of writing can or cannot represent. It intervenes on the
formulae of genre fictions, including the romance plot.

Brooks Bouson views the novel as a warning in the context of the
1980s emergent backlash against feminism and concurrent increase in
the visibility of sado-masochistic, violent and pornographic imagery
in mass culture. *Bodily Harm* is an 'exposé of the misogyny and power
politics underlying masculine culture in the "postfeminist'" 1980s'.[60]
Atwood explores ways in which a version of the male gaze transforms women into 'sexual commodities': 'If women are objectified
and marginalized by masculine desire, they are also, as the narrative
graphically depicts, bodily dissected and psychically damaged.'[61]

Brooks Bouson elaborates on the theme of psychic harm or 'mind-
rape' and argues that, contrary to Jake's claim that a man cannot 'rape
a woman's mind without her consent',[62] the narrative reveals the mind-
rape of women like Rennie who, through their culturally induced passivity and desire to please men, become collaborators in their own
sexual exploitation. Rennie's body is a blank sheet, a cultural text on
which Jake inscribes the narrative of male desire: 'Reduced to an erotic
object, she is both shaped and interpreted by the male gaze.'[63]

The reality and metaphor of surgery are linked to sadomasochistic pornography. Rennie feels wounded, and disassociated from her
own body when she tries to make love with Jake after her operation.
She imagines that her diseased, cancerous breast, with its scarred
flesh, bears the marks of the men who have probed and cut into it:

> Atwood has described *Bodily Harm* as an 'anti-thriller'; the intertextual
> use of murder mysteries, spy thrillers, and children's detective board
> games highlights the primary narrative of the novel, which concerns
> the gradual awakening of political awareness of a detached 'life-
> styles' journalist, appropriately described by Sharon Rose Wilson as a
> 'life-tourist'.[64]

Rennie's own compulsion to package and avoid reality, to trivialise
even personal crises by turning them into 'pieces' makes her hold

life at bay for much of the novel. She counters the threat of the anonymous rapist by attempting an article on pornography, and when faced with the medical diagnosis of cancer, she unsuccessfully attempts to reduce and escape her experience in the usual way: 'as she walked home she was still thinking in the ways she used to. For instance, she could do a piece on it. "Cancer, the Coming Thing." *Homemakers* might take it, or *Chatelaine*. How about "the Cutoff Point"?'[65]

Comparing *Bodily Harm* to short stories, particularly 'Travel Pieces', Stanley S. Atherton[66] sees it exposing the harsh realities of the Caribbean as far from an island paradise. The travel writer in Atwood's short story substitutes clichéd fantasy for the pollution and violence which readers would not want to know about, and Rennie does the same initially, avoiding action in the prison cell while Lora is violently beaten up.

After Lora's savage beating by prison guards, Rennie works up the courage to touch her battered body, so making herself aware that she is not exempt from pain and involvement. She resolves to report what she has seen on the islands, which involvement runs counter to her mother's insistence that she should look but not touch.

For Brooks Bouson, the relationship between the two central female characters is a commentary on power and social class. Lora's tale is important here because it is a testimony to pain and development, a parallel to Rennie's own bodily pain. Reparation takes place in the connection between the two women and is emphasised in the imagery of hands, symbolising healing. This female, positive-oriented development undermines conventional narrative plots, in which males are rescuers. Although the novel does not offer any final rescue by anyone, it does suggest development through Rennie's connection with Lora and her growing self awareness.

There can be no conventional happy ending, rather, according to Alice Palumbo, Atwood works with ideas of the recuperative power of storytelling in *Bodily Harm*, as she does later in *The Handmaid's Tale* (1985).

The postcolonial and Canada

Atwood rarely deals with the postcolonial or locations aside from North America and so the setting and the politics of this novel come under scrutiny. Writers and critics are divided on their views of the depiction of the Caribbean because of a general concern that the use of settings in cultures which have experienced colonialism or imperialism could repeat a kind of touristic, superficial reaction to difference. Such a reaction takes a number of forms: ignoring the difference, finding it quaint or lush, fertile, ripe for development, misunderstanding it, or refusing to engage at all. In 'Tale of Two Colonies', [67] Blaire Clark sees this as a novel about a mundane suburban Canadian abroad. Rennie and her 'struggling southern Ontario decent' Griswold background (Griswold is both an area, suburban and ordinary, and a complacent worldview) is strangely sophisticated, as is Toronto itself.

Some critics have found it problematic that men in the Caribbean are portrayed as stereotypically brutal in their treatment of women and point out that the island politics highlights gaps between culturally affected popular expectations, stereotypes and harsher realities.

Others, however, are more supportive of Atwood's engagement with difference, stereotyping and representation and recognise that the novel deals with the contemporary politics of colonialism, colonised people and the colonies and that Atwood exposes the ways in which the tourist gaze tends to idealise or stereotype, before revealing some of the more immediate, real problems of political unrest, brutality and poor medical care.

Men and women are interestingly divided over their responses to the Caribbean, political plot, or the women and body plot. Anatolia Broyard's 'And Toronto Too' relates Rennie's bodily suffering with that of the developing world and notes that 'Rennie begins to realise that we all live in a "third world" now', [68] while Roselyn Brown compares the body and politics, arguing that Rennie's confronting of the politics and depravity in the Caribbean 'puts her self-absorbed despair – or her narcissism – in larger perspective'. [69] She suggests that the fragmented narrative shapes Rennie's confusions and attempts to make sense of what is happening to her and around her. The unnamed reviewer of *The Westerly* provides an American perspective, criticising 'self righteous' Canadian life, but comments on Rennie's postcolonial viewpoint, and how she is forced into awareness with Lora's beating in a way which resembles responses to scenes in Inuit tales. [70] Rennie is implicated in the suffering and she grows aware not merely in terms of the content but the form, as a tourist who, enlightened after her experience, must become a citizen, forced to take responsibility when she returns to Canada.

Diana Brydon's fine essay 'Caribbean revolution and literary convention',[71] deals thoroughly with the expression of postcolonialism. She focuses on comparing the politics of colonialism, tourism and language with this novel and *The Prime Minister* (1994) by Austin Clarke (born 1934), finding both concerned with outsiders writing about outsiders. Atwood's novel considers ways in which suppression aims to silence journalism and how the Canadian writer's mind is blocked with journalistic illusions and forms when dealing with the Caribbean, despite the overt political oppression experienced there. *Bodily Harm*, for Brydon, combines 'images of the journalist who reacts but never acts with the tourist who sight sees but cannot see'.[72] She merges the museum, jail and tourist sites in arguing that tourists, bent on exploiting and consuming, are the 'new imperialists'. The novel's epigraph from John Berger's *Ways of Seeing* (1972), she suggests, enables us to see that the text challenges the stance of imperialist novels through a confrontation with the colonial 'heart of darkness'.

Brydon's later 'Atwood's Postcolonial Imagination: Reading *Bodily Harm*' updates this discussion, re-scrutinising *Bodily Harm* and arguing that it 'encodes its central character's efforts to come to terms with her repressive Canadian childhood and her breast cancer in the context of a Caribbean holiday disrupted by US interference in local politics'.[73] According to Brydon, Atwood's questioning of why the US feels justified in interfering predates much postcolonial criticism, such as 'Reading *National Geographic*' by Catherine Lutz and Jane Collins (1993), building on work by Tiffin, Lawson, and others. Brydon reminds us that Atwood's awareness of how literary institutions and the educational system promote colonialism leads her to become involved in decisions over what literature is taught and the ways it is discussed in Canada and how this could be altered to help develop a national sense of identity in opposition both to paternalistic British imperialism and the economic and cultural imperialism of the US.

It is a short step for Atwood from Canadian nationalism to involvement with Amnesty and PEN (http://www.internationalpen.org.uk/), the influential writing organisation which promotes literature in a variety of countries. Colonial habits of mind, Brydon reminds us, need to be questioned, deconstructed and rejected. This is the real challenge of postcolonialism. Globally, even institutional structures and commonsense assumptions about the world are implicated in imperial habits of mind. Investigating representations of the fractured Canadian subject would be useful in reading all of

Atwood's work, Brydon suggests. In *Bodily Harm*, Atwood speaks openly about such concerns.

The novel contributes to current debates about the future of post-coloniality and Canada's position within it, in a time of national migrations, when tourist travelling can be seen as the essence of, and one of the worst offshoots of colonialism. *Bodily Harm* reminds us of the human costs, lies, betrayals and the material suffering underlying what seems like freedom (for some). Linking Atwood to bell hooks, Brydon warns about travel as a new mode of imperialism,[74] and that while Rennie's experiences suggest these links, she lacks understanding herself and occupies a prison cell of the mind. For Brydon, hooks argues that much writing still speaks to continued fascination with the way white minds, particularly the colonial imperialist traveller, perceive blackness, and that there is still very little expressed interest in representations of whiteness in the black imagination, a critique which Helen Tiffin applies to *Bodily Harm*.[75]

Similarly, Marlene Nourbese Philip, a Caribbean Canadian woman of African descent, points out that 'in a racist, sexist and classist society the imagination left unexamined can and does service the wrong ideas of the time'.[76] Rennie is written through by such a society, as is shown when she comments on the meals which Paul produces and in her writing about tales of St Agatha and St Antoine, saints whose names are those of the islands.

There are some moments which invite reading in multiple ways, which may explain why critics are so divided about whether Atwood is merely reproducing another touristic critique or criticising such naïveté, and where her values lie, as differentiated from those of Rennie, her protagonist. Some moments presented as realistic, prompted by tourist arrogance about development and simplicity, are actually critical of such arrogance as naïve, complicit, destructive and dangerous. For example, Rennie's arrogant naïveté is exposed when she does not ask questions about the lack of a doctor or school, but focuses on a lack of American literacy in reporting Paul's misreading of a 'Long Life' milk carton. Rennie knows it merely represents the treatment undergone by the milk to preserve it rather than local belief that it will lead to a long life for them. Her misreading is a cultural confusion over the everyday and a form of cultural arrogance which fails to see beyond the quaintly foreign (and naïve). The issue in this instance must surely be that any kind of long life is unlikely in a place without a doctor. There are differences between the novel's perceptive comments and Rennie's blank spots. She criticises people for following their own leaders instead of taking the advice of Paul, but he turns out to be an American drug dealer and arms trader. Clearly, the real terrorists are America and Canada, who are propping up a corrupt commando government.

Rennie cannot find a language for communicating what she sees when beginning her stories of the island because they exceed the frame she brings to them. The novel is self-conscious about forms of fictions and reportage possible and uses Rennie both as example and mouthpiece of this critical view, especially when she herself rejects the tourist brochures and formulaic thriller fictions read in Paul's house. Even the rather artificial use of the future tense forces readers to consider the novel's own formulaic nature as a constructed fiction. *Bodily Harm* is:

> Atwood's indictment of the tourist mentality and the media who promote it. That indictment works satirically to imply that Rennie's approach to her Caribbean escape is part of a large trend of late twentieth century white culture. That pattern is built on denial.[77]

In 'Black Looks, Race and Representation', bell hooks comments that the black person is always seen as a terrorist, but actually it's not the black person, it's the whites who are that –

> one fantasy of whiteness is that the threatening Other is always a terrorist. This projection enables many white people to imagine there is no representation of whiteness as terror, as terrorising. Yet it is this representation of whiteness in the black imagination

And such a view as is sustained by travel to many different locations.[78]

Several critics find that the portrayal of the Caribbean, stressed as innocent, is never fully realised. While Helen Tiffin rejects enlightened views of the critical stance of the novel, seeing it as too complicit with Eurocentric attitudes towards colonised places,[79] Brydon argues that in order to understand the novel's postcolonial position, we must consider who Rennie is and whether the reader is prepared for the shift from tourist to reporter.

It eventually becomes impossible for Rennie, the tourist journalist, to emulate the stereotypes of holiday writing, or political writing, when she becomes more engaged with the events of the island and her own experiences on it. Rennie changes her vision and style and tries to find the language to express this.

Some critics refuse to see the novel as postcolonial and enlightened, arguing that it does not fully question hierarchies between first and third world, it suggests replacing them, feels claustrophobic, and does not try to be cross-cultural. Brydon finds Rennie hardly develops, and cannot provide a model for white readers about how to behave in a different cultural context since, instead of ignoring elements of cultural difference around her and misreading them, 'she's paying attention that's all'. For Brydon, the novel actually problematises some of the reading approaches which postcolonial critics take and *Bodily Harm* 'is neither counter-discursive nor cross-cultural' but is instead located in a small gap in '[the] apparently endless web of white cultural discourse. This is the kind of novel that challenges postcolonial critics to define their terminologies and rethink their methods. *Bodily Harm* exposes the limitations of simple distinctions between distant and complicit narratives.'[80]

Brydon also argues that its form and context lead us away from a rhetoric of subversion toward what Gayatri Chakravorty Spivak has defined as 'relearning of our privilege as our loss'.[81] Brydon refers to Edward Kamau Brathwaite (1984) and his critique of cultural ignorance and the damage it can do in universalising differences.

Atwood explores the role of the writer as recorder and commentator, as she explores the artist in *Cat's Eye*, the memoirist and a series of other writers in *The Blind Assassin*, and a writer of Gothic romances in *Lady Oracle*. These tales each explore the forms, possibilities and limitations of the writer and writing.

For Rennie, involvement is the major learning point. Her death is irrelevant, whether immediate in the prison or imminent from cancer. It is her vision which counts: 'Zero is waiting somewhere, whoever said that there was life everlasting; so why feel grateful? She doesn't have much time left, for anything. But neither does anyone else. She's paying attention, that's all.'[82]

This is a powerful novel of gendered relationships, the writer's role, and, unusually for Atwood, postcolonial issues. The next chapter considers Atwood's focus on a terrible future in which individual liberties have been lost and women are entirely defined according to their reproductive capabilities. In *The Handmaid's Tale* (1985), the first of her futuristic novels, the political, historical and cultural engagement seen in *Life Before Man* and *Bodily Harm* is expressed through dystopian and science fiction elements and blossom into what has been considered Atwood's most influential work.

5

The Oppressive Future:
The Handmaid's Tale (1985)

For those unaware of Margaret Atwood's immense reputation, the book they will have heard of, read or studied is *The Handmaid's Tale*. This was Atwood's first best-selling novel, establishing her reputation in the US and internationally.

The Handmaid's Tale is set in Cambridge, Massachusetts, home to the oldest US university, Harvard, where Atwood studied for her Master's degree. In a post-holocaust future world dominated by a fundamentalist regime, women are both idolised as the only potential source of humanity's future, and divided and ruled, their roles split, and their reproductive abilities their destiny. Language hides thoughts, freedom of speech is impossible, and women are divided against each other because of divided roles – wife, mistress/child-bearer, housekeepers, and the wives of the poor, Econowives.

The tale is told from the point of view of Offred, a handmaid or fertile woman in the service of Fred, one of the Commanders who rule the Republic of Gilead with military power. Offred is meant to be silent, so keeping a journal is forbidden, but her story is passed down to a future readership, and to us, from transcribed recordings. The narrative itself operates in three main time periods: one, the period of second-wave feminism, that of Offred's youth and her mother's activist involvement; Offred's own lifetime, in post-holocaust Gilead, the main substance of the novel; while a third is when Offred's tapes and personal testimony are discovered and put under academic scrutiny by Professor Pieixoto, which serves as an example of male intellectual control over history.

The novel differs from Atwood's previous and subsequent work, which is usually set in contemporary Canada, except insofar as it deals with male and female relationships of power, a common theme, particularly in the immediately preceding *Bodily Harm* (1981). *The Handmaid's Tale* has been widely studied and was turned into a highly successful film (screenplay by Harold Pinter, 1990). It is seen, variously, as science fiction and a dystopia which focuses on a religious fundamentalist regime, with practices reminiscent of Big Brother in *Nineteen Eighty-Four* (1949), and the reproductive controls and problematising of art in *Brave New World* (1932). It dramatises the destructive nature of fundamentalist regimes, and their controls over language. Since the story of Offred is our insight into these problematic times, it also illustrates the power of narrative and the strength of individual self.

Early reviews: a feminist text

Many of the early reviewers established a popular reading of the novel as a feminist text that debates issues of reproductive technology and women's roles. They also deal with it as a novel that explores the act of writing, reading and interpretation. It highlights Offred's (the handmaid) role as narrator constructing a tale set in the context of power over expression, which prevents free speech among the handmaidens and everyone else, and various contradictions playing on language or enforced silence. It is not a piece of science fiction, Atwood argues, because the 'seeds of everything it contains lie in the reality around us'.[1] This is an argument she returns to in later debates over *Oryx and Crake* (2003):

> It certainly isn't science fiction. Science fiction is filled with Martians and space travel to other planets, and things like that. That isn't this book at all. *The Handmaid's Tale* is speculative fiction in the genre of *Brave New World* and *Nineteen Eighty-Four*. *Nineteen Eighty-Four* was written not as science fiction but as an extrapolation of life in 1948. So, too, *The Handmaid's Tale* is a slight twist on the society we have now.[2]

However, latterly, she has redefined both novels as speculative fiction and comments that such works: 'can explore the consequences of new and proposed technologies in graphic ways, by showing them as fully operational', and: 'They can explore proposed changes in social organisation, by showing what they might actually be like for those living within them', as well as man's relationships to nature, to the universe, and the 'limits of what it means to be human'.[3] Feminist critics and readers embraced and argued over the book, which both confirms some of the worst nightmares of futures for women, and upon closer inspection, also undermines some of

feminism's more naïve arguments. Atwood prefers dialogue to dia-
tribe – this novel is not a feminist bible as such. However, as she said
earlier in an interview with Ellen Coughlin in *Books and Arts*:

> I think it is ridiculous for any woman in my position, who writes books
> and is a professional, to say she's *not* a feminist. I don't believe women
> who've been to school and have been to college and have jobs and then
> say they aren't feminists, because their whole mode of existence has
> been made possible by people several generations ago who chained
> themselves to fences. If feminism is dealing with women as independent
> entities, then I'm a feminist.[4]

But she is not, she says, a propagandist for the movement.

In an early review, Ken Adachi describes the book as 'intense,
compelling', celebrating its 'quiet intense hypnotic' grip and its similarities to work by Doris Lessing:

> one might call this a feminist theological novel; certainly it is didactic,
> densely infiltrated by myth, metaphor and history. Swift's *A Modest
> Proposal*, the Biblical Genesis, Orwell's *Nineteen Eighty-Four* and other
> dystopias come to mind, as do Doris Lessing's 'energetic satires on the
> totalitarian state as viewed from outer space'.[5]

Research for the novel is evidence of Atwood's fascination with
various tendencies and problems in late twentieth-century life. She
gathered materials on toxic waste, baby stealing, reproductive technologies, the American Right, fundamentalism and feminist protests.
She built up a fascinating mixture of influences, projecting a future
where experiments and casual ignoring of the environment led to
nuclear holocaust, toxic wastelands, and a new fundamentalist totalitarian regime. In trying to control, divide, rule and create, the regime
forces women into clearly defined roles based on their reproductive
value to society – women are their ability to reproduce – these sur-
rogates have no freedom or human rights and are little more than
baby machines to support patriarchal, despotic games.

Much critical writing about the novel relates Atwood's work to
feminist critique of reproductive technology. Other issues of concern are the trustworthiness of narrative, the partiality of record,
and the importance of being able to develop and express an individual subjectivity.

The Handmaid's Tale projects into a dystopian future some of the
problems and possibilities affecting women in the 1970s. Ironically,

in a future state where women are not expected to carry out a debilitating variety of roles, there is no sisterhood, only division and disempowerment. The text also deals with the controlling state and the silencing of individual self-expression. In an early review, Mary McCarthy identifies Gilead as a woman's world, ironically policed by men: 'Its ethos is entirely domestic, its female population is divided into classes based on household functions, each class clad in a separate colour that instantly identifies the wearer.'[6] Marthas (houseworkers) in dull green, Wives in blue, Econowives (working class) in blue and green stripes, and red for Handmaids, the childbearers for the sterile Wives. The Handmaids 'in their long red gowns and white wimple-like headgear, have something of the aura of a temple harlot'. The Aunts, in brown, are 'a thought-control force, part-governess, part reform-school matron'.[7]

Commanders govern households and use Handmaids to substitute for their sterile wives as childbearers. The three roles for women are matched by the three generations, that of Offred, her mother, the feminist, and her daughter. Offred's own body is not a place of safety – she feels that it is a swamp threatening to overwhelm her. McCarthy, however, finds Offred's mother unconvincing and part of the indictment of:

> 'excessive' feminism, which here seems to bear some responsibility for Gilead, to be one of its causes. The kind of doctrinaire feminism likely to produce a backlash is exemplified in the narrator's absurd mother, whom we first hear of at a book-burning in the old, pre-Gilead time – the 'right' kind of book-burning, naturally, merely a pyre of pornographic magazines: 'Mother,' thinks the narrator in what has become the present, 'You wanted a women's culture. Well, now there is one.' The wrong kind, of course.[8]

A major problem which the novel highlights is ostensible freedom – what does freedom really mean? The Aunts suggest it is freedom from (rape, sexism) rather than freedom to (do what you choose).

Lorna Sage recognises Atwood's critique of American values, seen earlier in *Surfacing*, and considers Atwood's Republic of Gilead as Middle America undermined by fanaticism, fuelled by fundamentalism, where traditional values mean everyone has one limited role, and all are under constant scrutiny, except for the 'Eyes of God', the secret police.[9] It is a world where those in power behave as though they had the power of God. They hunt down 'gender traitors', Baptists, guerrillas, Jews, Blacks (Sons of Ham) and send them for liquidation, expatriation or transportation to the colonies (radioactive post-nuclear war lands) to pick over toxic and radioactive waste dumps.

In this comparison between the post-holocaust colonies and the relatively safer Republic, Gilead seems like 'a vast garden suburb'. In her early, very English, interpretation, Lorna Sage has no illusion about the mixed feminist message of *The Handmaid's Tale*:

> [O]ne of the book's persistent polemical projections is the tendency in present day feminism towards a kind of separatist pit, a matriarchal nostalgia (Offred's mother, we discover, went it alone – 'A man is just a woman's strategy for making other women', burned pornographic magazines, reclaimed the night) that seems to combine with the language of conservation and 'back to Nature'. This, in turn, threatens to join forces with right-wing demands for 'traditional values', law and order, national and racial chauvinism.[10]

Sage is less keen on both Moira, Offred's radical friend, and the Commander, a mildly perverse ex-market researcher, arguing 'surely even patriarchal male sexuality can't feel this strange?' In the context of the difficulties of communication between the sexes in this novel,

'Offred's most difficult task is to persuade herself that her eventual reader – her real partner in crime – may be a man.'[11]

Strangeness culminates in a 'game of heterosexual Scrabble'. *The Handmaid's Tale* is a cautionary tale about gender relations and reproduction in the face of pollution and casual destruction. Fertility is the clue to the continuity (or not) of the species. Kate Fullbrook explores how *The Handmaid's Tale* functions as a dystopian feminist novel,[12] recognising it as a version of science fiction, as does Cathy Davidson.[13]

Jane Brooks Bouson sees the novel as a feminist dystopia containing a warning against a feminist backlash and the rise of the New Right, which in the 1980s sought the restoration of women's traditional roles. While the novel problematises notions of history and reality, it encourages readers to reflect on the oppressive realities of contemporary patriarchal ideology, employing tactics to counter and challenge assumptions of male power and superiority: '[It] reflects on the anti-feminist messages given to women by the fundamentalist New Right in the 1980s. Atwood delineates in chilling detail just what might follow: the virtual enslavement of women, their reduction to mere functions.'[14]

Brooks Bouson also considers the importance of language as a regulator in these oppressive times:

> [I]t also incorporates an antagonistic, feminist-dialogic speech which serves to partially contain and master the female fears it dramatizes. Describing how this tactic works, Offred muses that '[t]here is something powerful in the whispering of obscenities, about those in power ... It's like a spell of sorts. It deflates them, reduces them to the common denominator where they can be dealt with.'[15]

Religion and fundamentalism

The novel begins with a dedication to Atwood's ancestor May Webster, who was hanged as a witch (but survived – presumably proving she *was* a witch). The theme of religious intolerance reflects North American Puritan history, as Atwood comments:

> You often hear in North America, 'It can't happen here' but it happened quite early on. The Puritans banished people who didn't agree with them, so we would be rather smug to assume that the seeds are not there. That's why I set the book in Cambridge.[16]

Atwood argues that any takeover of America would be through religious persuasion or force. Religious fundamentalism and the perversion of religion in Gilead are themes taken up by Anne Kaler,[17] who sees the novel deploying both science fiction formulae and the strategies of autobiography and metafiction.

It is highly political and exposes the psychological, cultural and legal structures and constraints which repress people and enforce often unjust, absurd laws, rules and roles. Kaler notes that the sources of Atwood's dystopia surrounded her in modern America and in her reading. Significantly, Atwood's study at Harvard coincided with the Cuban Missile Crisis of 1962, a contemporary historical incident, which must have helped focus her views of American society, politics and potential imminent destruction. Studying with Perry Miller enlightened Atwood about the more grotesque aspects of the religious imagination in New England under its 'founding fathers', information which resurfaces in the ideological hierarchy of the novel. It taps into the repressive histories of early America. Cotton Mather (1663–1728), the historical Puritan leader, provides us with one starting point, since he invested biblical phraseology with a particular resonance when writing about a deceased 'Gentlewoman'. He mentions the women of New England as: 'Those *Handmaids of the Lord*, who tho' they live very much Conceal'd from the World, and may be called *The Hidden Ones*, yet have no little share in the *Beauty* and the *Defence* of the Land.'[18] Cotton Mather here employs a typically patriarchal sleight-of-hand, highlighting women's importance, but at the same time advocating their self-effacement and subordination, a device repeated later in Atwood's writing. Nicholson points out differences, however, since while in *The Handmaid's Tale*, fertile women are scarce, 'In colonial New England, however, the birth-rate was very high.'[19]

Handmaids are re-named as if possessions of Commanders, so Offred is 'of Fred'. New England women were renamed in ways which, as Kaler puts it: 'providentially reminded them of their feminine destiny. They had names such as "Silence, Fear, Patience, Prudence, Mindwell, Comfort, Hopestill and Be Fruitful".'[20] The upbringing of New England women, like the retraining of the Handmaids, included a rejection of mirrors, combs and any clothes which were more than functional. Each has reading restricted to the teachings of the Bible.

Gilead is named after ancient Palestine and Sharon Wilson explores a Biblical intertext where Offred, surrogate child bearer, is developed from the Biblical story of infertile Rachel, whose handmaid Bilhah bore children for her husband Jacob. An epigraph from the novel echoes Genesis 30:1–3: 'she shall bear upon my knees, that I may also have children by her'.[21]

Other intertexts are based in myth. Atwood studied with Northrop Frye at Victoria College, and his *Anatomy of Criticism* influences the use of mythical patterns. Frye found pastoral myth particularly prevalent in Canadian literature: 'Rather than the heaven-on-earth or more flat world the fathers of Gilead say, and perhaps believe, they are building, *The Handmaid's Tale* ironically depicts Frye's world of the nightmare and the scapegoat, of bondage, pain and confusion.'[22]

It is 'A Babylon rather than Jerusalem, it is an anti-apocalyptic world with its euphemistic language, metamorphoric wolf, sinister garden urban waste land, temple prostitutes, and even technological Behemoths.' More ironically, Gilead fulfils traditional scholarly definitions of 'hell' primarily because of its treatment of 'gender traitors', and non-white races, religious minorities and especially women.[23]

Genesis is a main intertext, in terms of sexual politics, but there are also satires on aspects of Islam, Puritanism, Mormonism and Christianity, particularly contemporary fundamentalism. In its consideration of oppression, *The Handmaid's Tale* returns to Atwood's depiction of the US as an oppressive neighbour.

John Updike focuses on the 'bemusement' of Canada, a 'fine old northern neighbour facing the US moral strenuousness, our noisy determination to combine virtue and power, and our occasional vast miscarriages of missionary intention'.[24] He is somewhat amused that the novel is set in the now liberal Cambridge, but unsurprised that escape to Canada still offers promise in the early days of Gilead, and refuses to see it as a humourless feminist piece:

> This novel could have been a humourless strident tract; but the poet in the author renders it quite otherwise. The narrative is light-handed, fitful, and gradually compelling, it assembles its horrid world with a casual meditative motion, and saves most of its action for the last few pages.[25]

Updike sees even the pervasive pollution described poetically and the manufacture of dishcloths and smiling buttons as touches which reduce the negativity. He says it 'does feel purposefully feminine', beneath the grim but 'playful details of its dystopia glows the vivid and intimate reality of its heroine'. It is filled with 'the heroine's irrepressible vitality'.[26]

Atwood takes cultural myths and investigates their roots, reverses, exposes and undercuts them. Irony, and mixing the rich detail of everyday life with the equally rich detail of myth and metaphor, make her work both realistic and fantastic.

Language and storytelling

The novel also asks questions about how history can be retold, and offers examples of storytelling through Offred's testimony. We are reliant for the story on Offred's taped record, rescued into an archive in a distant future, where her transcribed words are viewed by yet another male controlling authority figure, Professor Pieixoto, who treats her as part of an archive, undependable because her reports are told in the first person and only marginally interesting. They are a testimony to silencing, tribulations, repressions and life under a regime which reduces people to their functions: control, reproduction, service, and those who regulate those functions: the Aunts, and the thought police – the Eyes. At one level, *The Handmaid's Tale* is also about the writing process. Offred comments on her own constructions, saying such things as 'Context is all,' and 'I've filled it out for her ...,' 'I made that up', and 'I wish this story were different.' Her habit of talking about storytelling highlights the processes of constructing and representing histories and legitimated or repressed versions of events.

There is a tendency for dystopian novels engaging with the dangers of totalitarian society to focus on repression of thought and expression. *Nineteen Eighty-Four* (1949), *Brave New World* (1932) and other dystopian novels explore connections between state repression of its subjects, and that of their thoughts, through the perversion and oppressions of language. In a context where the Handmaids must remain silent, or speak to each other only in a limited, religiously inflected code, there are clear relationships between language, power and sexuality and the theories of Michel Foucault (1926–84), whose *The History of Sexuality* (1984) enlightens an exploration of these relationships in Gilead. Foucault relates language to power, surveillance and sexuality, showing that language and power can enable the expression of self and sexuality, or repress them. In Gilead, there seems to be only repression. If anyone speaks against the regime or even makes mistakes in a coded response, they find themselves policed by their colleagues as well as the Eyes of God, and could face incarceration and death. Surveillance predominates. Language is power and disempowerment depending on who you are. Stripping women of their permanent individual names attempts to erase individuality. Language also *excludes* by naming so that the sexually dissident, the feminist, is called 'Unwoman' and the many babies born with birth defects are rejected as 'Unbabies'. Ethnicity and religion exclude others through labelling, much as was the practice in Nazi Germany. Since this is a religious fundamentalist regime, the labels derive from the Bible, so Jewish people are termed 'Sons of Jacob' and Black people 'Children of Ham'. Definitions of difference provide a licence for exclusion and destruction. Thoughts must be veiled and unspoken. There are approved greetings for personal and other encounters, and those who do not produce the correct greetings fall under suspicion of disloyalty. The rituals of Gilead, which involve various persecutions, called cleansing, are given particular names such as 'Prayvaganzas', 'Salvagings' and 'Particicutions'. In Atwood's novel, language is coded, thoughts policed, and all sexual freedoms have been lost.

The novel is both a dystopian fiction, a satire of a potential future, and a feminist challenge to the forms of dystopian fictions which focus on masculine worldviews. Coral Ann Howells notes:

> This is *history*, a deconstructive view of patriarchal authority, which in turn is challenged at an academic conference two hundred years later by the male Cambridge historian Professor Pieixoto, who tries to discredit Offred's version for its lack of documentary information. However, by this time Offred has the author's support (in the pun 'Denay Nunavit') and she also has the reader's sympathy, so that history does not succeed in undermining history after all.[27]

The Handmaid's Tale is very much a female form of the dystopian novel because it focuses on women, reproductive technologies, and in particular on one woman, Offred, whose experiences under this totalitarian regime disempower her and reduce her value to that of reproduction. Although she is silenced, Offred's taped journal records the radical views which form as a result of her own gradual self-awareness. Howells notes: 'Though it shares many of the thematic features of traditional models of the genre, it subverts the masculine dystopian fascination with institutional politics or military tactics by focusing on the silenced Others in Gilead.'[28] There is no final version of the history of Offred and Gilead and the tone and ending have also provoked much speculation.

Marta Dvorak finds a variety of humour in the novel, and notes common critical devices, including the setting up of specious dialogues, where variously repellent and hideously comic speakers (Aunt Lydia with her long yellow rodent teeth is her example) speak against the view of the authorial narrative voice. This is a strategy which leads to caricature which is both amusing, and empowering to the versions offered by the narrator. Dvorak notices '"Metalinguistic play" which critiques the institutional linguistic practice serving to promote ideology.'[29]

Education is attacked as a vehicle for ideology and restraint. The Aunts teach silent obedience and, in Gilead, Harvard University is transformed into a place of repression, its buildings now a detention centre run by Gilead's secret police, 'the Eyes'. Salvagings (mass executions) take place in Harvard Yard, on the steps of the library, and the hooded bodies of executed dissidents hang from the wall circling the college. Palumbo notes: 'Harvard becomes a symbol of the inverted world that Gilead has created: a place that was founded to pursue knowledge and truth becomes a seat of oppression, torture, and the denial of every principle for which a university is supposed to stand.'[30]

The Handmaid's Tale can be read in several ways, each related to themes which run throughout Atwood's work. As a satire, it contains humour, and through that perhaps some vision, some hope, when wondering about how likely this dystopia is to become a reality. As a favourite of feminist critics, it provides an exploration of questions about the control of women's bodies, the intrusion of reproductive technologies and the ways in which language operates as power to repress self, control sexuality and limit freedoms. It also questions histories and the ways in which we construct them. Orwell's *Nineteen Eighty-Four* gave us the duplicitous 'Newspeak', where language is manipulated by ideology to be contradictory and undependable. Because Offred's tale is told as a past event, this suggests the death of both the regime and of any kind of Newspeak which might have covered up its worst lies and horrors. There is a future beyond the dystopia and this offers hope that its worst elements could be overcome.

The Handmaid's Tale is a powerful feminist critique of a potential future where women's freedoms are entirely eroded, but it also challenges and undermines many of the more rigid tenets of feminism, showing the views of second-wave feminism to be both insightful in places and limited. Critics debate the ways in which Atwood deals with issues alive for feminism. She shows how language can warp the way we see the world, exposing the potential for a regime to subject men and women to horrifying silences and destructive mindsets. However, Brooks Bouson suggests that in telling the story, Offred has a freedom beyond the enforced constraints of her position – and the projection of a way forward. In our reading of Offred's testimony beyond the limited interpretations of the Professor, there is some small hope for a future that perhaps might avoid some of the worst problems threatened in the contemporary world.

Postscript: *The Handmaid's Tale* (1990) – the movie

The novel was turned into a movie (108 mins), with a screenplay by the noted playwright Harold Pinter. It stars Natasha Richardson, Faye Dunaway, Aidan Quinn, Elizabeth McGovern, Victoria Tennant and Robert Duvall, and is directed by Volker Schlöndorff.

It is a powerful, harrowing film, beginning with the separation of Offred and her family, hunted down in the snow, trying to escape the regime. Nischik, writing on Atwood's genre work, tells us that the script underwent a number of radical adaptations as different film studios refused the film,[31] and Pinter's original screenplay. Teitelbaum explains that 'a film for and about women ... would be lucky if it made it to video'.[32] Many thought the film was too feminist and would harm the reputations of the actors.

The film had only a short run in 1990 but has been variously taught on literature and women's studies as well as film courses since then.[33] Nischik, like many of the original reviewers, found that Schlöndorff's much revised screenplay rather confusingly made it into a thriller. It misrepresents Offred, who oscillates between passivity and finding her own voice, as someone active and violent enough to murder the Commander. After a bloodbath, the film ends with Offred pregnant and awaiting her lover, Nick the chauffeur, to escape together to Canada. A potentially romantic ending replaces the original in which Offred's history is left as speculation and her experiences in Gilead the main focus. The next chapter considers other failures of sisterhood. Both *Cat's Eye* (1988) and *The Robber Bride* (1993) use memory and the Gothic to explore spiteful females and the importance of self-affirmation.

6

Feminist Gothic:
Cat's Eye (1988),
The Robber Bride (1993)

In both *Cat's Eye* and *The Robber Bride*, Atwood's exploration of female mischievousness and spite, and the use of narratives to shape versions of reality, take her work more deeply into favourite areas of concern. Both novels deal with representations and constructions of women, constraints upon their roles and the tension between artifice and authenticity. They also consider the constructions of narratives, ways that retelling or fabricating can enable us to manage events that might be puzzling, even life-denying. Both novels use female Gothic and reflective storytelling to shape histories and ultimately to own and affirm positive versions of identity.

Some critics, including Jane Brooks Bouson (1993) and Judith McCombs (1991), explore the creation of a version of history and the self in *Cat's Eye*, discussing how Atwood exposes the practices of female spitefulness in the characters and relationships. Eleonora Rao (1993), Suzanne Becker (1999) and Coral Ann Howells (1996) are more concerned with Atwood's development of the feminist Gothic, focusing on the rewriting of myths, Gothic settings and how the texts deal with multiple identities, immorality, abuse and cruelty. These are also novels of Toronto in terms of location and mores, as is the later *The Blind Assassin* (2000). *The Robber Bride* caused something of a sensation among Toronto society, as gossip columnists claimed to identify Zenia among society hostesses.

Cat's Eye (1988)

Cat's Eye is probably Atwood's most autobiographical novel, at least until *Moral Disorder* appeared in 2006. Its cautionary tale is 'women beware women', and it also concerns the artistic ability to project

and represent, to continue to explore mental images of displacement and disorientation, moving between the real and the surreal.
Through Elaine Risley, the protagonist, a female artist, Atwood
engages with the power of art to transform and manage, while
simultaneously breaking loose. In *Cat's Eye* she also offers a very
rare insight into the spirit of girlhood and the defences of the tal-
ented, isolated individual in the face of alienation and spite. Some of
the cruelties Elaine experiences have caused reviewers to liken the
novel to William Golding's *Lord of the Flies* (1954), in which a group
of British schoolboys stranded on a tropical island turn wild and
attack each other.

Early reviews

Early reviews tend to focus on the Toronto setting, the remembered
minutiae and the parallels between Elaine Risley and Margaret
Atwood. Philip Howard in 'Back on her home ground' reads it auto-
biographically as a 'gripping search for times past'.[1] It is also a novel
of relationships between girls and women, men and women. Mark
Glassman thinks many critics do not understand the book because
it is outside their experience, affected by segregated schools, when
only in the marbles season did the boys and girls play together.
Atwood, however, says that most women recognise it reflects a part
of their own lives in some way: 'just about every woman who has
read this book has said to me, "this is my story and I've forgotten or
dismissed it".'[2]

Alberto Manguel finds *Cat's Eye* reminiscent of a period. Atwood
works 'not by mimicry but by accumulation, to unload onto the page
an attic full of memorabilia ... pages and pages of games we played,
food we ate, clothes we wore, words we used, things we thought,
names we had'.[3]

It is 'a topological catalogue of the evolution of Toronto's tribal
customs of the forties to the eighties'. Elaine is 'obsessively reminiscent', and two-thirds into the book 'the accumulation loses its
composite nature', acquiring the shape of 'a huge collage that depicts
not only Elaine and Toronto's coming of age'[4] but the texture and
content of her childhood lost. However, while Toronto-based Ken
Adachi recognises real places – the parliament building, University
Avenue, and Queen Street – he distrusts the realism and finds this
so much detritus, wanting the ideas developed rather than the

details. In the midst of these wrangles about autobiography and realism, it is a good idea to remember that on the inside of the dust jacket is a disclaimer: 'This is a work of fiction. Although its form is that of an autobiography, it isn't me.'[5]

Remembering the past

The novel is a *Bildungsroman*, the story of an individual developing from childhood through maturity, turned into a narrative, retrospectively, making some sense of its stages, its rites of passage. While Charlotte Bronte's *Jane Eyre* (1847) follows the developing life of another increasingly self-composed and individualistic young woman, like James Joyce's *Portrait of the Artist as a Young Man* (1914), Atwood's novel is a tale of an artist recovering historical versions of self, developed, exorcised and shaped by her art. For Elaine Risley, this recollection and reinterpretation help her to make new sense from the events which have made her what she is. *Cat's Eye* is also the story of an artist, and one which relies upon the trickeries, revisitings and sense-making possible through an artistic management of events and of time. Successful painter Elaine Risley returns to Toronto, where she grew up, to be part of a retrospective on her work, and this stirs up her own retrospection, revising and attempting to understand her girlhood memories and the woman she has now become. It is a novel which has something to say to all its readers about ways in which we make sense of our lives (or fail in that attempt), and the importance of memory, revisiting and reshaping events, and the shaping, cathartic, expressions of art.

Claire Tomalin sees the book as a 'meditation on ageing and the ways it changes one's relations with people, places and the past'.[6] Sharon Wilson notes that Elaine's early childhood placed her initially in the 'back seat', safe behind her family's heads in the car, while she gradually learned to scrutinise behaviour, gaining perspective using her father's microscope, looking down on people from his lab as if they were snowflakes.[7] Because the family moved with the seasons and the father's job, it took years for her to settle into school and to engage with the social interactions of others. She had to try to define what was expected of her as a girl. But that was a small thing compared to the judgements of the legislative nine-year-old trio, Grace, Carol and Cordelia, who made Elaine Risley an outsider, and her life a hell. The worst act the girls committed was to send her down an icy ravine and leave her there, telling her mother she had remained at school. The life-changing effect of this was that Elaine learned never to want to be part of a coven of girls again; and to remove herself from any need for mixed constraints and comforts of such closed societies. However, during this isolating moment, inspiration came to her in a vision of the Virgin Mary, which helped her out of the ravine. Her mother, not believing the others, came to rescue her.

Friendship, family, gender roles and the construction of femininity are all important elements, argues Brooks Bouson. Family life is isolated but safe, and girlhood, 'a dangerous, threatening world where the female self is shaped and irrevocably damaged in the process'.[8] It is an ideologically inflected lesson in gender construction and moulding, which Elaine suffers, reflects on, and then learns to manage her own way.

> [It] describes the methods by which femininity is constructed in our culture. Repeating what has been done to them, Elaine's friends determine to 'improve' Elaine; that is, they attempt to coerce her to be a proper little girl and to mimic culturally prescribed feminine behaviour.[9]

But she resists and eventually develops, despite their cruelties and insistence on conformity. Clare Tomalin comments: 'There's a message here, of course, for feminists who see the female sex as perpetually benevolent, instead showing hierarchical and sadistic behaviour among girls.'[10] Mark Glassman interviews Atwood in 'Atwood's Eye', where she points out that most women would be aware of the relationships of little girls but that they don't understand how devastating these relationships can be: 'I think because we are used to thinking of women's important relationships as being with men.'[11] The novel focuses on recall and identity:

> Narrated in the first-person present tense and deftly structured by interweaving chronological instalments of present and past time, *Cat's Eye* is a lyrical novel of memory but also an anxiety-ridden narrative preoccupied with the notion of psychic vampirism: the invasion by and loss of the self to a malignant other.[12]

Judith McCombs comments that from the vantage of a 50-year-old Elaine, her interpretation of the paintings she did as a 25-year-old reveal her fears as a child.[13] One painting of falling women shows three women jumping from a bridge like the one over the ravine into which the girls, led by Cordelia, forced Elaine, trying to push her over the edge into mental instability. Images of falling women are conventionally interpreted as signifying a sexual act and this 'also represents her own romantic fall', another moment of fear and loneliness. However, turning to art helped her escape the childhood bullying, and the retrospective, of her life as well as of her art, high-lights its exploratory, self-expressive and therapeutic use. For Elaine, her paintings re-enact, make sense of and exorcise the past, the fears and the realities. One painting is of her brother falling from a plane, another of three evil hooded figures (the girls, her 'friends'). More positive images include the Virgin Mary vision from the ravine, and 'three magi, the Scottish teacher, the Jewish neighbour Mrs Finestein and the Indian Dr Bannerji, all of whom help her establish and paint versions of self'.[14]

McCombs points out that one of her artworks, the cat's eye por-trait, reflects a famous painting, Jan Van Eyck's 'Arnolfini Wedding'. Here, the artist appears in a mirror behind a couple who seem to represent fidelity but might just be posing. In Elaine's painting there are the familiar three tormentor figures with her in the mir-ror. McCombs reminds us of the mirroring of Marian in sunglasses in *The Edible Woman* (1969), where she invents herself as half her own size: a feminist reading of ways in which many conventional relationships demoralise and diminish women. But in *Cat's Eye*, the diminished one is eventually Cordelia, reflected back to herself shrunken in her own sunglasses as mirror.

Cordelia and Elaine mirror themselves for each other, reveal-ing darker sides, as Zenia does later in *The Robber Bride*. Although schoolgirl Elaine covered for her, dissecting the biology sections, Cordelia could still not pass the exams. One of the great gains of this strange relationship is that, in time, Elaine becomes stronger and more aware of her own talents. These are not in the sciences as her family would expect, but in art, and emerge as she draws biology specimens. When she sees a glimpse of Cordelia alive after her retrospective, Elaine realises that in those early years Cordelia offloaded her own lack on to her friend, tormenting her because she was herself denied and undermined. Sharon Wilson sees that even-tually Elaine and Cordelia change places. Cordelia has the abusive family life.[15] Her parents belittle her, her father undermines her, and she takes this lack of ontological security out on Elaine, whom she torments. But following the moment in the ravine, Elaine retreats into silence and self-assured separateness. Cordelia can never harm her again because Elaine turns into a harder woman, refusing to interact, and Cordelia, bereft of anyone to torment and manipulate, eventually deteriorates into an emotional instability and mental illness which is something Elaine is neither able nor willing to stop.

Artistic representation enables retrospective valuation, a distancing from events, and a development of different versions of reality, self and experience. Cordelia and the two other tormentors are genuine, but the novel explores the ways in which tormenters and tormented construct each other's versions of self. Elaine can escape this tormenting through avoidance, removing herself from their physical spaces, moving into other spaces, finding different friendships, and through refusing their versions of herself. She expresses herself through her art, digging through the layers of different periods in her life and revealing how people change and reconstruct versions of themselves and others.

While Brookner is very positive about the representation of childhood in the novel: 'The devolvement of childhood, its inability to gauge its own entitlements is beautifully conveyed and is all the more powerful being understated',[16] Carole Angier sees in these childhood recollections the genesis of cruelty: 'it's extremely bleak about humanity; it's about cruelty'.[17] Brooks Bouson also links the act of painting and Elaine Risley's life, the transformation of deep emotional trauma into a complex and coded work of art[18] and notes its similarity with other Atwood novels in undermining the romance plot.

Looking at the relationship between the girls, Carol, Grace and Cordelia, and the games they play, Anita Brookner identifies the only 'normal' child as Carol, since Grace is the daughter of evangelical parents who view Elaine as a heathen, and Cordelia, who maintains a hierarchical position of power and height, is clearly a psychopath, luring others into her magical circles.[19]

Time and age

Coming to 50 means coming to terms with age and change, parents dying, brother killed and love scaled down from passion to companionship. Time lends a certain perspective, and Atwood's reading of the scientific research of Stephen Hawking and others on the topic of time underpins the ways Elaine deconstructs both space and time. This, Angier says, is the point of the novel; that Elaine 'was really Cordelia; that reality is not what we are but what we accept, reject, forget, remember'.[20] In his review 'Physics and Psyche in *Cat's Eye*', Douglas Rice also involves Stephen Hawking's theories, where 'time is not alien but a dimension',[21] since Elaine sees her brother's information on time and space as important and so – 'the Einstein version of time where it speeds up in absence'[22] clarifies Elaine's surprise at finding how Cordelia has aged.

Atwood's originality is very much Elaine's originality – they both produce startling effects by a somewhat daring juxtaposition of experimental (image, patterns) and traditional (plot, character) devices. Peter Kemp in 'Childhood through alien's eyes' sees that 'skilfully *Cat's Eye* keeps altering its field of vision, from following into the ambiguous excesses of personal experiences through to scrutinising the phases of a woman's life'.[23] It expands into surveying the contours of a culture. The aesthetic and the scientific elegantly interact in its study of creativity and destructiveness, its harking back animated by nostalgia. By turns bleak, funny, sensuously evocative, he sees it as a disturbing, self-conscious manipulation of images.[24]

As Elaine wanders through the now open market city of her youth, remembering the dingy Toronto of 40 years ago, she recalls layers of her past: her at 8/9, her in her twenties. When she began the painting that exorcised the pain of her younger life, making it safe, she still could not exorcise Cordelia. Pausing in front of a cosmetic counter, she thinks she'd happily use anything to stop the progress of time, but only two things can – memory and art – and Atwood uses them both in this novel. Elaine sees herself as a piece of graffiti on the street: 'I have achieved finally a face that a moustache can be drawn on, a face that attracts moustaches. A public face, a face worth defacing. This is an accomplishment.'[25]

Not a feminist novel

There are many debates about whether *Cat's Eye* is a feminist novel or one which, by exposing female spite, is anti-feminist. Identifying *Cat's Eye* as a *Bildungsroman*, a portrait that incorporates transmuted autobiography in a 'most elaborate representation of the human self as complexly layered',[26] as we saw earlier, McCombs also sees it as feminist:

> profoundly woman-centred and feminist-oriented re-remembering and visions; in its learning, painful girlhood is of passage and its crotchety,

womanly, coming to terms with aging; in its portrait of the artist not as
a young man, but as a fifty-year-old woman, and in the private iconography of her paintings.[27]

It is both feminist and despairing of power politics wherever they
are played out, as Nischik comments,

> [It is] decidedly feminist not only in its woman-centered approach and
> oppositional appeal but also in its continuing critique of patriarchy and
> its politics of domination and subordination. That Atwood has the cour-
> age 'to turn the tables on her own kind' in *Cat's Eye* does not make her
> antifeminist.[28]

Claire Tomalin's 'What little girls are made of' identifies the spite
and cruelty in girls' lives with which *Cat's Eye* deals. When an
admirer tells Elaine that she loved her real work, it is guessed she
means its energy and cruelty, but Tomalin notes that Elaine has
moved on,

> [She] has grown uneasy about being co-opted by furious feminists,
> living with a man she likes, disposed to make friends again with the
> rejected husband of her youth, she doesn't want to shout a man down …
> she doesn't want to be either sanctified or burnt at the stake by the
> sisterhood.[29]

Elaine refuses feminist commentary and questioning, not surprisingly, given the lack of sisterhood she experienced as a child. For
Anita Brookner, the novel is about mourning and Atwood is able to
'turn the tables on her own kind' using the fiftyish Elaine Risley as
her alter ego. On the one hand, Brookner wonders if women in post-
feminism are going to stop taking things out on men and look back
at their own lives and those injuries, the remains from childhood,[30]
while on the other, Beverly Pagam praises Atwood for being beyond
feminism: stratospheres above the feminist bleating which are often
palmed off as important contemporary women's literature.[31]

Transformation, myth and fairytale

One of the novel's triumphs is its comment upon transformation
and its own transmutation of pain and life into art. Elaine's art helps
her deal ironically with and distance her tormentors, especially

Mrs Smeath. The recollection of her life, through her own layered storytelling, helps her pull the past and present together into some pattern. She notices literal and figurative amputations around her, the 'severed limbs' in ex-husband Jon's apartment, which remind her of her past and her own vulnerable childhood.[32]

Expecting to see Cordelia at the exhibition pinpoints her need to confront both past and tormenter in order to move into a fuller sense of herself.

Sharon Wilson traces a number of motifs and fairytale pattern-ings in the novel, which reveal this trajectory of recovery of self-worth and wholeness. She first aligns it with the popular motif of Rapunzel, where a beautiful young woman is kept in a tower by a witch, eventually letting her hair down for her prince to climb up and rescue her. This is a favourite Atwood representation of Canadian womanhood, and, for Wilson, the book demonstrates the Canadian 'comedy of manners traditions'. Like earlier works it 're-visions or transforms fantastic intertexts that influence the nov-el's images, characters, structure and themes.'[33]

Atwood uses magic realism to portray a symbolically dismem-bered character capable of fairytale metamorphosis. In this case, the metamorphosis affects not only vision and the self but 'conceptions of time and art'.[34] The fairytale intertexts are not merely Rapunzel, but the Snow Queen, in a version of which Elaine can remove the sliver of ice in her eye through her renewed vision, the cat's eye, the retrospective of her art.

Elaine humorously decides to wear vampire[35] and Hecate black for her exhibition. She watches herself in little metaphoric mirrors and frames others in mental photographs. As a visual artist, she lit-erally frames Mrs Smeath, Cordelia, her own partners Jon and Josef in vengeful 'eye for an eye' paintings.[36] However, because she has repressed pain by cultivating the alien vision of the cat's eye marble, she is uneasy, realising she must move on. The moment that Elaine Risley 'finally sees her life entire'[37] comes near the book's end. It is a painter's vision and one which can be used for revenge, as Brooks Bouson says, commenting on the treatment of love and men:

> In her refusal to overvalue love, the middle-aged Elaine asserts her own dialogic authority as she contests the notion that romantic affiliation is at the center of a woman's life. ... Not only does *Cat's Eye* demystify the ideology of romantic love, it also openly enacts a fantasy of female revenge.[38]

A novel about the vision of the artist and a dialogue with versions of feminism, *Cat's Eye* was a change in focus and tone for Atwood, moving towards magical realism to explore the mixture of geographical, cultural and historical reality, using layering of myth and the romance of imagination, which also govern our lives. This novel undermines naïve feminist readings about female friendships. Female metamorphosis and spite, the questioning of the fictions of romance, and critique of myths and fairytales as modes of exploring and expressing themes develop further in *The Robber Bride*.

The Robber Bride (1993)

The Robber Bride is a Gothic, magic realist novel that explores the lives of four women. Three of them, Tony, a military historian, Roz, a business woman, and Charis, a hippy working in a mind, body, spirit shop, are bound together by their relationships with the fourth, the endlessly metamorphosing, vampiric Zenia. In focusing on the relationship between women and their potential in the contemporary world in terms of self-development and response to constraints and construction, this novel furthers themes familiar from Atwood's earlier novels, most particularly *Lady Oracle* (1976). Zenia, like Joan Foster, constructs versions of herself taken from Gothic romances for women. The novel also resembles *Cat's Eye* in dealing with twinning motifs and with female spite. In *The Robber Bride*, Atwood considers possibilities for self-exploration and self-development. In so doing, she takes the four women, three of whom represent elements of contemporary versions of women's lives, while the fourth, Zenia, acts as provocateur and catalyst for their worst fears, insecurities and finally breakthroughs. Zenia's morphing and oppressive relationships bring out the worst fears of each woman, but engagement with her ultimately enables them to develop some personal strengths and choices.

The book begins as a Gothic, magical tale. In the Toxique Restaurant, the women – Roz, Charis and Tony – have gathered for a meal, when suddenly they catch sight of Zenia, whom they thought dead. Her return provokes each woman to recount her own history. Zenia is the hub around which revolves the lives and tales of the other women, their versions of reality, and the stories they tell themselves and us. Her personality and stability of self change and reinvent in her relationship with each of the other women. Ingersoll and others recognise her as a character we all know in real life: a manipulator.[39]

The Robber Bride is also a Gothic marriage tale which highlights the pleasures and dangers of male/female relationships and of sisterhood. The story itself derives from a fairytale by the Brothers Grimm, 'The Robber Bridegroom', in which a male robber, a kind of peasant Bluebeard, tricks a series of hapless brides into marriage then returns to his dreadful family. His mother colludes, the girls become victims, he hacks them to pieces and the family devours them. In Atwood's version, the robber bridegroom is replaced by a kind of robber bride, Zenia, a powerful, intrusive female, who is a villainess, the embodiment of female evil. Zenia is fascinating to the three women on whom she preys, and equally fascinating to readers. Atwood is aware of the roles feminists and other women expect her to play and gives short shrift to arguments that women are kinder than men, something exposed in both *Cat's Eye* and *The Robber Bride*. In her discussion with Stephanie McKinnon, 'In Search of Evil Women', Atwood emphasises that 'we know from real life that women are not programmed like a robot to be good'.[40] Really 'good' people might be quite dull, and in narratives without the more feisty and wicked, there would be no real plot or interest. She says,' I think the key is complexity and if all you can be is good you can't be complex.'[41]

In *The Saturday Review*, Sandra McKenzie identified Zenia's sexual vampirism, in, 'A landscape littered with the wasted bodies of damaged women',[42] and Gabriele Annan describes the book as 'a soap opera for moderate feminists'.[43] Maureen Nicholson in 'Unpopular gals', sees the novel as concerning 'the exploitation of vulnerability',[44] examining how those exploited can be complicit in their own exploitation. The feminist appeal is in the presentation of female friendships, a type of female sexual power, and skilled manipulation of the male characters. Nicholson argues that like most of Atwood's men, the boys here are 'a bit thick'. The book is popular, she claims, because of an interest in crime and the 'lurid'. Zenia is an 'apparently unstoppable force of nature that rampages its greedy way through marital and family ties, friendship and history'.[45]

Atwood's Gothic

Margaret Atwood is frequently noted for her use of the Gothic, which enables ironic twists and exposés of the false securities of the everyday world, using imagery of twinning, the monstrous, vampires, duplicity and the crossing of liminal spaces between good and evil, male and female, life and death. Many of the short stories and the earlier *Lady Oracle* particularly scrutinised and rewrote fairytales, myths and Gothic tales. Marina Warner, whose expertise lies in myth and gender, sees the 'usual onset of villains ... bad mother, wicked queen and the three little pigs, the phantasma-gorical world of the femme fatale'. For her, this is also the territory of Angela Carter. The women are 'casualties of the second world war and a variety of abusive domestic scenarios, child abuse, child beating'.[46]

Warner's own language is fantastic, Gothic and rich. She sees the men stolen away one after another by Zenia,

> the novel's hollow core, the incubus with implants for breasts who, like a weasel kills not to eat but for the pleasure of it, or, like a fox, always digs back doors and makes havoc at the feast these have provided.[47]

In Warner's view, basic causes of such destruction are the failure of family, of luck and of weak men.

The three women believe they have seen Zenia die, and her return initially both triggers their memories, and reinstates her power over them. Mark Lawson in 'Canadian Gothic' finds generic experimen-tation in the ghost story, arguing it elaborates, contrasts and devel-ops insights 'on the life choices available to women at the end of the 20th century'.[48]

Salman Rushdie describes the novel as brilliantly written, and witty. It explores: 'The best fears of our lives, a tale of small, private catastrophes, its villain unleashes nothing grander than domestic brand emotional violence.'[49] Zenia is heavily theorised and fascinat-ing, as Atwood intends. She explains: 'Your attraction to the Zenias of this world is that they are pure forms of all kinds of things that we unitarily suppress. And there was something attractive about a kind of outlaw figure.'[50]

In 'Bewitched, bothered and bewildered', Peter Kemp sees it as a 'witch fable ... flickering imitations of vampires, doppelgangers, macabre mixings, the fatal inviting of an evil spirit over the thresh-old are shown as events as sharply located in everyday actuality'. Atwood 'extends a vast web of conflicts: sex antagonisms, domestic infighting, warring aspects of the self, battles from medieval blood-baths, hi tech hostilities in the Gulf'.[51]

Scenes of hard-edged realism mix with 'Gothic phosphorescence shivers',[52] narrative excitement and wit.

Francis King finds Atwood's men, as usual, useless: 'Roz's husband, a class lawyer, endless philanderer; Charis' husband, an American draft dodger; Tony's husband, a wet academic'.[53] The scenes where Zenia looses her will on others are fun but 'disquieting', even 'frightening'; King notes that Atwood demonstrates with eerie skill ... the way in which victims acquiesce in – and sometimes actually will – their own exploitation.[54] In the *Financial Times*, Anthony Thorncroft sees this as territory covered by Daphne du Maurier's novels, such as *Rebecca*, in which a second wife is swept off her feet by a rich man, Maxim de Winter, who lives in a grand Gothic house, Manderley, and is haunted by the livelier, beautiful but sexually promiscuous first wife, Rebecca. In Atwood, however, this territory is 'lightly dusted with feminism'.[55]

Sherrill Grace's 'Atwood's postmodern fairytale' compares *The Robber Bride* to two earlier works, *Good Bones* (1992) and *Wilderness Tips* (1991), imagining Atwood writing fairytales for grown-ups with 'inchoate fears, and powerful desires that haunt our sophisticated urban worlds and power, like wolves, around the edges of our most secure, mundane-seeming lives'.[56] Bluebeard is a favourite, appearing in *The Edible Woman*, *Lady Oracle* and *The Handmaid's Tale*. Each woman repeats a useless father in her husband or partner so, 'behind each woman stretches a history of abandonment, betrayal, abuse and treachery'.[57] We are taken into the past of each – Tony's mother left her with an alcoholic suicidal father; Charis' mother abandoned her with her aunt and abusive uncle; Roz's father is a womaniser. Zenia, the robber bride, who holds them all together is compared to Eve, Lolita, Jezebel, Medusa, Circe and Medea, in 'gothic romance and fin de siècle iconography'.[58]

For Grace, it is a postmodern fairytale, one emphasising our need for stories, and which has parallels in the cruelties of the everyday world, so that, Grace reports, an unnamed Canadian reviewer tells us, 'even in the heart of Toronto with its chic restaurants, sophisticated domestic arrangements, drugs and fashion statements, some things never change'.[59] At the end, when Zenia has been finally killed and dismembered (told in several versions), Tony returns to the others, who are already telling stories about Zenia.

Shannon Hengen's review considers it a 'pot-boiler of a modern tale',[60] an explicit reading of fairytale in the modern world in which, as Roz realises, 'no matter what you do, somebody always gets boiled'. Hengen comments that 'we learn to sympathise for the downtrodden through fairytales and that we also learn to find solutions to our own problems'. Women who 'still remain caught between the traditional and pivotal woman's role of nurturer, and the new roles demanded of them in life in a difficult, complex world'[61] need some of Zenia's hardness or they get boiled, she argues.

Alice Palumbo's review is a very thorough integration of issues of fairytale Gothic and the feminist. She sees this novel as filled with typical Atwood elements: 'the use of Toronto and menacing urban settings, the constant reworking of Gothic and fairytale elements, and reflections on female friendship ... A macabre, sentimental and naive romance ... An overgrown Gothic.[62]

She uses Leslie Fiedler's definition of the Gothic in *Love and Death in the American Novel* (1960) as a 'series of genre clichés exaggerated to grotesqueness',[63] noticing that *The Robber Bride*, with its lost mothers, abusive fathers, damaged children, vicious upbringings, double characters and overlapping contradictions combines many versions of the Gothic: 'The Female Gothic, and nineteenth century American Gothic, the one looking at childhoods, the other the figure of the "transforming woman"'.[64]

Each woman finds a tale to fit Zenia. She is the original treacherous guest, as Tony reflects: 'People like Zenia can never step through your doorway, can never enter and entangle themselves in your life, unless you invite them in. There has to be a recognition, an offer of hospitality, a word of greeting.'[65]

Sandra Mackenzie notes the 'hypnotically intricate plot, the vividly realized characters, the impeccably detailed settings'[66] of the lives of the women united by having attended the same college and being wounded by Zenia. Zenia is an 'amola pedato' who lies and cheats, steals their men, dumps them and ruins lives. The men, though, are 'emotional cripples' and are interchangeable. A familiar Atwood landscape, it is 'littered with the wasted bodies of damaged women and the menacing shadows of the men who wounded them either by their distance or their presence'.[67]

Atwood has argued that the fairytales we grew up with all feature handsome princes, but that there are others with violent, different roles for men and women. Talking to Val Ross[68] in the Rivoli restaurant, which Ross feels could be the model for the Toxique, Atwood declares that the only real-life person in *The Robber Bride* is Saddam Hussein, who is mentioned in conversation in the novel, and that she allied herself with each character: with Roz, interested in interior design; Tony, because she is diminutive; and Zenia because 'of course I'm Zenia-like. She's a liar, and what do novelists do? They lie.' Atwood also notes that readers need to see Lake Ontario as a motif – 'lots of things disappear into Lake Ontario: Tony's mother's ashes, the identity of Charis ... it's all part of the final scene.'[69]

A feminist novel?

Christopher Gully, interviewing Atwood, asked about the reception of the work as not feminist, to which she replied that not all men are devils nor women angels and that she had never met a feminist who believed that to be the case, although some believed all men to be devils. He argues that: 'The treacherous little girls in *Cat's Eye*, and Zenia, the monstrous villainous, main character in *The Robber Bride*, whom Atwood says could be modelled after Madonna or Cher, have conformed with her feminist stance.'[70]

Atwood acknowledges that the book has some sustaining relationships in it. However, Judith Timson says, '[It] has as its central theme an idea that feminism was duped ...: there are female predators out there, and they will get your man if you are not careful, even if you are.'[71]

She sees Zenia as 'a double agent, every woman's worst nightmare',[72] and finds the jokiness of Toronto detail doesn't quite fit the sifting through the detritus of each woman's past. 'Up on a pedestal or down on our knees, it's all a male fantasy', muses Roz. 'Even pretending you're not catering to male fantasies is a male fantasy'[73] but the combination of the trite and dark does not please this reviewer.

A Gothic fantasy, the novel investigates versions of sexuality, gender roles, male/female relationships and female/female relationships. It is meta-fictional, playing with and commenting on the power of language, of memory and history. History is not fixed and dependable but clearly a construction – Tony, the historian, constructs and rewrites, replays it in her lectures; versions unravel; and history, seen as a construct, pinned down by military tactics, nonetheless evades real comprehension. Skilled in dramatic representations of self, of disguises, Zenia produces lurid versions of herself and her history for each woman: a Russian, a refugee, a child prostitute. History is shown to be a construction.

Twinning is a significant motif throughout. The novel explores Otherising and ways of coming to terms with versions of self and reality. Charis' repressed Other is the more violent, abused Karen, who returns when she is destabilised. Roz's twins, Erin and Paula, tell different versions of fairytales and construct life differently. Following a disturbed childhood, Tony reverses words to control them, a language which gives her ritualistic power. The three words by which the women define Zenia illustrate their different natures: inspirational (Tony), peaceful (Charis) and kaput (Roz). Zenia, their mirror image/opposite, threatens each differently: 'she makes me sick of myself', says Charis, 'What is she doing here on this side of the mirror?'[74] For Tony, Zenia's influence means menace, chaos, cities, flame, towers crashing down, the anarchy of deep water.[75] Alice Palumbo sees: 'one long act of exorcism'. Each woman tries to exorcise her past through her relationship with Zenia so

> Tony sees her life, and her interactions with Zenia, using the rhetoric of history, while Charis sees her own relationship with Zenia through New Age prophecy, and Roz through the language of mystery novels and fairytales. Zenia wreaks havoc with the lives of each of the women.[76]

Zenia herself is each woman's alter ego, bad twin, a sustained fiction, and Atwood indicates that what is more important than the facts of her life is the impact she has on others. If a familiar feminist fiction is that all women are good, their problems caused externally, by cultural constraints, then Zenia as fascinating and deadly undercuts such naïveté. She seems witch-like, vampiric, a female monster. However, her role exposes the flaws and internalised constraints of each woman's life, their dependence on deceptive, selfish, weak men, their vulnerabilities. The damage she does to them comes from these weaknesses, and ultimately feeds into their strengths and survival as a community, and as individuals.

A Canadian novel

The Robber Bride is a Gothic exploration of the damage people do to themselves and each other, located in the streets and houses of Toronto, but internationally familiar. Carole Ann Howells identifies contemporary Canadian social history in the novel's chronicle of changing cultural fashions in post-war Toronto, ending with a street map placed over a map of medieval Europe, while world events swirl around the narrative. Arguably, there is a new awareness here of Canada in a globalised context. Atwood, the shape-shifter, transforms her favourite genre, the Gothic, and demonstrates that her writing 'is both canonical and post canonical, nationalistic and postnationalistic, realistic and postmodern'.[77]

In a later critical essay, Howells both places the novel in its historical context and expands other arguments about definitions and expressions of what it means to be Canadian. She places this Gothic novel with those in which Atwood deals with history, place and contemporary issues from a Canadian perspective, such as the earlier *Surfacing* and *Bodily Harm*. The novel, she argues, primarily:

> addresses English Canadian anxieties about changing representations of national identity, focused at a precise point in time and place: Toronto in 1990–1991, while that city is itself situated in the international context, with events in eastern Europe and the Gulf war whirling around. Atwood's concerns with late twentieth century Canada's malaise have shifted off anxieties about the country's survival expressed in *Wilderness Tips* (1991).[78]

In *The Robber Bride* she is asking, are we really that different from anybody else and, if so, how? What do distinctively Canadian identities – personal and collective – look like in the 1990s, and is Canadian identity always in the plural, to take into account cultural differences and revised narratives of Canada's national heritage? Howells finally suggests:

> *The Robber Bride* is a ghost story or rather a story about exorcising ghosts, in an attempt at a realistic reappraisal of Canadianness in the 1990s and a more honest recognition of the differences concealed within constructions of personal and national identity.[79]

Using postcolonial theory, she explores how Atwood's 'fictional representations' of subjectivity reveal the non-fixity of identity, and how her narrative strategies uncover secrets hidden in the past, thus deconstructing myths of white English Canadian authenticity, and showing how 'difference is a crucial fact in any identity construction'.[80] Zenia's foreignness labels her not just Other woman but Other, maybe an immigration threat. However, she actually enables the women to move on and change, thus offering the positive side of multiculturalism. Zenia tells her stories and the others tell theirs, upon which she capitalises.

The comic

The novel is postfeminist, Gothic and also comic, ironic, a fine example of Atwood's wordplay and lively imagination. Sandra Martin
sees *The Robber Bride* as 'playful with razor blades', which are always
a 'tantalising and potential wounding business'. Atwood is uncon-
ventional, challenging readers with 'what do you think about?'
The title is compelling and 'grisly', Grimm's fairytale 'shamelessly
appropriated, combined with various body parts and peccadilloes
associated with contemporary Canadian sirens'.[81] She likes two
scenes, where Tony is talking about Saddam Hussein, comparing
him to Caesar crossing the Rubicon, and the women discuss a range
of lipsticks referencing famous rivers fatefully crossed – Tennyson
(a bright, cool red), the Jordan (a rich, good-time red) and the
Ganges (a blazing orange). The St Lawrence (a fire and ice hot pink)
is dismissed because 'saints won't do'.[82] A second favourite scene
is where Tony is in the basement, early morning in Toronto, in the
new house, replaying military battles on the sand table bought at a
garage sale – moving spices around to create the combatants: 'cloves
for the Germanic tribes, red peppercorns for the Vikings, green
peppercorns for the Saracens, white ones for the Slavs'.[83] Zenia is a
figure straight from Atwood's unpopular girls, fairytale and myth.
In the next chapter, the exploration of *Alias Grace* (1996) focuses on
yet another Atwood female liar.

7

No Nearer the Truth:
Versions of Fictionalising:
Alias Grace (1996)

Alias Grace retells the tale of a convicted nineteenth-century Canadian murderess and *cause célèbre*, Grace Marks, who probably killed both her employer Thomas Kinnear and Nancy Montgomery, his lover and housekeeper, with the aid of her own lover, James McDermott. Grace was a poor Irish immigrant, and she could have been cajoled, tricked or seduced into taking part in the murders, or perhaps they were her idea in the first place. As a woman, she was sent to prison, while McDermott was condemned to death. The difficulties of fixing the truth at the time, and then in history, is as much the subject here as Grace Marks's crimes. Unravelling what might have happened exposes a wealth of Victorian obsessions about women's innocence, sexuality, and spiritualism. The case of Grace Marks fascinated Susanna Moodie, pioneer, diarist and prison visitor, as it has Atwood since. First Moodie, Atwood and then the reader piece together newspaper reports, ballads and testimonies to try and determine exactly what did happen and how guilty Grace actually was. In Atwood's novel we match the documentary evidence and response against Grace Marks's own tale, but still get no nearer to any final truth and, as Atwood frequently reminds us, those who tell stories cannot be trusted. *Alias Grace* combines a range of Atwood's fascinations. Canadian history, murder mystery, women's roles and performances and the art and function of storytelling come together in this tale of a poor, immigrant Irish maidservant escaping poverty into household service, who might or might not be a dual murderer. Grace is a consummate role player, storyteller and performer, so we are left quilting versions together and never really finding the 'truth'.

Alias Grace has received a great deal of critical attention since its publication. Two main areas of interest recur. One concentrates on the problematising of fixing, articulating and proving history and the facts of any events, given the questionable status of all forms of records, from journalism to first-person narrative, or ballad to police record. Another is concerned with historically contextualising the representation and treatment of women.

Early reviews

Readers and reviewers found the tale sensational, mired in nineteenth-century misogyny in its representation of Grace, and rich in humanity – a fascinating story which ultimately refuses to close itself down. Several reviewers like the Victorian qualities of the novel, its interest in the psychological, its construction and representation of women, and its dealing with the lack of dependability of historical records, testimony and memories. Some take a feminist approach, while others focus on the Gothic qualities. Some include interviews with Atwood which show her playing with language, ironic, constructing a public self, and aware of representing a Canadian consciousness, Canadian issues, locations and history. Despite Atwood's insistence that the tales she tells do not resemble her own life, several reviewers seek similarities between Grace and the author (role play and construction of identity).

Most recently, *Alias Grace* has been compared with the range of Atwood's work in terms of issues of identity, Canadian qualities and women's roles. Most critical books on Atwood came out before *Alias Grace* was published but latterly twentieth- and twenty-first-century critics, comparing *Alias Grace* to the prize-winning *The Blind Assassin* (2000), focus on the Canadian qualities, and the unreliability and jigsaw puzzle nature of contrasting history and testimony. Both novels are partly personal testimony, partly layered palimpsest text of documentary, journalistic, literary, personal and historical records. As such, *Alias Grace* is seen as postmodernist in its focus on the fragmentary nature and undependability of history and memory, its intertextuality, and problematising of 'reality' and the 'self' as unitary. Popular fictional genres can be seen as cultural indices, and this novel incorporates elements of crime fiction, journal and diary writing, and a horror novel plumbing the psyche and revealing trauma through imagery and memory.

Early favourable reviewers focused on the detailed, factual recreation of nineteenth-century Canada, and the reopening of the historically notorious murder case, which caused divided responses at the time. Hilary Mantel takes a historical approach which establishes the colonial history of the case. Mantel looks at Grace's origins, history and linking her life with Grace's crossing of social boundaries. Grace escaped her brutal father, into domestic servitude.[1] When offered a job by good-tempered, pretty Nancy, Grace perceives that Mr Kinnear's household is not as straightforward as it seems. He crosses various boundaries in his relationship with Nancy, his mistress, for whom he buys gold ornaments and jewellery. Grace's location at the edge of the town and forest is already on a boundary, and her boundary crossing awakens Grace's sexuality, her desires for a better life.

Frank Davey's observations of Atwood's treatment of class undermine any simple reading of this as an example of the hard lives of working-class immigrant women.[2] Grace has a middle-class mother, her Aunt Pauline runs a dry goods business and Davey suggests her intelligence reveals itself through her control of her story and hiding of details, rather like the middle-class origins of a lost child reveal themselves in Dickens. Simon Jordan, the neo-Freudian doctor who attempts to psychoanalyse Grace, but actually becomes obsessed by her, tries to see himself outside class. Davey compares him with John Fowles' Charles in *The French Lieutenant's Woman* because he is an example of someone on the cusp of social change – vulnerable as well as questioning. For both these men, the link between their conservative ways and their sense of new knowledge is negotiated through a relationship with a woman. While Davey does not extend the discussion, this could be seen as contributing to the realignment of *Alias Grace* as a novel which characterises women's time (as described by Kristeva), and an undermining of patriarchal or phallocentric narratives. Grace's shifting tale speaks of a working-class immigrant woman, whose life would have remained silenced in record and narrative. The very shiftiness of the tale she tells and those told of her emphasise the constructedness of all history and its partiality, since public record and accepted history are more likely to be that of those in power: middle-class men. Grace's narrative challenges readings of lives of the past, as does the shape of the novel, which resembles a quilt, patches making different patterns, depending on the point of view of the interpreter.

For Rosario Arias, the historical elements bring 'the past to life' and give us a 'portrait of mid-nineteenth-century Canadian society in the full description of the voyage from Ireland – Grace's homeland – to Canada', including the hardships which followed, Grace's mother's death and poverty, with 'minute details of house-keeping as well as accounts of Spiritualism and Mesmerism, very popular in both the United States and Canada at that time'.[3]

Arias sees it as a version of what Linda Hutcheon terms 'histo-riographical metafiction'[4] (fictional constructions of history) and focuses on ways in which Atwood deals with the reconstruction of the historical novel, as well as problematising the fixed nature of history.

Some reviewers have emphasised ways that the novel contributed to the developing Canadian literary scene and others, including Lindsay Duguid, emphasised the psychoanalytic and psychologi-cal focus, who discusses the interest in hypnotism, séances, and in storytelling at the novel's heart. She notices how people:

> dabble in séances and mesmerism and crude theories of 'neuro-hypnotism,' unleashing terrible demons. It is these wild imaginings which seem to go to the heart of the mystery, though Grace herself pro-poses a metafictional solution: 'When you are in the middle of a story it isn't a story at all, but only a confusion.'[5]

The credibility of the spiritualism offers insights into an under-standing (or not) of Grace and her fictions. Peter Kemp argues that Atwood presents us with both the terrors of the period and its Zeitgeist, the spirit of the age – the way it lives and breathes: 'The way in which fustiness and rawness mingle in the mid-19th-century provincial Canadian society is pungently conveyed.' But the novel goes further than detailing historical moments and Grace Marks's tale, offering a Gothic texture in its details which reminds the reader of the murders at its heart. Kemp notes the governor's wife's parlour has furniture 'done out in "the colours ... of the inside of the body – the maroon of kidneys, the reddish purple of hearts, the opaque blue of veins, the ivory of teeth and bones"'.[6]

Like Kemp, Francine Prose identifies Margaret Atwood's achieve-ment in writing what appears and sounds like a nineteenth-century novel with 'the physical heft and weighty authority of a 19th-century novel. In its scope, its moral seriousness, its paradoxically ponder-ous and engrossing narrative, the book evokes the high Victorian mode', and laced with Gothic 'spooky plot twists'.[7] However, she is unconvinced about the need for such a wealth of historical detail and research.

Prose compares it to work by Charlotte Brontë (*Jane Eyre*, 1847), Daphne du Maurier (*Rebecca*, 1938) and short stories by Alice Munro. This is partly because of its very credible, authentic creation of a voice for Grace, which provides insights into the daily lives of the servant classes, so that with 'startling authenticity, Atwood conveys the delirious joy that a fresh red radish or a newly plucked chicken offers a woman who has survived on prison fare'.[8]

Like Munro's characters, Grace is trapped in her role in a small town, but Atwood's text adds a Gothic tinge to the historically realistic. The everyday feel of haunted places and objects is brought to life in a threatening manner. This could be seen to mirror Grace's own parallel text of seemingly straightforward recall with infusions of suppressed guilt. A washday description is riddled with decapitated creatures and ghosts, so we sense Grace is haunted both by the murders and possible violent urges and madness, which are never acknowledged in her first-person narrative. Prose is unhappy with the novel's use of dissemination and research, however, seeing it as 'a crash course in Victorian culture', because it introduces information on spiritualism and the middle class's 'quasi-religious faith in progress, its mounting discomfort with the gap between the theology and science'.[9] This is a lively review but mistakes as pretentious scholarship Atwood's deliberate use of the recorded weight of history, evidence and research, which accumulates around a historical event and/or a person. The offering up of all the details which we need to contextualise and interpret Grace and the murders deliberately indicates that no amount of ponderous excess can ever bring us or any other historical or contemporary researchers any closer to what really happened, what the 'truth' is. Unravelling the truth, or failing to do so, is explored further below.

Feminism and the treatment of women

Many reviewers took a feminist approach. According to Catherine Pepinster, Atwood's quarrels with second-wave feminism are a response to a rather too straightforward take on gendered representations and politics:

> This latest novel is a far cry from green-spined Virago volumes in which the heroine copes with the infidelities of double-dealing men. Atwood

is suspicious of such labels, such as feminist writer, which has been attached to her since she published *Surfacing*.[10]

Carol Angier, however, considers the novel a feminist treatise resembling *The Handmaid's Tale*.[11] Grace answers (or evades) the questions posed her by Simon Jordan, who has conventional gendered fantasies and hang-ups about his own early relationships with servant girls. Jordan mistakenly perceives Grace as a maiden in a tower (the Rapunzel figure) who needs to be rescued, but Grace cleverly manages her interactions with him. Sometimes she tells him what he wants, sometimes she shows incomprehension. She survives 'the projections of a nation, and escapes to marriage and freedom', while Simon Jordan ends up suffering a form of psychosis, the main victim of the fantasies in which he invests 'cut down by a cruel irony: sex brings him as close as it brought Grace to madness and murder, and he ends as she began, an amnesiac prisoner'.[12]

Love and sex are problematic here as in all Atwood texts. Angier concentrates on the love between Kinnear and Nancy Montgomery, that between Grace and James McDermott, and on ways in which men construct and represent Grace. She compares Atwood's tale to myths, fairytales and nineteenth-century texts, such as *Jane Eyre*, exploring engagement with constructions and representations of women, sex and psychology. However, Christopher Lehmann-Haupt reads the relationship between Simon Jordan and Grace Marks as a thwarted romantic fiction, ignoring the voyeuristic and rather lascivious subconscious responses Jordan develops while psychoanalysing her.[13] Lindsay Duguid connects with the popular Victorian myth of the beautiful, wronged, trapped woman, filtering out the topical fascination with sex and death. No single narrative sums up Grace, whose candour deceives us. We can never discover the truth: 'Our interest, like Jordan's, is partly in whether this is actually a case of madness, or promiscuity, or plain murder.'[14] For Duguid, Atwood gives us 'a sinister femaleness'. Grace is both deceptive and perhaps a victim, while the other women are simultaneously seemingly beautiful and innocent but also disgusting:

> under their crinolines, the do-gooding ladies are 'delicate and white, like wobbly soft-boiled eggs'; a servant's thighs are imagined as 'greyish, like boiled sausages, and stubbled like a singed turkey'; when she sleeps with the son of the house, Mary stops smelling like 'nutmeg or carnations' and reeks of 'salt fish'.[15]

Unravelling the truth

Part of the story's fascination is the link between love and violence, the ultimate uncertainty of Grace's exact role in the murders.
Another is the representation of this, the ways in which different
versions of events are presented in history through document, ballad and memory, brought together here in the novel like patches in
a quilt – with themes, and different patterns. When Atwood found
that Moodie's records of visits to Grace in Kingston Penitentiary and
Toronto Lunatic Asylum were factually flawed, she set about searching through other contemporary historical records and produced
a fiction which mirrors the confusion of reported and recorded
versions. Atwood's addition – Grace's own narration, thoughts and
memories – simultaneously reveals and puzzles. We can appreciate
how Grace is both a victim of, and manipulates, the naïvetés and
obsessions of her times.

It seems that far from being an innocent, bullied or tricked by
her lover into murdering her boss, Grace might have been playing Bonnie to McDermott's Clyde. Atwood was not satisfied with
Grace's skewed legacy, so she dug deeper, as do several critics who
are fascinated with murderers and how they are reported.

David Wiley uses interview material with Margaret Atwood in
his review, comparing the story to other notorious cases: Lizzie
Borden, the subject of a popular tale and song, who killed her family with an axe, and the more recent serial murderer, Ted Bundy,
who mutilated and killed women.[16] Wiley also relates Grace Marks's
tale to the O. J. Simpson trial in terms of its public fascination, and
recognises that the love rectangle in the Kinnear household provides much interest for contemporary readers. Thomas Kinnear
is probably a 'remittance' man, a younger son sent abroad to find
his fortune. When he has an affair with his housekeeper, Nancy
Montgomery, she becomes pregnant. As his fortunes grow, he
employs two more servants, James McDermott, the valet, and Grace
Marks, who are only there for just three weeks before the tragedy
takes place. Wiley sees the tale as no more complex in its origins
than an episode of *Rikki Lake* or *Jerry Springer*, two US television
programmes which rely on sensationalism and exposés, but Grace's
tale is fatal in its consequences. Grace falls for Kinnear, who loves
Nancy. McDermott's motives are unclear, and in an attempt to
make sense of them, Susanna Moodie wrote a little Victorian play
in which McDermott tells his version, identifying Grace as the

instigator because of her love for Kinnear. When McDermott kills Nancy, Grace feels the event is over, but McDermott has another plot in mind. Wanting her for himself means killing Kinnear.

Christopher Lehmann-Haupt digs more deeply into both the stories which constrain people culturally and ways the mind hides details, which psychoanalysis attempts to uncover. Form and psychoanalysis are linked in the recurrence and patterning of symbols and leitmotifs. Apples emphasise the Garden of Eden motif. Grace deals with conventional beliefs that, as a woman, she is paradoxically bound to be both the author of original sin, like Eve, and also too delicate to have committed sin. When Simon invites Grace to retell her story, revive her memories, he brings her fruit and vegetables:

> the apple Simon offers Grace initiates an intricate symbolic working out of the Eden myth that ultimately resolves itself in Grace's theory that only one tree existed in Paradise, 'and that the Fruit of Life and the Fruit of Good and Evil were the same'.[17]

Lehmann-Haupt falls into a rather conventional fictional trap himself, however, when he reads the novel as romantic fiction, believing that the readership expect Simon and Grace to fall in love because of the intensity of their time together.

Quilting

Quilting, a woman's form of artistic expression, lies at the heart of the novel's structure, representing construction, patterning and hidden or revealed themes. Atwood is very thorough in her research. Her deliberate use of quilting, one of Grace's pleasures, offers a kind of patchwork shape to the novel, which indicates ways in which we read patterns into events to make sense of them, leads the reader into trying to determine 'the truth' and yet enacts the difficulties of constructing a single final narrative. The storyline, feminist comments and romance are each differently figured in quilting motifs, and Peter Kemp notes that quilt patterns give the chapters their names: 'Jagged Edges, Broken Dishes, Pandora's Box – take their names from 19th century quilt patterns'.[18] Maureen Freely reads quilting through a feminist, psychoanalytic approach.[19] Such an approach can lead us to appreciate Grace's own self-defence mechanisms through the protective cover of her role as a seamstress working on a quilt for the governor's family, and the patterned versions of events which she reveals or constructs as if individualised quilting pieces, in response to Simon Jordan's questioning. Atwood does not change historical facts about Grace, but invents other elements to fit into her quilt, notable among which is the creation of Simon Jordan, a 'protopsychologist'. Scrapbooks and albums, another type of collection, and the jigsawing of events, are mentioned in the early stages of Grace's dealings with Jordan, accentuating the sense of the novel as both album and quilt, and emphasising how he, like the reader, tries to piece together a coherent narrative. While she talks to Simon Jordan, he 'works hard to unravel her defences'.[20] Ironically, Jordan is more likely to come unravelled than Grace. As a son without an inheritance, he must make a name for himself, and he establishes trust by writing down all she says, proving himself a good listener. Jordan, however, lacks the structure of Grace Marks. His life spirals out of control and we, as readers, try to piece it all together, as we also do Grace's narrative. The nature of the collections and quilting patterns reveal a great deal about those who construct, use and try and patch them together, and we cannot trust his interpretations. Rosario Arias uses criminal defence, arguing that the novel gives us the voice of the culturally silenced, poor Irish woman, and that quilting suggests revelation, hiding Grace's own tale in the midst of others' versions. Arias sees Grace and Atwood constructing the tale against:

> male discrimination, and against the shadows left in cultural records. In having Grace's viewpoint, the narrative questions the (mis)representations about her and lets us hear the voice of the traditionally silent and dead.[21]

Both the prison governor's wife and his daughters are devoted collectors. She collects newspaper cuttings about notorious criminals to 'frighten' her acquaintances, but the daughters' tastes run more to sentimentality, with scraps of cloth from their dresses, magazine pictures, written expressions of undying love from female friends, and a scarf to remind one daughter of a young woman who drowned in the lake. Grace Marks dwells on the meaning of these collections, and her own contributions to the album quilt of the novel represent the same themes of crime, friendship, love and death.

Grace imagines the leitmotif of the Garden of Eden and Tree of Paradise as quilting patterns she can reproduce. These images seem to characterise her own position, since they suggest both the dangers of seeking forbidden knowledge and ways in which Western society consistently blames women for Eve's original sin. Margaret Rogerson suggests that Grace has asserted the wholeness of her life story in the Tree design, but, because she speaks in a quiltmaker's dialect, her meanings are unclear, perhaps even to herself.[22] For Arias, the novel is a linear collection of quilt block patterns. Grace uses third-person dialogue to narrate the murders, suggesting you might consider events from different perspectives.

> if you looked at it one way it was closed boxes, and when you looked at it another way the boxes were open, and I suppose the closed boxes were the attics and the open ones were the windows.[23]

For Peter Kemp, the contours of the patchwork parts reveal Grace's feelings and the varied textures of events and records: 'the "flaring colours" of the quilt segments signal the importance of the bed as the place of domestic dramas: births, sex, sickness, death, dreams, nightmare.[24] Hilary Mantel compares Atwood and Grace as expert quilters. We must patch together versions of reality and events since:

> [C]onsciousness, is fragmented and can be rearranged, she suggests; your perception of the past is likewise a thing of shreds and patches. And this tale of memory, murder and possession is also a novel of ideas, where intellect and passion are finely hand-stitched, revealing their ultimate effect only when some 500 pages are shaken out and the dazzling design shows, in all the glory of its pattern, texture and colour.[25]

Among others, Ingersoll identifies the quilting metaphor as the main structuring device in the novel: 'the patchwork trope functions as the organising principle of others' narrative'.[26] He positions the 'traditional novel', which offers a 'seamless' version of the story and characterisation, with both early novels – Thomas Sterne's *Tristram Shandy* – and more contemporary works such as Flann O'Brien's *At-Swim-Two-Birds*, which each expose the constructedness of narrative as they do that of our own narrative histories. The novel is one among many, which could also include Doris Lessing's *The Golden Notebook*, that offer multiple perspectives and potentialities, multiple readings of a constructed text, and in so doing undermine the sense that there can be a single version of any history.

Alias Grace builds on Linda Hutcheon's definitions of history as graphical meta-fiction,[27] which recognise ways in which post-modern writing reconstructs the past and retells the stories, some of which have been fixed in documents or memories showing them to be deconstructions. Several texts (including Pat Barker's *Regeneration* trilogy) build on and explore a 'theoretical self-awareness of history and fiction as human constructs ... made the grounds for[a] rethinking and reworking of the forms and contents of the past'.[28] Murray discusses the quilting in *Alias Grace* as an example of what we realise, that even in reconstructing versions of the past we are always constructing, there is no fixed point of truth,[29] so 'the patchwork quilt comes to represent the determining paradox of the novel: that of making present meaning from traces'[30] of the past including *The Journals of Susanna Moodie*. Murray traces Atwood's use of sewing and scissor work in her poetic reconstruction of Susanna Moodie's own writing (*Roughing it in the Bush* and *Life in the Clearings*), through the forbidden pleasures of sewing in *The Handmaid's Tale*, to the unstitching of history by historian Tony in *The Robber Bride*, who indicates that you can unravel history by picking at any thread. This is how Tony begins one of her more convoluted lectures, the one on the dynamics of spontaneous massacres. The metaphor is of weaving or else of knitting, and of sewing scissors. On the one hand, Grace is a competent seamstress and, as Murray notes, her sewing offers a certain control and repetition, but against this mechanical control is set her desire to please Simon Jordan in selecting some elements from her ragbag of a past history to put together into a story for him to please him. Desire, Murray suggests, gives Grace the power to choose how to present her history – and Jordan, too, tries to patch it together to suit his own version of her. Grace, Murray argues, recognises the importance of quilts in the 1840s as a trousseau item and as indicators of the difficulties of women's lives, childbirth and child rearing. Grace then situates herself as representing the hardships of women's lives. While one quilt pattern represents broken dishes, remnants of the teapot Grace's Aunt Pauline gave her mother, which fell and broke on the journey, producing fragments, the other, called 'Attic Windows', suggests different perspectives, as Grace notes:

> that is the same with all quilts, you can see them two different ways, by looking at the dark pieces, or else the light.[31]

Murray comments: 'The act of interpretation is quite clearly implied in this passage. Grace's discourse communicates variability of perspective and therefore suggests the diversity and the instability of positions offered to "the one who looks".'[32] In discussing the relationship between the quilting metaphor and that of contrasting readings of events and of the narrative, the quilt, Murray notes, is both a whole patterned piece and fragmented, so suggesting both unity and its lack, its temporary partiality.

Finally, Grace's understanding of male dominance is echoed in her choice of other quilt patterns: 'she acknowledges the phallic dominance of patriarchy'[33] – 'On my Tree of Paradise, I intend to put a border of snakes entwined.'[34]

Ingersoll mentions Julia Kristeva who, with Judith Butler, exposes the ways in which women are themselves performative, constructions in a male gaze and a patriarchally constructed narrative. Grace is reconstructed by the documentary, journalistic and balladic versions of her life, and redescribed by Simon Jordan. It can be argued that the quilting or patchwork nature of the ways in which she tells her tale undercuts the socially and historically dominant modes of constructing and representing women's lives. Ingersoll moves beyond earlier readings of the quilting metaphor and exposes ways in which the first person narrative status itself is undermined by the fragments and the way they are combined together. When readers reach Part IV: 'A Young Man's Fancy', a combination of letters to which Grace would not have had access in Part VI, and a third person narrative about Jordan in sections VIII, X and X1, among other fragments, the first person narrative is undercut. Ingersoll sees Grace as 'bent on subverting the novel's form and the move towards standard'.[35] Her Tree of Paradise pattern offers a version of an untrustworthy relationship with the man who earlier exposed her. Using the work of Barbara Jonson and Teresa de Lauretis, the 'effort at avoiding a tempting impulse to define a single female narrative paradigm',[36] the text emerges as a masquerade, actually deconstructing what we expect in a traditional narrative.

Quilting also captures Grace's own personal version of a romantic fiction. However, what she ends up with is a potentially problematic marriage 'to a man whose testimony helped put her behind bars is reflected in the second-hand and potentially unlucky "Log Cabin" quilt under which they sleep.'[37]

Storytelling and murder mystery

A version of Scheherazade, the legendary woman storyteller in the *Arabian Nights* (1706), who told tales to keep herself alive, Grace compels Simon Jordan to listen, while simultaneously enthralling readers by the mysteries which are drawn from her tale (and his): 'By focusing on Grace's story, she echoes the major obsessions of her fiction: women's identity, the relations of the sexes, the nature of consciousness itself.'[38]

States of consciousness, confusions, the need to fix identity, and searching for truth underpin the tale, problematising the belief that there is any fixed, discoverable truth in the first place. Simon, interested in unconscious mental processes and wishing to open his own asylum, hopes to encourage Grace to remember, to 'open her up like an oyster'.[39] But Grace is too amorphous. He merely discovers a version of her history constructed to fit his obsessions. Her experiences of sex, love and child bearing are conditioned by her poverty and class position, while his grow from his own position of privilege, chasing after the maids in a wealthy home.

Tom LeClair uses the language of seduction and guilt, seeing the writing characterised by a 'coiled discipline'. He aligns form with content and views Grace's story as 'criminally seductive' and 'the most telling displacement yet of Atwood, the subversive artist and ideological outlaw'.[40] Nicholas Basbanes focuses on the murder as a form of explosion from social containment, comparing Grace's tale to the tale of Lizzie Borden, and interspersing quotations from Atwood, who considers it more as a mystery about a murder than a murder mystery: 'In a murder mystery you have to come up with the solution, or the readers will rise up against you. You can't just end it by saying, "Well, I don't know."'[41]

Atwood emphasises how dangerous it is to trust any single version of history, in this case Susanna Moodie's, or Grace Marks's. Spiritual and mystical concerns were popular in the period, when in an attempt to find 'the truth', nineteenth-century Canada turned to spiritualism, séances, table-tapping, mediumship, and trances, something Atwood also explores in *Lady Oracle*. Arias suggests the novel is as much a tale of possession as detective fiction,[42] while for Alison Moore science and spiritualism collide:

> This is the age of scientific disciplines and unbridled mysticism – studies of the brain and drawing room table-rapping séances, electromagnetic

therapies and mesmerism. This is a novel about gender and power and the upheaval of superstition in the face of what may or may not be provable theory.[43]

In taking a clinical interest, Jordan hopes to map the unconscious, but Grace Marks, whether mere serving girl or clever manipulator, sends everyone around her into a free fall into the unconscious. Jordan's questioning provokes a version of Grace's tale which we should find difficult to trust, warns Moore, who links it with contemporary 'false memory' syndrome which, she suggests, resembles the states of amnesia Grace claims when unable to recall details of the murders. Jordan is bewildered by Grace and encourages her to remember the murder and its causes, but transference takes place. The dreams he wants Grace to remember so he can record and analyze them spring instead from his own suggestible unconscious. He imagines Grace's sexual dominance but discovers himself acting this out with his own landlady.

Nineteenth-century Scheherazade, and woman under threat, Grace Marks keeps both her story and herself alive, and out of prison, through this weaving of fascinating versions filled with patterns and gaps, a series of versions of her own tale of the incidents of the murder. Grace Marks's storytelling fascinates not only Simon Jordan but the reader, and Atwood's construction and compilation of traces and versions also fascinate us, focusing us on ways we reconstruct the past and the present and how we, too, stay coherent and alive through storytelling. Atwood is a historian of the popular and the imaginary as well as of real events. As readers, we attempt to construct the fuller picture of events of Grace Marks's tale in context, taking into account others' interpretations, including Jordan's, and what influences these interpretations. It is a multi-layered text encouraging a multi-layered interpretation.

At the time of its publication, Atwood said her fascination with Marks and with the notion of making marks on paper, recording things, inspired the novel. In the 1996 Charles R. Bronfman lecture in Canadian Studies at the University of Ottawa, 'In search of *Alias Grace*: on writing Canadian historical fiction',[44] she comments that fiction relates the history of the individual to more general history. Canadian history and literature were largely missing in her schooling and the new generation of post-war writers ignore history in the main and yet: 'we were, however, relentlessly contemporary: history, for us, either did not exist, or it happened elsewhere, or if it was ours, it was boring. Their history was "anaemic".'[45]

She speaks of the 'lure of time travel, which appeals to the little cultural anthropologist in each one of us', and how she initially believed all she read in Moodie's account of Marks, 'a scowling, sullen teenage temptress', from the visit to the penitentiary in 1851. McDermott was a 'dupe' driven by lust for Grace. Atwood believed then that 'non-fiction' meant 'true': 'I did not question it.' The story fascinated her, but waited its time. In the 1970s, she wrote a television script, tried to turn it into a theatre piece, but it became too far-fetched. In a hotel in the 1990s, suddenly it came to her when she was staring at notepaper:

> The past is made of paper; sometimes, now, it's made of microfilm and CD-ROMS, but ultimately they too are made of paper. Sometimes there's a building or a picture of a grave, but mostly it's paper. Paper must be taken care of; archivists and librarians are the guardian angels of paper; without them there would be a lot less of the past than there is ..., we owe them a huge debt of thanks ... There is – as I increasingly came to discover – no more reason to trust anything written down on paper then than theatre.[46]

No one really tells the 'truth', it is all constructed. Eventually,

> despite Atwood's crystal-clear vision, she leaves the story as muddy as history itself. And that's the point. There's no way to recover Grace Marks fully, and with *Alias Grace* Atwood has done her the greatest service a novelist could do: She's left her intact and in peace.[47]

It is a powerful historical tale which gives a voice to the silenced working-class woman, and to a particular period in Canadian history, but it also emphasises the difficulties of determining historical facts, bound as we are with interpretations and fictions. Nevertheless, Atwood counsels, the past belongs to us, because we are the ones who need it.[48]

In the next chapter on *The Blind Assassin* (2000) and *The Penelopiad* (2005), women's constrained lives and the power of fiction are again the main focus.

8

Rewriting History and Myth: *The Blind Assassin* (2000), *The Penelopiad* (2005)

Both *The Blind Assassin* (2000) and *The Penelopiad* (2005) continue Margaret Atwood's fascination with storytelling and the fictionalising process. Each novel explores ways in which narrative strategies can construct, cover up or expose family secrets and maintain myths. Each deals with roles expected of women, some fulfilled and some undermined and ironised. Penelope, faithful wife of the journeying Odysseus, reveals the plots and fictions which kept her and her court busy, her myth intact. Iris Chase Griffen both strings together various versions of the story of her own life and that of her sister, Laura, at particular moments in Toronto society, and offers alternatives through the formulae of different kinds of fiction. Both women weave stories which present different versions and undermine any final reading.

The Blind Assassin (2000)

In the Booker Prize-winning *The Blind Assassin*, 82-year-old Iris Chase Griffen carries out her own 'negotiating with the dead', struggling to get to the end of the writing of the novel, 'letting the blood' of her last days to bring the dead back so she can tell their stories. One of these stories is of her sister Laura, alleged author of *The Blind Assassin*, the announcement of whose death starts the novel and invites readers' attention for what can be seen as a 'whodunnit' – with a vengeance. Elaborating the initial mystery: 'Ten days after the war ended, my sister Laura drove her car off a bridge',[1] the novel can be seen as a 'line' (a piece of fiction, a lie, a version), like *Alias Grace*

132

(1996), dependent on a fallible narrator. In fact, *Alias Grace, The Blind Assassin* (2000) and *The Angel of Bad Judgement* (Margaret Atwood Papers) all came from the same Atwood 'UR source', or initial set of ideas and writing, showing her fascination with the ways in which people try to narrativise, tell stories and construct truths. Iris's terrible cover-up is exposed first to herself and then to the reader, as we pick through the layers of the texts, and put together a reading of the photographs of her past and that of Laura. Sharon Wilson tells us they 'seem to indicate a paradoxical but not uncommon direction for a postmodern writer: increasing historical documentation that compounds textual gaps and coexists with growing magical realism'.[2] Both *The Blind Assassin* and *Alias Grace* are period pieces and about research: the attempt to construct meaning or truth about both personal and public pasts. Both novels are puzzles about the inconsistencies between appearance and reality: the appearance of piety and propriety versus hidden murder, abuse, rape, and other violence. Like a Greek tragedy.[3]

Atwood and, through her, Iris, cast doubt on the ways we can rearrange memory and story so that photographs resemble war memorials, they memorialise, but are critiques, and evidence passions, pain and attempts to heal. Because the tales, photographs and other documents are assembled before us, we see that reading them as 'the truth' is rather arbitrary. Attempts at verification only undercut the possibility of determining what really happened. In this respect, Wilson points out that the novel is a metafiction which rearranges time and events to suit the aesthetic and neatening purposes of the narrator.

The role of the narrator and the interpreter of 'reality' or history are favourite Atwood topics. In her focus on the texture of the lives of the Chase sisters, as scripted by Iris, she uses a variety of popular fictional forms, including sci-fi with a political message. Atwood also focuses on constraints on women, and on female narrators. Women are sacrificial victims, society hostesses hiding secrets and tolerating bullying. Iris's language has a socially superficial surface of respectability, but what she really thinks, what she reveals only appear gradually, in the cracks, silences and nested boxes of memoir. The novel exposes ways in which different versions of records, and different fictions each construct different stories, and how difficult it is to piece together any viable route through. What is left is intertextual reading, splicing the versions and producing a different pattern. Throughout Iris's tale we believe her straightforward

version of her own marriage to Richard Griffen. It emerges as a
society cover-up of a relationship based on conformity and control,
and on the abuse of Laura, whom Richard made pregnant, then banished to have an abortion. Finally we learn that Iris's own daughter
Aimee was the child of the political radical Alex Thomas. Laura's
story is a gothic tale of woman silenced, incarcerated and misrepresented, who finally reveals all through forms of secret superscripts
over the public version of the lives of the Griffens, their relatives and
contacts. The Iris and Richard tale is a gothic marriage tale of conformity and hidden abuse. Society successes represent their lives in
public photographs and journalistic records, but they hide the violent oppressive relationships underlying such performed, conformist versions. Like the versions of Grace Marks's story in *Alias Grace*,
the palimpsestic layers of journalism, public record, private journals, codes, photographs and fictive, embedded tales come together
as an alternative version, though no final truths can be proven and
there is no dependable narrator. Some of 'the truth', as Iris reveals it,
helps us to piece together earlier hints about how little Laura ever
wrote, and so we realise the bestselling novel was Iris's not Laura's.
The Blind Assassin reveals its nested fictional versions and its public
narratives, sets science fiction side by side with memoir and gothic
romance, and produces as many hidden as revealed stories.

Early reviews

Early reviewers are interested in time, memory, the gap between
official, managed versions of family histories, fictions and the possibly real events. Barbara Mujica speculates that time is the blind
assassin in this novel: 'the blind force of evil lurks everywhere in
Atwood's novel; we are all potential blind assassins. But the most
heartless assassin is time. Atwood is obsessed with time,'[4] while
Roberta Rubenstein sees Atwood as 'a fiendishly clever manipulator of the reader's knowledge'.[5] Reviewers comment that versions of
the constructedness of life appear in romantic stories of love, sexual
involvement, class difference, politics and wild imagination. For
Lorna Sage, the novel is a detailed family saga:

> The story of the rise and fall of Canadian captains of industry, repre-
> sentative lives, and wives. It is a garrulous account full of circumstantial
> detail: clothes, weather, class conflict, real estate, photograph albums,

gossip, secrets and lies, set off with dry, present tense awareness of mortality and materiality.[6]

The Blind Assassin mixes the fictional with the semi-fictionalised autobiographical records and intersperses versions of what happened, or what people might be like, with constructions and representations from journalism and other public documentation. It is clear that we and our society are all in the fictionalising business. Records, representations and interpretations are constructions of the concretely experienced real or the real of the imagination.

Memory, history and fiction

As an octogenarian, Iris recalls her and her sister's lives as children, growing up in the 1920s in a large nineteenth-century house named Avilion, after the 'island-valley' in Alfred Lord Tennyson's 'Idylls of the King' (1859). She narrates the romantic story they were told about the meeting and love of their parents and their mother's work in the war. Following this romanticised version and harsher events, their hard-drinking, physically and emotionally war-damaged father returned from the war, took up disreputable wanderings in the old town, and their mother died from a miscarriage. There are many missing or dead mothers in Atwood, as in many other contemporary women writers, and these girls certainly lack consistent care. Their father consigns them to a series of ineffectual governesses and tutors, a paedophile, bully and a dreamer, and no-one can really control or guide Iris and Laura. They develop apart from the working-class children in their father's button factory, aware of the need to wear the right clothes, yet wishing to be beyond the boundaries of social niceties, looking askance at its constructed versions of behaviour and life. While Iris grows up more conformist in order to keep the family economically stable, Laura is troubled by taking everything literally. They are surrounded by people who fictionalise or problematise the relationship between words, values and shared realities, especially the housekeeper Reenie, Iris's old nursemaid, 'a starchy font of home truths and old saws',[7] who deals in clichés and idiomatic expressions. Laura, the more vulnerable, less stable of the sisters, believes herself the cause of their mother's death.

Memory and memoir have been used before to effect by Atwood in *Cat's Eye* (1988), in a retrospective exploring the artist Elaine

Risley's return to Toronto, the location for spiteful childish experiences; Grace Marks in *Alias Grace* also tells part of her story, as
does Jimmy/Snowman in *Oryx and Crake* (2003), and Offred the
handmaid in *The Handmaid's Tale* (1985). Atwood explores the
human need to shape, weave, fictionalise, try out versions of self
and events and share them, while she also undercuts any hold on
certainty or the possibility of any grasp of the real. Iris needs to set
a few stories straight or perhaps to construct a palatable version
of repressed events and memories. Memory and time reveal, suppress and offer alternatives. Within Iris's recall of their childhood
and young adulthood, and set against political events of the 1930s
through the Depression and up to the Spanish Civil war, is nested
Laura's (it seems) novel *The Blind Assassin*, a romantic fiction which
made her famous. It seems based on a relationship between a
young woman very like herself and a man who resembles the war-
orphaned, political radical, Alex Thomas, whom the girls housed
and protected.

The third boxed narrative within Laura's romantic fiction *The
Blind Assassin* is the science fiction tales of 'the Peach women of
Aa'A', 'The Lizard Men of Xenor' and 'The Blind Assassin of Zycron',
a tale which the male protagonist, the Alex figure, of Laura's/Iris's
romantic fiction, tells his female lover in their snatched moments
together under trees, or in borrowed rooms. Here they construct a
world that bizarrely echoes the extremes of their everyday world,
but also enacts and criticises the suppressive representations of
women in myth and culture. It provides insights into the male sci-fi
narrator's versions of and tastes for life, and women.

His tales are of politics, and the controlling power of myth to
manage both class and gender relations. He peoples them with
muted beautiful women, sacrificed in lieu of the daughters of the
upper classes, and blind assassins, working-class heroes of sorts,
driven by the agendas of politicians to murder the girls, and victims
of beliefs concerning society's continuance. This is a land populated
by tyrannical Snilfards and subjugated Ygnirods (Alex's bolshevism
shows through this division). In Zycron, no one really believes
in the myths any more but they seem to need to perpetuate their
paraphernalia. Girls continue to die, assassins to murder, and kings
to rule, rather pointlessly and vacuously. These pulp sci-fi tales are
really fantasy versions of the lives and experiences of the two Chase
women. In Zycron, women grow on trees and, like Laura and Iris,
they have constrained lives ruled by social and cultural mores.

Molly Hite focuses on the fate of the women in the sci-fi tale and on one particular virgin, singled out for ritual and sacrifice, who has her tongue cut out to prevent complaint or cries against the High Priest who comes to cut her throat and sacrifice her:[8]

> Thus, tongueless and swollen with words she could never again pronounce, each girl would be led in procession to the sound of solemn music, wrapped in veils and garlanded with flowers, up the winding steps to the city's ninth door. Nowadays you might say she looked like a pampered society bride.[9]

Referring to the Greek myth of Philomela, who was raped and had her tongue cut out to prevent her naming her attacker, Hite comments:

> Margaret Atwood's novel *The Blind Assassin* is about the conjunction between pampered society brides and these sci-fi Philomelas: mute girls, swollen with words. That is, it is about haves and have-nots, marriage, love (which is not the same thing), sacrifice, and stories, told and untold. Within the novel, stories produce anguish and arousal, charges and vindications, guilt and vengeance.[10]

This is an unpleasant fictional universe. As the narrator notes: 'In Paradise there are no stories, because there are no journeys. It's loss and regret and misery and yearning that drive the story forward.'[11]

Alex Thompson's science fictions are very one-sided, but like the rest of these narratives, multiple versions question fixed truths of 'history', the reliability of narrators and the fixity of identity. The different formats of sci-fi, murder mystery, fable, diary/journal, novels and journalism present very different renderings of experience, history and people's lives, each of which can cast some light on constructions and interpretations of events, each limited by its own genre.

Elaine Showalter sees the interrelatedness of the boxed tales, each dealing with virgin sacrifice.[12] She comments on ways in which, in the frame narrative of the Toronto society marriage in the Depression, told in retrospect by Iris Chase Griffen, Laura and Iris are both differently sacrificed, while *The Blind Assassin*, the posthumous novel-within-the-novel of two illicit lovers, ostensibly told by Iris's suicidal sister Laura, is hard-boiled and stylised. The third novel, also called *The Blind Assassin*, the pulp science-fiction story, which the unnamed lovers tell each other between sexual bouts and which explores the extraterrestrial world of Zycron, the home of the Lizard Men and the Peach Women, is cruel, exotic and cynical. Showalter sees blindness and the corruption of innocence running throughout each tale. Stories within the sci-fi story indicate relationships between myth, class, sex and power. In one repeated, developing tale, children are forced to make carpets until they go blind. One of the assassins falls in love with a victim. In the second, inset tale in Zycron, the Peach women of Aa'A grow on trees. This is a paradise which Showalter presumes is for men, which you can't leave, and therefore, the novel suggests, can only be hell.

Ingersoll discusses ways in which the novel plays on the idea of 'lines' and selling us a line in Iris's tale. He compares the novel to a crime fiction or whodunnit:

> Her repeated troping of the flow of the words from her body as a 'line' can suggest two equally important (and less than positive) implications: either Iris is 'feeding her readers a line' with the bait of a revelation to come when they are 'hooked,' or she is spinning out the thread of a web in which unwary readers will eventually become trapped.[13]

This emphasises the 'textuality' of the narrative, its constructedness. Atwood's choice of title, he argues, seems a gesture toward modernism, teasing readers into suspecting everything is metafiction, a fiction commenting on fiction, and wondering who the real 'Blind Assassin' might be. Wendy Roy's later essay also sees the novel as a mystery, in which Iris and Laura are sold into a form of white slavery.[14] For Iris, this entails marriage to Richard, the subsequent silencing of her tale, hidden marking on her well-clad body, while for Laura it is incarceration for mental health problems (read, abortion of Richard's child). Clues in Iris's narrative link her and Alex to the protagonists of the embedded modernist novel. The two narratives are just as firmly connected by their parallel emphasis on societal sanctioning of the sexualising and silencing of women. Roy suggests that in its sexual power and rawness, the short fragmented novel of love and desire is reminiscent of Elizabeth Smart's (1945) Canadian modernist classic, *By Grand Central Station I Sat Down and Wept* (to which the fictional critics in *The Blind Assassin* also compare it). Sharon Wilson sees it as a Gothic tale, like *The Robber Bride* and several Atwood short stories.[15]

David Punter characterises the Gothic as: 'A way of imagining the unimaginable, whether it be the distant depths of history or the even more distant soundings of the unconscious. The gothic is a distorting lens, a magnifying lens.'[16]

In this novel:

> The protagonist needs to find the hidden coded message to gain knowledge of the unspeakable: here represented by the tragic and gothic story of her sister's life and *her* sacrifice. When Iris does find, and manages to interpret, the messages – hidden in old notebooks and hand-tinted in her wedding photos – she is faced with a horrific story: a story that 'had been there all along, right before my very eyes. How could I have been so blind?'[17]

Another Gothic theme emerges as we realise Richard and Winifred had Laura confined in an institution as if mad, and

> here, the gothic theme about the madwoman is turned even more gothic as the reader learns that the clinic is an abortion clinic. Consequently, Atwood's novel also included the 'marital gothic,' since Richard sexually abuses both his young wife and even younger sister-in-law.[18]

Brooks Bouson explores the text as a puzzle composed of many retellings of a story: 'Atwood, through repetitive retellings of the story of women's sexual victimization, probes the cultural – and historical – repetition of sexual violence against women, showing the link between institutionalized misogyny and the sexual traumatization of women.'[19]

Continuing the theme of women's oppression and silencing, Helena Hyttinen exposes manipulation and control of events, in particular, of women's lives (a topic explored throughout Atwood's earlier *Lady Oracle*). For her, the novel takes issues of representation into a discussion of ways in which Atwood uses popular and established fictional genres: 'Atwood is hence highly involved in scrutinizing not only social and political structures but also the structures prevailing within the realm of literature, from a perspective that highlights power structures and gender discourse.'[20]

She also identifies Gothic characteristics: 'Among the many genres Atwood intricately uses and transcends in her novel *The Blind Assassin* we find the Gothic romance with its key characteristics of mystery and betrayal, of lies and the unspoken, of the unspeakable, and of buried life.'[21]

'Laura's' novella destroys Richard's reputation and eventually his life but still silences Laura because it is taken to represent her secret life.

Atwood is herself close to popular culture as a guest on talk shows and author of a string of bestsellers. She read a lot of pulp magazine fictions as a child, from romantic fiction, to sci-fi, to political allegory, and she uses them in the novel. As Sharon Wilson notes, this provides a record of and comment on North American popular culture:

> Atwood's works incisively record, investigate, satirize, and paradoxically celebrate North American popular culture. In addition to household appliances and other objects we may see every day, she uses both urban and wilderness settings, styles of clothing and home culture.[22]

Both Iris and Laura belong to the past. There effectively is no future generation. Aimee, Iris's daughter, dies of drugs and self-neglect, and Laura's daughter, an unknown quantity, was aborted or disappeared. Here the book becomes self-conscious in an entirely modern fashion. Futures lie with readers and we can no longer rely on assumptions about place or the family.

Issues of ageing and dying are to be expected in the tale of an octogenarian. Iris, with her damaged ear, feels she's racing towards a motel room aged with mildew. The fate of the text is dependent upon the ways in which it is read and interpreted and some of the best writing is seen as saved for the end, when the elderly narrator confuses past with present, sister with sister, life, death and love. The last pages reveal the love affair between Iris and Alex, a confession, like Offred playing Scrabble with the commander in *The Handmaid's Tale* (1985).

Elaine Showalter, in 'Virgin suicide', points out similarities between the pulp fictions and Iris's life: 'cruel, exotic and cynical, married off to a business man, she realises her husband would enjoy her suffering "my job was to open my legs and shut my mouth"'.[23] Showalter sees this as *The Handmaid's Tale* turned inside out, in which the female narrator is obsessed with memory and truth but unreliable and secretive. Atwood, she argues, deploys a gothic architecture of basements and attics, a décor of trunks, torn photographs and elaborate costumes; her heroines are sacrificial virgins legitimated by religion, myth and fairytale.

The Blind Assassin is a novel of factual detail, but, ironically, unreliable truths. Some reviewers do not like the detail, arguing that

Atwood sometimes operates with the indiscriminate retrieval of an Internet search engine set to 'display all'. Thomas Mallon finds her detail excessive. Initially, Iris seems determined to get the tale told through clippings, but this evolves into self-aware, highly constructed language which Mallon dislikes:

> Adding to an extraordinary stock of rhetorical irritants is Iris's tic of etymologizing or parsing the obvious: 'That's my trousseau, I thought ... It sounded like trussed'; 'I considered the word warn'; 'Laura had finally snapped. Snapped, she said, as if Laura was a bean.' One also comes up against Atwood's peculiar tendency to mint similes whose vehicles are more obscure than what they're describing: 'yeast fermenting, going straight to her head like warm helium'.[24]

Unlike other reviewers, he criticises ways the form and expression develop, and finds the chattiness irritating.

Karen Stein traces Gothic elements, plot devices and narrative strategies in the novel, in which the protagonists vacillate between 'hiding/revealing, and speech/silence', struggling to 'discover how to live in a dangerous society'.[25] Iris unravels clues and unpicks themes, captivating then revealing her story, wielding it 'like a weapon, captivating her readers and gaining justification and revenge against her husband and sister-in-law'.[26]

As Hytinnen notes, there is a multitude of voices through time and space so:

> The role, function, and identity of the narrator *and* the arranging narrator(s) remain a haunting mystery to the readers. The incorporation of tales within tales is skilfully carried out in order to have the multiple tales enter into dialogue discourse since they not only intersect but also interact with each other as well as with other texts, thus inviting an intertextual reading of the novel.[27]

Most recently Ellen McWilliams focuses on the novel as one of Atwood's female *Bildungsroman* and in so doing explores ways in which Iris constructs versions of her own life in her hiding of Laura's, and assemblage of documents, photographs and fictions. The novel 'replaces conventional narrative of cohesive, singular development, with sometimes outrageous narratives of multiple identity'.[28] Atwood as a postmodernist writer is seen as 'coming of age' in a way that is similar to that of Canadian writing itself. Her writing here is essentially political and related to *Lady Oracle* and

Cat's Eye since both artist and writer share an interest in the changes and paradoxes of 'writing a life' and draw attention to the processes of evasion, subversion and illusion that are at work in all narratives of self, but necessarily most dramatically manifested in those self-consciously committed to writing women's lives.

Iris is a 'puzzle' of self in a narrative showing the 'mode of mutually dependent literary selves'.[29] The novel offers an 'intrusive and audaciously unreliable narrator', a 'stealthy manipulation of a literary persona'.[30] McWilliams sees the novel as a 'fusion of interpolated fictions'.[31]

In the next novel, *The Penelopiad*, another woman's story is revealed.

The Penelopiad (2005)

Atwood's *The Penelopiad* is another tale of woman as storyteller, constructing and weaving her own versions of events. Here, Atwood revisits Penelope – faithful, waiting wife of Odysseus, her warrior husband in Homer's *The Odyssey* (ancient Greek epic poem from the eighth century BC). Penelope wards off suitors but has different versions of events and her own life to those commonly received through Homer's retelling of the historical myths.

The Penelopiad is part of the 'Myths' series, commissioned by Canongate, in partnership with other European publishers. Authors Chinua Achebe, A.S. Byatt, David Grossman, Milton Hatoun, Su Tong and Victor Pelevin were invited to take a myth of their choice and rework it in a contemporary way.

This novelette is a post-feminist reinterpretation of a mythic relationship. Atwood loves short fictional forms, their aphorisms and punchy one-liners, their ability to rework a myth or behavioural nonsense in a few words. Some of this is explored in Chapter 3 on her earlier short stories and in Chapter 10 on *The Tent* (2006). *The Penelopiad* is filled with opportunities to hear the silenced women, to unpick woven versions, and discover some everyday trials of being not only a faithful wife, but a mythic representative of certain outdated values, hiding truths about the testing times and boredoms. Penelope reveals her secrets, and the silenced of history and myth, her twelve maids, also tell their own stories. In *The Odyssey*, the maids collude with the suitors, sleeping with them, and are eventually hanged for their experiences, but here they emerge as lively and devious, supporting Penelope in her tedious years of not merely waiting for her husband's return, but warding off greedy men determined to take his place and lands.

Catherine Taylor sees the tale as social commentary, with its sour teenaged Telemachus and the sisterly unities among the women. Penelope, left behind on 'inhospitable' Ithaca, waits for ten years for the return of her husband, hero of the Trojan War, while:

> Telemachus develops from a suspicious child into a disgruntled teenager and slow-burning sociopath, and Penelope, having through sheer hard work successfully maintained Odysseus's kingdom, is importuned by scores of would-be suitors eager to siphon off her wealth.[32]

The maids are significant. Complicit in their mistress's plans to foil the suitors, they are hanged by Odysseus on his return, as part of his 'bloody revenge'. But they are not all guilty, and this seems a brutal misplaced revenge. The image of their execution 'for a little while their feet twitched, but not for very long'[33] is distressing. Taylor notes that Atwood uses poetry, burlesque, mock trial and, less successfully, dour sociological tract. Penelope is a survivor, Helen a beautiful rival, and Helen seems more fun, while the afterlife has some come-uppances for Odysseus and his wife: an eternity of wandering through fields of asphodel, haunted by their unexpiated guilt.[34] *The Penelopiad* gives Homer's Odyssey a female voice.

Atwood has a wry sense of humour. We find Penelope commenting on herself, Odysseus, suitors, men in general, and on her fashion-conscious, rather contemporary cousin Helen, in a very modern manner, after death, in which she learns about high-heels and bustles, and how dangerous the world is.

Most reviewers find the book fun, a new version of an epic tale giving a women-oriented worldview. However, they also see it as quite lightweight, preferring the parts about rivalry in the afterlife/netherworld where Penelope and Helen meet again. Simon Goldhill calls it a lightweight 'bourgeois sitcom' and sees the choric maids as:

> resentful but vivacious victims of the hero's desire for patriarchal order because they act as a chorus line singing sea shanties, popular tunes and ballads, kicking their legs (when hanged) as if in a musical rather than in violent punishment.[35]

The style and form are in many ways a new move for Atwood, into pastiche, which is familiar in her short stories. Goldhill, however, does not underplay the role of comedy in commentary on modern life, finding the ending 'surprisingly poignant', as Penelope confesses that unlike Helen, she is unwilling to risk going back to earth to try life out again.

> Others also find it a fun book. Rebecca Ascher-Walsh, in *Entertainment Weekly*, comments: 'She channels Penelope by way of *Absolutely Fabulous*; one can imagine her chain-smoking and swilling wine between cracks about the weakness of men and the misery they visit upon women.'[36] Others find her lively, witty, even 'spry', the work formally daring: 'Pragmatic, clever, domestic, mournful, Penelope is a perfect Atwood heroine ... What gives her narrative its moral problem and its emotional centre of gravity are the choric songs, lightly burlesqued, that intersperse it.[37]

It is a burlesque novel, jokey, anachronistic, with Penelope a modern Canadian heroine.

Coral Ann Howells finds 'A whiff of scandal' in this woman-centred version of Homer's *The Odyssey* , and suggests that images of shape-changing and surreptitious returns from the dead remind us of Atwood's fascination with the Gothic, so *The Penelopiad* might be seen as Atwood's Gothic version of *The Odyssey*, while her description of the play script version as 'an echo of an echo of an echo of an echo'[38] (*The Penelopiad: The Play, v*) could be read as either very Gothic, with its whispered continuities, or as very postmodern with its deferrals and indeterminacies.

Howells sees it as a 'shape-changing text,' since its first appearance in 'the book version' in 2005 was followed by a staged reading in a London church (Atwood played Penelope), a lay script Atwood adapted first performed at the Swan Theatre (2007), after changes negotiated with the director, Josette Bushell-Mingo.[39]

Howells argues that Atwood challenges *The Odyssey* and flouts epic conventions:

> instead of war she deals with domestic relations, shifting the action indoors, and dismantling the epic model by transforming it into a double-voiced female confessional narrative, interspersed with song-and-dance routines, a burlesque drama, an anthropology lecture, and a trial scene, videotaped by the maids.[40]

So the different generic conventions for storytelling are explored and doubt cast on any single version: 'Atwood is highlighting the malleability of myths and openness to revision.'[41]

The undercutting of form and the trustworthiness of story are accompanied by undercutting Homeric epic language as Penelope uses a 'very postmodern scepticism towards tales of heroism and the sacred'.[42] She also undercuts Odysseus's physical and moral stature noting his 'short legs' and 'how can I put this? – his unscrupulousness'[43] and removes the supernatural elements of the mythic through her ironic storytelling seen as a 'low art' practised by old women, beggars and children – but also by Odysseus and herself.[44]

Formally, she notes: 'Unlike Penelope's carefully crafted monologue, the maids' stories are multivoiced and fragmentary as Atwood reimagines their lives through a dazzling variety of narrative forms, alternating between poetry and song, prose, and burlesque drama.'[45]

Shannon Hengen tells us that in 2007, in collaboration with the UK's Royal Shakespeare Company, the Ottawa National Arts Centre very successfully adapted *The Penelopiad* for the stage in a cabaret style, building on the previous adaptations of *The Handmaid's Tale* and her earlier 1993 piece *Penelope*, which grows from the 'Circe/ Mud Poems', in *You Are Happy*. Atwood explained to radio journalist Carol Off in a CBC interview about the staged rendering of *The Penelopiad* that the origins of myth are always both oral and local, that myth is shaped from the beginning by its method of delivery *and* by the time and place in which it is told.[46]

Hengen comments that Penelope's opening warning "Don't follow my example," 'is beckoning us to relive experientially and individually Penelope's neglect of her disadvantaged maids and then, as an audience, to discern the instances and effects of similar neglect in our time.'[47]

As with this tale from Homer, more recent Atwood work has been produced in a cabaret style, mixing choral song, monologue, dialogue, and dance.

Media accounts detail the collaboration between two powerful women: Phyllida Lloyd, British director of the opera version of *The Handmaid's Tale*, and Margaret Atwood, which initiated *The Penelopiad* as opera and coproduction.

Hengen provides the playbill which introduces 'the Penelope Circle' of nine Canadian women donors who recognise the importance of Canadian artists involved in *The Penelopiad*. Each gave leadership gifts to enable young women to act as their protégés, to champion *The Penelopiad* project.

Conclusion

Both *The Penelopiad* and *The Blind Assassin* deal with the retelling
of old stories, the remaking of old myths and the alteration of fixed
versions – a female insider's version of events. Iris Chase Griffen
reveals the hidden secrets of her life with her sister and the oppressive husband, the 'truth' about authorship, and versions which
the narrative might take to interweave fantasies and truths. In the
rewritten myth of Odysseus, Penelope uses images of weaving suitable to her history and brings to life the cat fights with Helen, the
everyday irritations and tedium of suitors, court and married life,
while the book gives a voice to the murdered maids. Each novel suggests that fictions, histories and myths are merely versions of events:
constraining, liberating or damage-limitation exercises. Elizabeth
Hand points out that of Penelope, as of other women in myth, it can
be said: 'Atwood doesn't exactly give her a makeover, but she gives
her a voice, at once plaintive and wise.'[48]

The makeover is itself a re-telling, a cosmetic version of truths
which can never quite be reached. In *Oryx and Crake* (2003),
another storyteller, the last man alive, constructs a tale of pre- and
post-holocaust.

9

Writers, Readers, Constructions of the Real and the Future: *Oryx and Crake* (2003)

This chapter looks at the novel *Oryx and Crake*, although the novel's focus on preservation of the species and preservation of language is also the concern of Atwood's lectures/essays *Negotiating with the Dead* (2002), which preceded the novel by two years. The themes and characters are revisited in *The Year of the Flood* (2009), which is discussed in Chapter 11, and we are promised a third novel in the trilogy.

Oryx and Crake is set on the East Coast of America (Atwood, with her scathing Canadian view of the US, likes to use it for her dystopias. *The Handmaid's Tale* is set in Cambridge, Massachusetts). *Oryx and Crake* opens in the year 2025 when most life on earth has been destroyed by a holocaust caused by unscrupulous, unethical genetic engineering and human carelessness. There is one main female character, the Asian ex-child porn star Oryx, and two main male characters, Jimmy, and his more intelligent friend Glenn. Jimmy is the protagonist and, it seems, the last surviving human. Much of the novel retells the tale of events up to Jimmy's desolate endangered existence in the present of 2025, then looks at his daily semi-existence in the polluted world. Jimmy/Snowman and Glenn/Crake were brought up in the Compounds, a protected zone guarded by the CorpSeCorps, a form of secret police, and removed from the violent, impoverished and less healthy pleeblands, a wild, lawless place where ordinary people live, outside the Compound. They led a regulated life which removed all will and energy from Jimmy's more radical mother, who moved from a job in science, to depression and eventual escape, and probably death. Left to their own devices, the young men visited Internet porn sites and played endless video games, which largely focused on destroying virtual people and worlds. Not surprisingly, neither developed any sense of morality or empathy for others, but for the highly intelligent scientific Glenn, nicknamed Crake after the red-necked Australian bird, this led to a godlike sense of power, an amoral lack of humanity, the creation of drugs and false medicines, and more or less accidentally, the destruction of most of the human race.

Oryx and Crake was published in the same year as the fiftieth anniversary of Crick and Watson's discovery of the double helix structure of DNA, which details and maps the code of all living organisms. For a novel focusing on the damage we might do to our planet through genetic engineering and the substitution of a virtual destructive reality for one which might grow and change organically, this is a significant moment. In this novel, a sole human survivor, Jimmy/Snowman (Abominable Snowman is how he sees himself – part myth, part terror, part sub-human and definitely isolated), surveys a post-holocaust world of strange creatures, hot sun and debris. His position is one of liminality, as he is probably the last human alive, tasked with caring for creatures, Crakers, an engineered, gentle race, who have some relationship to him as human, stranded in a post-holocaust moment, caught between states of being and probably about to starve. Coral Ann Howells points out that 'death hangs over the novel from the start'.[1] Snowman's storytelling role is divided between his public myth-making of the Crakers and his private monologue – addressed to whom? – 'Any reader he can possibly imagine is in the past',[2] though an article and subscript identify that the narrative has been produced for Oryx to read (an address later embedded in the unpublished version).[3]

Early reviews

Early reviews debate whether this is a science fiction novel, how it relates to Atwood's earlier dystopia, *The Handmaid's Tale* (1985), which she saw as a kind of 'bookend' to this new work, and the treatment of gender and language. For Ingersoll,[4] *Oryx and Crake* is a survival novel, replaying Atwood's interest in science fiction from her earlier *The Handmaid's Tale*, of a kind with Mary Shelley's (1797–1851) *Frankenstein* (1818), George Orwell's (1903–50) *Nineteen Eighty-Four* (1949), and Aldous Huxley's (1894–1963) *Brave New World* (1932), particularly through the use of the survivor, protagonist Jimmy/Snowman. His scientific, logic-oriented friend Glenn/Crake is a kind of Dr Frankenstein.

The novel's doom-laden, futuristic dystopian vision resembles both *The Time Machine* (1895) by H.G. Wells (1866–1946) and *The Island of Dr. Moreau* (1896), which is probably a closer comparison because of its focus on genetic splicing and engineering. Atwood's animal–human hybrids ('pigoons', created at 'OrganInc Farms' – a name that neatly encapsulates her vision of the future) acquire 'human cunning with no diminution of animal savagery'.[5] Atwood is exploring a brutal world ravaged by climate change and populated by genetically modified animals and hubristic scientists, says Tara Pepper.[6]

Critical appreciation of the novel focuses on the ways in which it identifies links between science and the arts, alerting us to the threat that we lose our creativity, passion, imagination and humanity at the expense of humankind itself. These issues are the matter of both ecological and science fictions, since each warns about genetic engineering and climate change, and science fiction can project forward to and enact the repercussions of ignoring such warnings.

The tone is 'dark, dry, scabrously witty, yet moving and studded with flashes of pure poetry',[7] although Natasha Walter finds the need to inform us about the future world sometimes leads to a rather dull tone, as she finds Atwood's style 'simply a vehicle for imparting information' and finds that 'it can begin to grate. The narrative voice becomes almost like a tour guide, always there at your elbow, to explain and clarify.'[8]

Oryx and Crake is a last man narrative. Snowman scavenges for food, taking refuge at night in a tree because the other genetic successes, the pigoons and rakunks, might otherwise tear him to pieces. The aggression of the human and animal world was spliced into the genetic make-up of these new creatures to disastrous effect. 'Snowman's liminal status is underscored repeatedly in the text.'[9]

> But those rules no longer apply and it's given Snowman a bitter pleasure to adopt this dubious label. The Abominable Snowman – existing and not existing, flickering at the edges of blizzards, apelike man or manlike ape, stealthy, elusive, known only through rumours and its backward-pointing footprints.[10]

Jimmy/Snowman's head is filled with a series of voices, overloaded as the airwaves. In order to grasp his sense of location and being, he shifts in his storytelling between the dangerous present of predatory experimental creatures in the world – wolfogs, pigoons – and ways of trying to stitch something together from the past, his childhood and upbringing, which might make some sense of it all. He is vulnerable, human man stripped down to his basic, insect-bitten, homeless humanity and left with little more than his memories, lost hopes and, most importantly, his creativity, his ability to tell his story and play with words. Lisa Appignanesi comments:

> In Jimmy, Atwood has created a great character: a tragi-comic artist of the future, part buffoon, part Orpheus. An adman who's a sad man; a jealous lover who's in perpetual mourning; a fantasist who can only remember the past.
>   Like Winston Smith and Offred the Handmaid, Jimmy believes in the power of love. For him, it's too late.[11]

She sees the Crakers 'the ultimate in genetic engineering' as hope. Jimmy's loss of love, of Oryx, makes him a tragic figure but he is also rather cornered into responsibility, as a kindly nurturer to the childlike Crakers, who need his leadership and his confirmation of the God-like roles of both Crake and Oryx. As a focaliser, someone from whose point of view the story is focused, Jimmy provides a way in for readers and, in so doing, ensures some kind of continuity and existence for himself and his tale.

Science fiction?

There was much debate in the critical and literary world, including discussions on the Fantastic in the Arts discussion list (at www.iafa. org), about whether or not this novel is science fiction. Atwood's claim that it is not science fiction[12] caused a furore among sci-fi and fantasy writers, and critics have different views, as they did over *The Handmaid's Tale*. She argues that it has 'no intergalactic space travel, no teleportation, no martians'.[13] But, taking the part of critics who see science fiction as projecting forward the fears and promises of the present into an alternative world, and/or a future time, this does not mean it cannot be so categorised – or cursed. Atwood argues 'it invents nothing we haven't already invented, started to invent'[14] and insists she is writing speculative fiction, rather than science fiction. She explores the distinctions. Atwood comments that writing about the future is usually termed science fiction or speculative fiction, and that the terms are fluid. She identifies both *Oryx and Crake* and *The Handmaid's Tale* as fitting these descriptions but suggests that she really sees science fiction as taking place in another world, or concerning things which have not happened/have not yet happened. She says:

> I like to make a distinction between science fiction proper and speculative fiction. For me, the science fiction label belongs on books with things in them that we can't yet do, such as going through a wormhole in space to another universe; and speculative fiction means a work that employs the means already to hand, such as DNA identification and credit cards, and that takes place on Planet Earth.

Atwood has also ensured that her research enables her to imaginatively grow both the ecological and human disasters from real events and trends. The University of Toronto, Thomas Fisher rare book library 'Brown box', is testimony to an accumulation of well-documented research, 'so there's nothing I can't back up'.[15] She has clipped news items from papers and popular science magazines, collecting images, ideas and reports, and 'noting with alarm that trends derided ten years ago as paranoid fantasies had become possibilities, then actualities'.[16] She used a similar research method with her clippings file for *The Handmaid's Tale*. In this second dystopian novel there is also a webpage in her Acknowledgments, citing references consulted.[17]

In the first novel, humankind's betrayal of life and the land leads to a totalitarian state in which women are treated as reproductive others, whilst in *Oryx and Crake* it seems unlikely that there will be any procreation at all following this particular holocaust, itself engendered by a valueless playfulness and lack of consideration of humankind, Crake treating the world like a kind of eco-oriented computer game. Everyday behaviours of everyday humans are equally at fault. Natasha Walter recognises Atwood's wicked sense of dark comedy and notes she 'has a lot of fun imagining the havoc that might be wreaked on the gene pool if scientists were constrained by nothing except the profit motive.'[18] The sterile and restricted world of the novel's opening was caused by poisoning the planet and undermining values that could lead to a sustainable lifestyle for most people. As Brooks Bouson points out, Atwood 'draws openly on the discourse of environmentalism as she emphasizes the effects of global warming on the future world',[19] in which the waters dry up, meat becomes hard to find and once lush areas turn arid.

North of Caution: A Journey through the Conservation Economy on the Northwest Coast of British Columbia (2001),[20] a book produced about and through the conservation economy on the northwest coast of British Columbia, was one of Atwood's sources influencing this contemporary and futuristic eco dystopian novel. She also used *Biomimicry: Innovation Inspired by Nature* (1997).[21] *Oryx and Crake* is a tale about ecological disaster and the survival of humans in their most basic form.

> *Oryx and Crake* projects a world defamiliarised not through military or state power but through the bias of scientific knowledge, where genetic engineering has created transgenic monsters and humanoid creatures in a post-apocalyptic scenario much closer to conventional science fiction.[22]

Howells quotes Bill McKibbens' views, that science fiction writers have taken technologies and 'dreamed up a galaxy of dystopias, each more unpleasant than the one before'.[23] In this, this novel differs from *The Handmaid's Tale*, which is both national rather than global in its reach and focus on fundamentalist religious regimes and the technological control of women's bodies. The earlier novel locates its events in a dystopian future world and offers a narrative where vision is limited, unique, and questionably verifiable (like most narratives, one could argue).

Moral and ethical issues

Surfacing (1976) introduced readers to Atwood's concerns with ecology and consumerism, while *The Handmaid's Tale* raised issues about individual freedoms following a holocaust, a disaster, the terrible repercussions of human selfishness, greed, ignorance and violence. Brooks Bouson considers her focus on environmentalism and biotechnology in which the planet uses up its resources, and people turn their backs on not only the environment but whatever helps sustain human life. This discourse is exposed and countered by that of *North of Caution*. The arid infertile planes, the deadly sea filled with 'ersatz' rubbish from a consumerist society and the scorching sun are all indicators of global warming fuelled by ignorance and a refusal to live in natural harmony with the environment, an apocalyptic setting found in a whole raft of novels and films of the early twenty-first century, including *The Day After Tomorrow* and Cormack McCarthy's *The Road*. Atwood indicts a blinkered removal from moral engagement evidenced in the hubristic game 'Extinctathon', which enacts in virtual play space the death of millions of species, matched by their actual deaths in the world outside the Compound. The wilful, godlike arrogance of biotechnology, in which danger-ous, genetic, experimental, spliced creatures prey on whatever is left living, is somewhat tempered in her critique when the same biotechnology also produces the gentle Crakers.

Daniel Mendelsohn [24] finds Atwood engaged, but her protagonist treated unsympathetically, arguing that, 'For Atwood, the greatest preoccupations have been sexism and class injustice.'[25] Although morally and politically outraged, this novel deals with abuse of nature itself 'by a culture whose intellectual sophistication has out-paced its moral awareness'.[26]

Atwood's mordant vision of our future pictures 'an era when cor-porate greed, allied with technological hyper-sophistication in the realm of genetics has led to the unbridled and unprincipled use of new technologies',[27] leading to extermination. He sees Snowman/Jimmy as 'an oddly vacant protagonist, he remains an intellectual and psychological cipher',[28] which means he is not a good vehicle for the book's moral insight.

Shuli Barzilai sees the novel as constituted as if in a dialogue with Shakespeare's *Hamlet* because of what she reads as the death of the father figure (Crake), love of the mother figure (Oryx) and the ways in which Jimmy tries to recover versions of the past and make sense of them,[29] a similar view to that of Brooks Bouson.[30]

Mendelsohn likens Jimmy to Robinson Crusoe, economic man at the beginning of capitalism, because he is in a wasteland, a casta-way, making lists to structure his life.[31] Castaways might send mes-sages in bottles, but this is beyond Jimmy/Snowman, who is not so sure there are any readers left. The audience he imagines, a potential rakunk friend like his departed pet, Killer, places us as readers in an odd position. Atwood uses traditional strategies of imaginary audi-ences to firm up reality and continuity and to authenticate narrative, which is consistently undercutting its own ontological security. Even castaways ensure readers, but Snowman cannot hope to find any, since the Crakers cannot read.

Coral Ann Howells sees *Oryx and Crake* as significant in Atwood's ethical engagement:

It offers Atwood the opportunity to explore what it might mean to be human and in so doing to compare the creative and the scientific approaches to life, undercutting some of the myths about gender, and intellectual orientation in the process so she is implying that the creative imagination is a distinctively human capability shared by scientists and artists alike, and that it is not gender specific.[32]

As a fiction writer from a family of scientists, Atwood is well aware of the creativity and the potential destructiveness of each, and equally able to engage and play with their discourses. She names the biotechnologically spliced pigoons and rakunks, wolfogs, and so on, and can imagine the fatal results of experimentation with the Blysspluss pills. The major human fault which links the culpable evils which Atwood takes to their logical conclusion is a failure to connect actions with their effects, a moral vacuum, a distance from which Rennie in the much earlier *Bodily Harm* (1981) also had to be jolted. The blinkered destructiveness of biotechnology, and of ignoring the environment, are here combined with Jimmy and Crake's moral blinkeredness when cruising pain and porn sites on the Internet without compunction or even interest in whether what they enact and sell is real. Brooks Bouson points out, Atwood 'conveys her uneasiness as she describes the degradation of culture in a society where violence and pornography have become cheap, and readily available, forms of entertainment'.[33]

For Jimmy and his friend Crake, family was also far from nurturing and Jimmy's own lonely, threatened existence is bare of any relationships of care until he takes some responsibility for the Crakers. Eleanor Rao focuses on representations of home, nation and self, processes of inside and out, in which Jimmy's 'isolation and temporal displacement makes him the ultimate outcast, compelled to "live", albeit surreptitiously, in the past, a past which is polluted by evils, dreams, memories and nostalgia'.[34] For her, Atwood offers only imaginative memory. Home is already a contested space constructed from privilege and power, a 'compromised site'.[35] As Sarah Appleton suggests, there is an inner alienation exposed here:

> The dystopian reference in the novel also points to another kind dystopia: the self created dystopia of a damaged psyche. A novel such as Ken Keesey's *One Flew Over the Cuckoo's Nest* articulates the self construction of a personal hell.[36]

Jimmy is also, as Eleanor Rao notes, a foreigner who is always alone, haunted by his memories, a refugee, a diasporic presence. He is defined by his loss of the beautiful ex-video porn star Oryx, and by his nostalgia. In this liminal space between past and future, Jimmy finds he is alone in his ability to use more complex language:

> He is a state of suspension between two dimensions: a past he cannot recover and a future which is unimaginable ... His sensitivity to language also aligns with this solidity of identity, his hold on the world, partly conveyed to us through his need to narrativise – tell stories to make himself feel real. Words reassure him as he repeats those no longer used *'succulent. morphology. purblind. quarto. Frass'.*[37]

In a crisis, his relationship with language changes and loses its connection with the real world: 'When the sense of temporariness and pointlessness overwhelms him, language loses its "solidity"; it becomes "thin, contingent, slippery"'.[38] This becomes exacerbated when Jimmy turns into Snowman. For him, signifier and signified, in this case the words and the real world, are disjointed, and as a result, language loses its ability to evoke any meaning at all.[39] His need to hear a human voice as well as imagine a reader or listener is so great that he hears Oryx's voice in his head. Howells comments that he hears old voices, only waking when a slug seems to reply using language. Like Offred in *The Handmaid's Tale,* Snowman is vulnerable and tells stories in a bid to claim his own identity. He delights in language and word play, but he is now the only creature to keep language alive. '"Hang onto the words", he tells himself'.[40] What he fears is that, unused, words will pass from meaning entirely, a far cry from his job in advertising, copywriting, where he was a 'word serf'. The novel can be compared with other dystopian fictions, Lewis Carroll's *Alice in Wonderland,* and Chuck Palahniuk's *Fight Club.* In one, adult reason is lacking, and in the other, as Sarah Appleton notes, a young man, 'disenchanted with the sops and impotency of corporate consumer life, psychologically creates a violent and powerful alter ego who commands the position of anarchist'. Palahniuk gives free rein to a constructed version of events, allowing his id and superego to act out 'violent and pleasurable fantasies of power'.[41]

The inclusion of distinct points of comparison with Jimmy's narrative and these classic and well-known texts indicates for Appleton that Jimmy's tale is a fabrication. But Jimmy seems to stay alive through creating and recreating his own history and his current world. He is basic, storytelling man.

Even when he is in a state of insecurity about continuity, and the meaning of what might be being conveyed, Jimmy/Snowman's narrative presumes a readership. The omniscient narrative renders his thoughts and feelings with free indirect discourse, so it seems as though he is more a vocaliser, one who speaks, than a narrator. As several critics have pointed out, Snowman's narrative is a form of therapy to make up for his earlier ignoring of the horrors Crake was developing.

His re-telling his tale constructs it both for the reader and for himself, although there are many gaps. Home, displacement, identity, and the losses of communication dominate. These are words which have gone out of use, indications of loss of human life and values, and casual and careless engineering in Crake's manipulation of what it means to be human in a reductive sense. Crake manipulated human life, built upon computer game playing. This virtual version of what it means to be human lacks familial care or sense of relationships and values and reminds us of the ways in which the Internet distances events through the medium, offering everything but removing real engagement. Latterly, Crake developed BlyssPluss pills, which seemed to offer limitless sexual pleasure and libido without reproduction, but ironically they lead to infertility.

The game Jimmy and Crake play, Extinctathon, is an ominous indication of the ways in which such ethics-free meddling can lead to the loss of civilisation, of life. When eventually Jimmy/Snowman revisits the location of the final explosions and deaths of Oryx and Crake, after the wiping out of the human species, he is at last able to confront his own culpability. He watches violence and deaths on the screen as he'd watched the games earlier, only earlier the distancing made it unreal, and placed him in a safe space. Now it only does so momentarily. Then he realises that the Internet version was in fact not a copy of the real, but the real itself. In this world, personal relations were just transitory, originating in the illicit pleasure enabled by voyeuristically moving between different Internet sites which reveal nameless and stereotypical Asian girls as sexual objects for delight and abuse. In a glimmer of an eye, Oryx appeared as a young girl entrancing Jimmy, then Crake, the two becoming rivals for her affections.

Jimmy's liminal existence, caught between past and future time, alone and starving, offers opportunities in the dystopian fiction to project forward problems of current behaviours. These include genetic engineering, the loss of subtlety of language, and the lack of communication produced by the abuse of a plethora of electronic medium opportunities, the distancing of the human, and the loss of the ethics of engagement with the shared world. The human race was destined to disaster because it was fictionalised in a game in which God is scientist and Internet game player.

In conversation with Ingersoll, Margaret Atwood says that while she aims to shock readers about potential dangers inherent in our present world, which could easily develop into a dystopian future, she also includes 'something which isn't supposed to be there in order to surprise the reader'.[42]

Howells identifies a trend in Atwood's work. Her focus is on the 'human particularity'.[43] Atwood takes pains in both *The Handmaid's Tale* and *Oryx and Crake* to ensure 'how to make the story real at a human and an individual level'.[44] Later, Howells considers Atwood's forms: sci-fi dystopia, wilderness tales, survivor and castaway narratives. In this dystopian satire on the American Dream of consumerism and technology replacing social and moral engagement, she asks: 'What does it mean to be human?' Howells argues that Atwood explores fictions of masculinity in which Crake is a representative of an 'urge toward male mastery through reason and science', while Jimmy represents an 'alternative "feminine" allegiance to the life of emotion and imagination'.[45] Both are kinds of artists: 'Crake as amoral creative genius or as magician aspiring to be God, while Jimmy/Snowman is the "word" man ("an adman who's a sad man", as one reviewer commented), a storyteller with a sense of moral responsibility.'[46]

They are a double act which complicates our perceptions of gender roles, although Oryx seems a stereotype – victim, pornographic performer and finally a kind of mother/goddess figure to the Crakers. The lens through which Oryx may be viewed is one which refuses simple versions of manhood, and encompasses previous Atwood constructions of duplicitous interpretations of women. Like Grace and Zenia, her image cannot be fixed. She remains a mysterious figure existing behind the screen onto which male fantasies of the feminine are projected, even in her relationship with both men, her phone call admitting accidental collusion in pushing the deadly BlyssPluss pill and then her God-like function after death. Appleton explains further that Oryx is a kind of outlet for Jimmy's emotions although Oryx, as Jimmy's id and *eros*, is surprisingly devoid of emotion, and she dismisses the horrors of her past. Thus, it would seem that even though Jimmy has compartmentalised his selves, he still doesn't have the capacity to find an outlet for his emotions.

However, Oryx as id is incapable of having any emotions of her own; she can only act as a conduit for Jimmy's repressed emotions – if he allows it.[47] The novel ends with Jimmy 'poised on the brink of his decision: will he or won't he rejoin humanity?' Appleton sees it is a conundrum in which Jimmy will choose life.[48]

Carol Osborne agrees with the positive ending, and comments that this supports Atwood's stressing of Snowman's

> psychological need for a narrative in which to ground his new identity by ending the first section of the novel, occurring in present time, with Snowman's admonition to himself to 'Get a life' (p.12) and beginning Chapter Two with the formula of the fairy tale: 'Once upon a time, Snowman wasn't Snowman. Instead he was Jimmy. He'd been a good boy then' (p.15).[49]

Like Snowman, we as readers recognise the power of constructing our own narratives.

These twin sides of human beings: reason and emotion, art and science, male and female, are troubled in the novel. Each is contained in all of us, so our responsibilities perhaps can be likened to those realised by Jimmy when:

> Only after the disaster, when he returns to the ruined Paradise dome, does Jimmy/Snowman finally confront the dimensions of his own complicity, recognising Crake as his own demonic double, 'Darker than dark, and some of that darkness is Snowman's. He helped with it'. (p. 389).[50]

In *Negotiating with the Dead*, Atwood likened the creative writing process to a journey to the Underworld in quest of a lost love or forbidden knowledge, where the writer negotiates with the ghosts of private and collective memory as well as with literary tradition: 'because the dead control the past, they control the stories. Snowman's journey back to Crake's ruined Paradise dome is a version of that same quest, though he claims that he is going in search of his physical survival'.[51] Some critics question the inconsistency of Crake's leaving Jimmy as the sole guardian of his progeny, given Crake's desire to eliminate the very features of humanity that Jimmy represents. But as Carol Osborne argues, this is an example of Crake's under estimation of Jimmy and his 'over-estimation of science's power to squelch the humanistic impulses in a newly created species. Despite Crake's efforts, his progeny retain the capacity to dream, to sing, to enjoy stories, and to develop religious rituals'.[52] The Crakers defy the constraints of their maker, and evolve. And so does Jimmy.

Some critics see glimmers of hope:

> The novel is not so totally bleak because the Crakers are starting to develop towards the end in ways unplanned, 'the Crakers are starting to have free will by the end of the book. They are already doing art, which they aren't supposed to have been able to do, and developing a religion.' Not the type that Crake the designer of this world, or his best friend Jimmy would wish 'but nonetheless a religion it is'.[53]

Finally, however, there is a possible future. Having constructed himself as the last man standing, Snowman realises he hears human voices and approaches the humans on the shore, ending with a familiar narrative scenario. Perhaps, as Howells puts it,

> [He is] rehearsing old plots from narratives of European colonialism and the Wild West only to discover that none of them fits his present situation. Is his role that of peacemaker, negotiation, or killer? He cannot finish the story although he knows it is 'time to go' (p. 433).[54]

The novel ends with potential harmony, and hope, built Osborne argues, from Atwood's research into the beliefs and practices of First Nations Canadians and the Aboriginal concept of dream time, all of a part with her environmentalism. It 'reveals the deep roots of the "saving graces" she emphasises in her novel. The indigenous people of Australia see all life and all phenomena as part of a vast system of relationships, all connected'.[55]

Jimmy does more than fulfil Crake's plotline of his role in saving the Crakers, and heads off on his own to seek other survivors, 'He has relinquished the old routines, in which he had become mired, observing them "entering the past"' (p. 372).[56] The lecture series and the dystopian fiction each negotiate in their own way with the dead, the influences and mistakes of the past. Each also deals with Atwood's fascination with fictionalising and the power of published or oral narrative, to affect the ways in which we see, project and construct worlds.

In Atwood's next short fiction collections, she focuses on ways in which storytellers construct versions of events, how we live by following the trail of certain myths and tales, linking a series of tales into a lifestyle in *Moral Disorder* (2006).

10

Re-Telling Old Tales: *Moral Disorder* (2006), *The Tent* (2006)

In these later works, Atwood returns to several of her familiar themes and forms. In *Strange Things: The Malevolent North in Canadian Literature*, a collection of critical essays dealing with fiction and the fictionalising processes, she replays versions of tales of the Canadian wilderness, the fascination with lost causes and pioneering journeys, adventure and mythic forest creatures, reprising the interests of the earlier *Survival* (1970). Similar tales surface in her story sequence *Moral Disorder*, where the protagonist, Nell's, father retells and inhabits them in his ageing mind. There are 11 tales, which feature both recollection and thoughts about the future, sometimes highly reflective and speculative, but never sentimental. *The Tent* is a collection of short, flash fictions rehearsing the storytelling forms and habits with which people make sense of their lives, explain the strange, build promises of the future, and speculate about how it could be otherwise. These fictions also consider the fictionalising processes themselves and evidence Atwood's endlessly ironic, parodic, intertextual, subtle, occasionally sarcastic satire.

The back to nature theme appears in *Moral Disorder*, as does the fascination with the ill-fated Franklin expedition, while in *The Tent*, narratives of exciting adventures, rescues, daring and survival are dealt with ironically, highlighting their functions as ways in which people idealise their world. These three texts are linked in their focus on the stories with which people construct and represent their lives, the urban and natural myths which constrain or shape us, whether personal life histories in *Moral Disorder*, familiar tales of a particular location, mindset, and people in *Strange Things*, or more broadly in the legends, myths and narrative shapes of hope and despair which structure representations and formulations of ways of seeing and living found in the flash fiction of *The Tent*.

Moral Disorder (2006)

Moral Disorder is a series of short linked fictions with autobiographical elements. Here, Atwood reworks scenarios familiar from *Cat's Eye* (1988). There are in all her works elements of the self and presentations or performances of what one remembers, fears and hopes reworked into fantasy, the Gothic, different perspectives, different genres, inventions, explorations, allegories and representations. We are alerted to the autobiographical in this collection because of the trajectory of Nell, the protagonist's, life, which maps some of what we know about Atwood's own life. However, nothing is quite so simple. Atwood reminds us that although it might use the formations of life writing, nonetheless, the stories are written in the third person, and many of the details do not match those of *her* life. This is a fictionalised version. Reviewers such as A. S. Byatt (2006) and latterly critics including Ellen McWilliams (2009) explore the ways in which Atwood, as in the earlier *Lady Oracle*, and *Cat's Eye*, raises issues of the constructedness, the artifice and performance of what seems to be almost a personal diary, a *Künstlerroman* (story of the artist or writer) and a female *Bildungsroman* (life story), but like even the most seemingly faithful traceable life stories, actually exposes its own constructedness. In this it resembles Iris Chase Griffen's story in *The Blind Assassin*, and that of Grace Marks in *Alias Grace*. We might like to trace this consistent theme through Atwood's works, and through the comments of critics, some of whom seem to take *Moral Disorder* at face value as a revisiting of Atwood's own past. However, while there are many similarities between what we know of Atwood's own life and that of Nell, there are many dissimilarities too. This is a construction, a fiction. Nell is not herself a writer. The novel/linked stories also focuses us on issues of the fallibility and selectivity of memory in returning to order and making some probably time-limited and ephemeral sense, as Nell orders her life in the retelling. Ageing and loss of memory, the precariousness of age, all emerge as themes through the first tale of Nell and Tig ageing, Nell's mother's illness, and the ageing of Tig's ex-wife, Oona, along with the old horse and various other deaths. The childhood memories of awaiting a new sibling; the scientist father and travelling between the bush and the city; varieties of students around her father's experiments with bugs; her scientific, fishing, mathematical brother, and the relationship in later life are all fascinating variations on previous relationships found in Atwood's earlier work.

However, the final discovery that the mother's horse has the same name as the protagonist, Nell, probably undercuts our security in mapping moment by moment onto Atwood's life. Much of these rather gentle and exploratory stories break new ground with their subject matter, particularly the treatment of relationships in middle age, with which the book starts and ends.

Early reviews

Reviewers celebrated *Moral Disorder*, some relating it directly to Atwood's life and some commenting on the ways in which an established writer has a rich vein of work and life from which to draw in maturity. *Moral Disorder* is not dealing with world-shattering events in the way that *Oryx and Crake* (2003) or *The Handmaid's Tale* (1985) are. It is much more reflective, gentler. Because of its realist nature, it receives similar descriptive reviews to those for the earlier *Life Before Man* (1979), where reviewers seem somewhat stuck with re-telling the tales rather than debating what the whole might argue, or represent. *Publishers Weekly* sees it as a patchwork which tacks back into a life: 'An intriguing patchwork of poignant episodes, chronicles 60 years of a Canadian family, from postwar Toronto to a farm in the present.'[1]

The Washington Post's Book World (washingtonpost.com) reviewer A. S. Byatt is more reflective about Atwood's plundering her stores of memories and previous work, seeing an inability to make total and neat sense of it all:

> A young writer, like a young woman, has a narrow strip of experience from which to contemplate an unknown future, empty and waiting for its form. An older writer, reminded of mortality by aging knees and dying parents, has the consolation of seeing everything in rich detail, meaningful and apparently pointless together.[2]

The short story sequence covers Nell's life from middle age, mid-sixties, then back and through childhood up to middle age again. Like Atwood, she grows up with her parents and lives between the bush and the city. There are early thoughts about the coming of her new sister, Lizzie, who later becomes schizophrenic, and Nell doubts her own ontological security at many stages. Told in segments, stories which focus on 'particular gritty or glittering episodes or problems', it tracks through each decade from the 1930s to the present, balancing 'the apparently random – disorderly – events and memories against the sense we all have that a life as a whole has its own shape, possibly a destiny'.[3] Not that that destiny reveals itself – though episodes, references and moments are reminders of each other. Yet there is, as in life, only the patterns one might place upon events by a desire for narrative and order, which is why, perhaps, *Moral Disorder* is such a good title: attempts at order are essentially both necessary and flawed. One reviewer notes that the title is taken from a novel abandoned by Atwood's husband, Graeme Gibson. One of its great strengths is the way in which it matches the shape of memories and narrative we might form about a life. Byatt notes that some tales are in the first person, some in the third. This format is:

> a perfect shape for contemplating life and death. It is like our memories: There are things that persist in refusing to be forgotten, are as clear as the day they happened, whereas all sorts of more apparently significant things vanish into dust or persist only in old newspapers and fashion magazines. A life, unlike a biography, does not unfold in a neat progression. Nor is it entirely incoherent.[4]

The selectivity, then, is an attempt to make sense, a pattern out of the incoherence of a life, which, in the event, emphasises the variety discovered by Nell. One reviewer notes that Atwood displays: 'the same intellectual fearlessness and wit of her other books, but this time tempered with a compassion and richness of portraiture'.[5] They suggest that following the stories of Nell resembles:

> staying up all night every decade or so with an old friend. Each intense encounter builds on a shared and cumulative history between character and reader, and Atwood's magic is such that we not only sense Nell's psychological development over the course of these stories, but we mature ourselves as a consequence of reading them.[6]

Maturity

Ageing is a framing device for the collection as a whole. *Moral Disorder* begins with 'The Bad News' and the couple in middle age, Nell relishing her slow satisfaction of the familiar, yet poised on the edge of fears that their comfortable existence is constantly threatened by the ravages of ageing. The stories trace a relationship between Nell and Tig, where Nell is the younger, second wife and Tig the writer. There are several rites of passage. 'The Bad News' starts with a new day: 'It's morning. For now, night is over. It's time for the bad news.'[7] It is a new if tentative beginning (night will return), but with the threat of bad news dissipated into merely recounting what the newspapers contain (where all news is bad news), as read by Tig/Gilbert, whose announcements about occurrences are weighted with depths of destruction. 'After this long together'[8] is really the theme here, as is the tenuousness of their security together in middle age, not because one will leave for someone else, but because of the inevitability of approaching age and death. Words like 'not yet, so far, so good' pepper the tale, which moves with a certain amusing, ironic tone, over recall of two dead cats, the familiar routines and the threat to their repetition due to ageing. They worry about their appliances and their own body parts and of particular concern is the working order of life. In this respect, she compares herself to the cat, Drumlin, who first lost her mind and then died, knowing that there won't be another cat now to keep her company after Tig dies (relying on the generally earlier death of men). Nell imagines:

> This has become my picture of my future self: wandering the house in the darkness, in my white nightdress, howling for what I can't quite remember I've lost. It's unbearable. I wake up in the night and reach out to make sure Tig is still there, still breathing. So far, so good.[9]

Nischik finds the story 'existential', it is 'exuding a sense of loss – of vitality, of reckless optimism – and a sense of fear and anxiety'.[10] Their security is both comfortable and threatened. The juxtapositioning of everyday items and actions undercuts statements about feeling safe, and, in this way, Atwood uses poetic strategies, the signification of objects, and realistic domestic detail to carry more weight than mere description, signalling insecurity in the everyday:

> 'We're lucky', says Tig. I know what he means. He means the two of us, sitting here in the kitchen, still. Neither of us gone. Not yet.
> 'Yes, we are.'
> I say, 'Watch the toast, it's burning.'[11]

The burning toast is an indicator of their tenuous hold on routine and life. They talk of the ancient Romans and paralleling their different worlds only serves to both reinforce the familiar, now turned into the historical, and the threat – since wherever these Romans are was clearly later invaded, lost, and they are dead.

More urgency is immediately evident in the next tale 'The Art of Cooking and Serving', the start of the growing up sequence, as Nell awaits the birth of the younger sister, the unplanned child Lillie, who is felt as a threat, a familiar scenario. Joyce Carol Oates talks of the development of the theme of the younger sister, first seen in *The Blind Assassin* (2000). She is predicted to be a menace, and turns out to be emotionally unstable and depressed:

> Atwood's narrator feels a helpless sort of sisterly responsibility. The depressed sister speaks obsessively of 'leaving': 'I should just check out. I'm useless here. It's too much effort,' which the narrator interprets as: She doesn't mean my house. She means her body. She means the planet Earth. I can see the same thing she's seeing: it's a cliff edge, it's a bridge with a steep drop, it's the end. That's what she wants: The End. Like the end of a story.[12]

But other reviewers have noticed how much fun this sister is in her word play and behaviour. She is edgy, reminding us of a wilder version of Laura in *The Blind Assassin*, someone poised on the edge of a ravine, perhaps. Her threat is activated, however, when the mother catches her thyroid disease from the sister's hamster, then develops Alzheimer's. This relates to the themes of ordering, memory and ageing, explored below. But while the seeds of destruction are potentially all around, so are notes of amusement and the richness of life's diversity.

> The book is full of wonderful details: the way in which the narrator as a teenager smeared her face with frozen Noxzema face cream before doing her homework (she had a theory that it would 'stimulate the blood flow' to her brain); the way in which her sister argues with the drivers of other cars, all of whom she calls Fred; her recipe for 'nuts and bolts', a vile-sounding hors d'oeuvre.[13]

Nischik comments on how few of the stories focus on the theme of gender so central to Atwood's earlier work, but that it is appropriate that this one and 'My Last Duchess' do, as these periods are crucial for gender socialization, especially given the stories' setting in the 1950s and 1960s, when gender was a particularly prominent social issue.[14] Nell considers gender colour schemes, knitting and roles for girls, in a series of events which aim to socialise her into being a conventional little 1950s girl.

Throughout the stories Nell, as focaliser (the person whose viewpoint we follow) and protagonist, is aware of the inevitable gap between how she felt in the past, how she remembers feeling, the difficulties of recalling and storytelling – and how easy it would be to change and elaborate details. There are few moments of sentiment and some reflections on the ways in which life remembered can be framed as something finished and neat or something artistic, when it is actually messier than that. In the stories of Nell and Tig this takes place within a creative reflection, life transmuted into art.

Like Nell's refusal to turn the beauty of the snow around her into art, to photograph it, because it looked too artificial – 'Atwood, too, works hard to circumvent cheap emotion or consolation.'[15] Boddy finds the stories unsentimental, 'they're rigorously anti-sentimental and, at their darkest, they're also at their funniest'.[16]

One character, Oona, Tig's wife/ex-wife, is variously depicted as formidable, manipulative, and then dependent, an example of the many different projections and interpretations of self and three-dimensional people there can be. Oona is a 1970s cookery and 'good-life' guru in a kaftan, author of the *Femagician's Box of Tricks*, a nice take on feminists engaged with 'mind, body and soul' and power games. Oona sets Nell up to take Tig over from her, thus freeing her to go her own way and leaving Nell to cope with Tig's sons at weekends. Oona manipulates their needs, arrivals and departures:

> Oona had her fingered for the position of second wife, or if not a second wife exactly, something second. Something secondary. Something controllable. A sort of concubine. She was to serve as Tig's other company, so that Oona could get on with the life of her own she was so determined to lead.[17]

Oates sympathises with Nell as someone who is manipulated, and who has moral disorder forced upon her:

> Poor Nell, who doesn't even cheat at solitaire! In the heady 1960s, where 'all games had changed at once and earlier structures had fallen apart and everyone had begun pretending that the very notion of rules was obsolete,' Nell finds herself in approximately the position she'd been boxed into at eleven: caretaker.[18]

Since the recollections and the bringing together of memories and interpretations are all Nell's, we might wonder with Oates, Byatt and McWilliams among others about how Nell can make sense, or different sense of her life as she reviews it through these tales and re-orderings. The whole novel/set of linked stories asks questions about ageing, memory and making sense, when each attempt to do so, to bring order to the disparate versions and fragments is only a partial version. Nell ages in the text and so too does Oona, offering an example of that very tenuous hold on what matters and one's sense of identity with which the book opens and closes. Oona loses money and confidence and needs a manageable house, which Nell finds for her using the advice of Lillie, concentration camp survivor turned real estate agent, who is always intensely imaginative about what can be done to hideous or uncomfortable houses.

Houses are significant. In this house where Oona dies in the kitchen, Nell calls in a 'Feng Shui' expert, who discovers a channel where entities come and go. When the house is sold to two gay men, they mistranslate the entities as 'aunties' and find it all amusing. Joyce Carol Oates contrasts the alternating narratives of pain, everyday real events, and advertisement, which set up a familiar Atwood debate between narrative, cosmetic representation, artifice, and the deeper complexities of messy lives.

Growing up and defining identity

After the initial tale about maturity and ageing, the collection goes back to Nell's childhood then moves chronologically forward through her life. As a child, Nell has a vivid imagination and feels she watches others as if from the height of a balloon. In 'The Art of Cooking and Serving', her self-absorption leads her to expect praise for the knitting of baby garments for her new sibling, a creative act she sees as far superior to that of her mother. Nell's focus is on her own world, casting herself as the starring role and her mother as somewhat irritating, absorbed elsewhere, 'a listless, bloated version'[19] of her usual self. Nischik emphasizes the way in which Atwood exposes the complexities of familiar relationships:

> Whereas this distancing between mother and daughter in puberty is a usual developmental step, giving birth to a child is rendered in rather unusual problematic terms in this story, thereby also working against any kind of euphemistic motherhood myth.[20]

When she finally refuses to look after her sister all the time, she feels freed as an adolescent who can eat popcorn and go to drive-in movies.

Linked stories 'The Headless Horseman' and 'My Last Duchess' follow Nell in the 1950s through relatively conventional middle-class adolescence, but expose her imaginative inner life. In the tale 'Moral Disorder', Atwood focuses on familiar territory in terms of time and place and uses rural Ontario, a location also found in short stories by Canadian, Alice Munro. Nancy Schiefer considers the farm segments, and how the story develops through Nell's life, where characters reappear, grown older, their influences on her reviewed at each stage.[21]

Schiefer finds the farm elements tiresome but at times they are also hilarious, with the activities of Gladys the horse, who has a mind of her own, screaming peacocks, and the naming of the cows. Nell oscillates between versions of her existence. She tries to define herself, and is never sure whether she is living a hippy life, as the mistress, farm woman, developing an idyllic existence with items from the past, or some other version. Around her the fruit ripens and falls and she realises she is caught up in the farm rhythms of life and death. One of the saddest sentimental moments is when the besotted lamb which follows Nell around has to be slaughtered. This is the contradiction of farm life. The lamb returns 'in a white oblong cardboard box, like a dress box. Neatly arranged in wax paper were the tender pink chops.'[22] Nell feels like a cannibal. The death of the lamb, however, reminds us of the theme of death and dying running throughout *Moral Disorder*. The life cycles in *Moral Disorder* have resonance for a broad readership, since everyone grows up and grows older. They also concern a woman with a great imagination who tells stories of her past, sees herself as a character in various versions of life, each based on genres and different forms of interpretation. Each version is always partial, not fully encompassing the experience of life itself, each a way of managing events but of not closing them down. According to an anonymous *The Booklist* reviewer, Atwood's wry, amusing use of language enables readers to move beyond a particular life and comment on the variety, pain and ironies of human lives more generally. Everyone can find something here to resonate with their worldviews and the narratives by which we structure our lives.[23]

Many of the tales also consider the importance of narrative as a controlling device. Schiefer celebrates the clarity of representation and the way in which Atwood offers 'skillfully crafted stories which echo W. H. Auden's observation that successful art demands clear thinking about mixed feelings',[24] for readers to develop further and map into their own lives. Narrative offers a way of constructing fictionalised versions and visions for Nell's father, fixed on tales of fatal treks to the Far North, and for her and her sister, making sense of their growing up and their mother growing old. Like much of Atwood's work, this emphasises the way we construct narratives to make sense of the world, and the constraints of those narratives. The collection appears to be a semi-fictionalised autobiography but with broader meaning. Ellen McWilliams expands on this theme (2009). The text is 'recuperative' and returns to familiar territory for Atwood: families, memories, relationships, the constructedness of even seemingly autobiographical narrative, but juxtaposes her motifs in ways which make them seem new, and orders her themes and concerns in a new way, '[it] represents a confluence of the preoccupations, interests, and commitments'[25] familiar to her oeuvre. It is a new 'collage of selfhood',[26] takes its title from an unfinished novel by Graeme Gibson, and by sitting part way between novel and short stories admits the influence of both James Joyce (most probably for *Dubliners*) and Alice Munro, fellow Canadian woman writer also concerned with relationships, Canadian settings and the 'minutiae' of life.

Locations are also important in Atwood's work, and McWilliams notes how here, as in much of her earlier work, there is a tension between entrapment and escape, where I would argue some of the entrapment is in repetitive narratives which limit the worldview of characters, as much as in spaces and roles which limit development. 'The Other Place' focuses on limits imposed by patriarchy, a theme McWilliams relates to that in *Lady Oracle*. Here it is a kind of limitation of a 'dream' self, where the 'promise of safety from the constant change of life proves less than satisfactory as it comes to represent isolation rather than security'.[27] So space, as well as narrative, relates to self. Houses represent identity and place, a sense of history still alive, and animals and their actions remind us of human experiences.

The Tent (2006)

No one could accuse *The Tent* of being a work of everyday or semi-fictionalised realism. Here, Atwood moves to more myth-oriented, sometimes Gothic, always ironic form and tone, familiar from *Good Bones and Simple Murders* (1994), and some of the more wry, fantastic musings of *Oryx and Crake*. *The Tent* is a collection of very short stories, witty aphorisms, and flash fictions, which engage with familiar Atwood interests and themes.

Early reviews

Early reviews were divided. Anita Sethi sees here 'the dark subject matter of growth and decay'[28] and doubts they would be published if written by someone less well known, since they are 'surplus jottings, writing exercises, gloomy off-cuts from the creative process'.[29] They are concerned with narrative development, the ways in which myths, legends, established narratives, storying lives and writing enable ways of controlling reality and keep reality at bay. Sethi finds it claustrophobic and Atwood's language idiosyncratic. The stories show us 'the human consciousness in conversation with itself' and 'the nuts and bolts of the tortuous creative process'.[30] However, 'Atwood's talent struggles to breathe inside these claustrophobic prisons.'[31] Others, including Kate Washington, find familiar Atwood interests, including 'scary dystopias as well as nods to 20th century feminism and its discontents in "Winter's Tales" and the long poem "Bring Back Mom: An Invocation".'[32]

Fictionalising

Hermione Lee relates this collection to Atwood's long-term interest in genre fictions and in re-telling versions of histories, so that, like Angela Carter or Stevie Smith: 'Atwood likes turning old fables on their heads and looking underneath for cruel motives and ironic relevance.'[33] It goes with her pleasure in genre-hopping, so she moves easily here between Greek myths, children's tales, and spoofs of action-packed science-fiction stories, like the one about the giant sponge taking over Florida and ultimately all humanity ('a sponge on the rampage is a formidable foe').[34]

She reworks old stories and versions of how individual, and national, lives and histories can be represented and distorted.

The fictions of travel, its trickeries and opportunities, the ordinariness of lives and the necessity for complex situations to make life interesting, the duplicity of politics and politicians and the mischievousness of animals appear here, deriving from and building upon a variety of genres, forms and perspectives from legend, myth, romance, crime fiction and science fiction through to confessions. The tent of the title refers to a safe space in which, hidden and secure, it is possible to retire and write and so also reminds us of Atwood's continued focus on the writing process, although usually she explores this through a figure who is creating a fiction. Atwood also problematises what short stories can deal with and how they can deal with it. In this respect, Nischik finds these short fictions part of Atwood's radical move to counteract or invert what is normally considered 'better'.

> [It is] part of a general tendency in Atwood's oeuvre to expose conventions (e.g. 'bigger is better' or 'significant is big') – that is, the social, psychological, linguistic, and mythical structures that underpin everyday perceptions and judgments – and to question their values and functions.[35]

Looking back over earlier short stories as well as *The Tent*, Nischik sees many offer a challenge to familiar forms of short fiction. They are part of Atwood's experimentation, pushing the boundaries of form. She has 'employed new textual formats for her challenging explorations and rewritings, short texts that are hard to classify and have few genuine forerunners in Canadian literature'.[36]

Atwood calls these short texts 'flash fictions' and, as with her other works, almost all of them have already been published in a variety of magazines. There is an early collection of several in *The Times*,[37] where she first writes 'Three Novels I Won't Write Soon'. 'Chicken Little Goes Too Far' was written in support of WWF Canada, and the original holograph sold during a WWF 'auction for nature'. This is an example of how, throughout her writing life, Atwood has notably supported, written about and for, and so helped fund ecological ventures to help save animals and the planet. The focus on sustainability is central to 'Thylacine Ragout', a story which seems to concern a possibly mythic, now extinct Tasmanian creature but which Shuli Barzilai researches and finds real, hunted to extinction. Barzilai discovered the Thylacine disappeared because of colonisation. 'In the story, "they named [the Thylacine] Trugannini, after the last fully Aboriginal inhabitant of that island".' Trugannini also existed, was mistreated by colonisers, eventually died and her death 'became synonymous with the extinction of her race'.[38] According to one reviewer, '"Thylacine Ragout" becomes a critique of power politics, colonisation and much more, as well as of science, humanity (as superior to Nature and in its will to control it), human values, etc.'[39]

This reviewer sees 'Faster' also as a piece among others 'concerned with the irrationality of human beings, with what we have done to our planet, with human greed' so identifying Atwood critique and irony of ecological and human damage.[40]

Voice and identity

Atwood's wry critical voice reminds Heather Birrell of a 'crone' able to be openly critical: 'The narrative voice throughout *The Tent* most closely evokes the archetypal character of the crone. Unlike the pure maiden or nurturing mother, the crone feels free to speak her mind, embracing the seedier, darker emotions and dystopic visions that accompany the end of life.'[41]

The voice attacks in 'Gateway', 'Time Folds', and 'Encouraging the Young', (who it believes should never be encouraged). Julia Keller notices other voices, and, in interview, explores Atwood's use of source material in forming and expressing versions of her own life. 'Written people always have at least two personalities', she says, hers, the writing self and the other self. 'And you can add more within that.'[42]

Atwood told Keller that when warning Americans that too many bad things would make people overlook the good, she said she's not courageous:

> If you're a writer it's not easy not to write ... writing is as much about the spirit haunted world of the past as it is about the future. It's a descent into the dark avenue of the underworld to pry loose treasure that must be ferried to the surface forthwith. And ghosts are cosily at home in the darkness.[43]

This could be termed her 'poltergeist as muse' theory. Many of these tales are about storytelling and the power of narratives to control perspectives, worldviews and lives. The first, 'Life Stories', is a parody of a life story in which the narrator discards stages of her life, significant people, pets, events, and is left with a neat, lighter self, just 'I'. She throws away all scrapbooks and pictures, 'I'm getting somewhere now, I'm feeling lighter. I'm coming unstuck from scrapbooks, from albums, from diaries and journals, from space, from time.'[44]

There is a group of stories about identity and being, roles to play, clearing junk, being someone who fits someone else's ideas, investing in fake dreams, wearing clothes to impress, being dominated vampirically by one's own performance voice, the falsity of photos, and unravelling names of animals, of things, tracking back to the moment before the creation and God's first word in the void as yet 'unspoken'. Some stories concern carrying out clichés, such as 'encouraging the young'. Trying to avoid being the wicked owner of the constructed gingerbread house, Atwood uses fairytale, Gothic imagery, Hansel and Gretel, but refuses the role of witch since:

> I won't fatten them in cages, though. I won't ply them with poisoned fruit items. I won't change them into clockwork images or talking shadows. I won't drain out their life's blood. They can do all those things for themselves.[45]

Other stories use myths and legends which make the mythic familiar and contemporary. 'It's not easy being half-divine' places Helen of Troy in an ordinary neighbourhood, not quite famous, as a child with an unnamed famous father, very aware of the power of her looks. She is 'mincing'[46] and preening, annoying other children. The struggles surrounding her infidelity and the threats of her powerful husband are all translated into everyday North America in tone, location and end result. Making the mythic everyday familiarises it, reminding us of its narrative powers. Atwood uses contemporary colloquialisms, teen talk, and street talk, so in 'Salome Was a Dancer', a teenager comments on the way Salome 'went after' the 'drooling', 'creepy' Religious Studies teacher[47] in order to protect her marks at school. Her reaction to his badmouthing her as a slut is to cry sexual assault, and so his life (not headless in this instance) plummets socially. Salome ends up stripping in bars and is 'whacked' in her dressing room by heavies sent round by her stepfather.

Some tales act out clichés, sayings, and fictional strategies which shows how they control expression, each speaking for themselves, with their own voice. Sometimes she tests out stereotypes, so, in 'Plots for Exotics' the character steps into the world of metafiction, asking to audition for a character in a plot, but as an 'exotic' the options are limited. Her attempt at re-empowering herself fails. She offers to be in the plot factory and write plots: 'I could do a whole plot with nothing in it but exotics. Exotics wall to wall. Then I'd be the main character for sure, no question.'[48] This emphasises the power games played in the literary, publishing and entertainment businesses. Elsewhere, Atwood examines the narratives which manage cultural awareness, so 'Post-Colonial' critiques colonialism's genocide and disenfranchisement. The tone is ironic and amusing, indicating ways in which native people were misunderstood, killed off, and latterly celebrated, their names joined to those of the once invaders, so that finally it is difficult to tell whether they are postcolonial themselves, or about to be invaded by others who see themselves as different and superior. Wordplay exposes the power games embedded in the 'post'- of postcolonial.

Atwood's humour is very effective when she adopts voices, perspectives and plotlines from a variety of sources. 'Our Cat Enters Heaven' gets inside the head and the dreams of the cat entering the afterlife. The best surprise is that God, too, is a form of cat, sitting in a tree. God in cat's heaven crunches irritating angelic birds and is happy for the cat to do the same. The laws of the human world have all been translated into something more palatable for a devious, mischievous, slyly vicious cat. 'Every once in a while God would reach out with its large furry paw and snatch one of them out of the air and crunch it up. The ground under the tree was littered with bitten-off wings.'[49] The cat is reunited with his cut-off testicles – which he always thought were going to be lying around somewhere – and God agrees to let him tease irritating pink human souls. He needs reassurance that he is safe with this favourite game: 'You mean, play with them? Said our cat. I used to get in trouble for that.'[50] God explains that it is a 'question of semantics'. The cat is clearly in his heaven, free to catch, play, crunch, and be his cat self. It is whimsical, amusing and wry.

Atwood's playfulness gives us constants of genre-based popular fictions in 'Three Novels I Won't Write Soon'. In 'Warlords', she indicts men as prisoners of some mythic toughness, infused by motifs and roles of serving warlords in some kind of action. The humour derives from the anachronism of the role, the plot and their everyday lives. In the most mundane and everyday of activities, she says, one can imagine them ready to take up the battle, futile though it will nevertheless eventually turn out to be. 'To be a warlord – that's a boy's dream everywhere',[51] though most will be merely sacrificed supporters. Those who have given up being warlords or working for them have no other occupation. Wasted, they hang about hoping for action:

> Look over there. See that ropy-muscled old guy raking the lawn? The other one sweeping the sidewalk, the third hauling the trash? Warlord survivors, all of them. They're branded with invisible tattoos. Behind their eyes the embers smoulder. They're waiting. They're ready for the call.[52]

The juxtapositioning of heroic and banal effectively exposes the myths by which they live.

'Take Charge' is also metafictional, using a single plotline with various contexts and genres to work through a series of moments lampooning heroism and strategies of managing others. The supporter delivers a terrible message about an attack at sea, on the ground through tank fire, in cyberspace with a worm virus from outer space, and finally in a kind of myth – space. The heroic leader barks out orders, the supporter cannot act because he is wounded, the heroic leader damns everything, and gets on with it himself, ending with 'well, do your best'. The replay of the scenarios is amusing, the settings stereotypical, the heroism of manfully taking charge the butt of the wit.

Atwood explores the power of fiction, the pull and shaping of narrative, whether for reflective exploration, fantasising or shaping lives, in the linked sequence of tales: *Moral Disorder, Strange Things*, and the flash fictions *The Tent. Moral Disorder* also charts Nell's growing up, family, ageing, her relationship to Tig and to her own parents. Nell has the last word here but it is one which could comment on Atwood's work on fiction, storytelling, the power of shaping, lying, fantasising, and understanding through recall or imaginative representation. In *The Year of the Flood* (2009), end of the world storytelling continues from some of the flash fictions with the second in the dystopian trilogy which began with *Oryx and Crake.*

11

The End of the World?: *The Year of the Flood* (2009)

The Year of the Flood has received mixed reviews internationally. This may be partly due to its post-apocalyptic, sustainability theme and its mixture of the homey arts and crafts, its quasi-religious tone, and its sometimes cartoonish characters. Atwood creates a very thorough fictional world, with immediate immersion in insider jokes, invented or other appropriate names, and an adventure, survival narrative. The main characters are Toby, escapee from brutal employment, a herb grower with the Gardeners, then a worker in the AnooYoo spa; Ren, a younger, pole-dancing trapeze artist and sex worker; Adam One, the leader of God's Gardeners; and Zeb, Ren's street-fighting eco-warrior stepfather. The novel opens in Year 25, historically the same year as *Oryx and Crake*. It is the moment of a divided society and a divided city. It is also a time suffering from the results of an ultimately deadly, reckless experimentation with biotechnology, coupled with a widespread social lack of any investment or belief in sustainability, ecological balance or natural harmonious existence.

Toby and Ren recall their lives up until that moment. They are survivors of the 'Waterless Flood', a fatal body-dissolving sickness brought on by the 'BlyssPluss' pills which were marketed by Crake, the game-playing scientific friend of Jimmy/Snowman from *Oryx and Crake* (2003), the first novel in Atwood's apocalyptic dystopian trilogy. *The Year of the Flood* gives us the pleebland, the wild lawless areas, rather than the policed, safe, sanitised Compound of *Oryx and Crake,* and a female- rather than male-oriented view of the world. Each novel starts in the 2025 wasteland and the surviving characters meet up again at the end of both. We are promised a third novel. Atwood explains: 'I returned to this world because people kept asking me what happened two minutes after *Oryx and Crake* ended ... I didn't know. So in order to find out what happened, then I had to go back and write another book.'[1]

Early reviews

Reviews variously both celebrated the novel and disliked it. Positive reviews, such as that by Gillian Beer, tend to see it as a 'fearless' brave book.[2] Beer and others recognise its often upbeat, blackly comic, eco-religious engagement with the horrors of the end of the world, when genetic engineering, technology-inspired hubris and a complete deadly disregard for the delicate ecological balance of the world, in which we are but one part, lead to street violence, sadistic and pornographic treatment of women, dehumanisation, and a wasteland of the soul as well as of nature.

Not every reviewer finds it easy to manage the structure of the novel. Robert Allen Papinchak finds it less 'compelling or engaging as the first novel. The problems begin with the narrative structure. It takes some effort to work out who is who, what is what, and what's going on, as well as when and where.'[3]

There are two main time frames. One gives the past histories of the main characters and their back stories, detailing their lives and escape from the 'Waterless Flood'; the other is set in the present apocalyptic world where survivors eke out an existence threatened by genetically spliced 'pigoons' and 'liobams'. Each character is isolated until the end when they rediscover the vestiges of a community. Gillian Beer's take on this is to recognise that it 'dips into the years before the disaster, moving back and forth so that we often grasp consequences before we understand impulses.'[4] I think this engages us all the more with the horror of the situation in which the survivors find themselves. As if equally taken by surprise that such devastation could result from human ignorance, selfishness and hubris, we, too, as readers are trying to piece together what really happened, what led to these dire consequences. While in *Oryx and Crake* we rely on the structuring of Jimmy/Snowman's personal narrative version, here we have the stories of several people seeing and experiencing events from different points of view, and the structural oscillation between their stories and the more formal structuring device of the hymns of the God's Gardeners starts to let us patch together a sense of the sources and origins of these devastating consequences, as well as some of the sense of the energies, agencies and worldviews which could lead to hope and reconstruction, a form of a potential rebuilding programme based on a mixture of self-reliance, eco-awareness and community ethics. Toby, Ren and the others are similarly patching together some interpretation and way forward.

In the *San Francisco Chronicle*, Joan Frank describes how in the near-past an unscrupulous health company peddles sickness: 'HelthWyzer, a pharmaceutical monsterglot that deliberately poisons people with tainted vitamins, then sells them an ineffective "cure," thus profiting two ways'.[5] The armed secret police, the CorpSeCorps, violently control everything, including those who dominate by thuggish violence – such as the terrifying Blanco. Street battles and hostage taking, sudden disappearances and violent deaths are everyday occurrences in this dysfunctional city and its suburbs, while God's Gardeners, dressed in suitably humble sackcloth and unmodish clothing, tend a rooftop garden, talk in biblical language and seem to have biblically based beliefs and behaviours. All fear the Waterless Flood. Here, Crake/Glenn is a maverick street runner, a kind of drug dealer connecting the gated town and the pleeblands, where adults and pleebrats (children) live in slums. The Gardeners live in rooftop garden areas, and Blanco, his men and others run sex entertainments or fast food outlets, such as SecretBurgers, using dubiously sourced, disgusting ingredients, which probably include the bodies of the disappeared victims of CorpSeCorps.

Some reviewers are concerned about the mixture of Anglican-inspired names, the God's Gardeners' hymns, which are sung about events and issues, and feast days that are, Atwood notes, inspired by William Blake, Emily Dickinson, John Bunyan and the hymn books she used during a year of family burials. Each chapter starts with a homily or sermon, from Adam One, and there are Gardeners' hymns and a variety of creature and event-related religious days.

Jane Shilling sees it as a remarkable invention, but one in which she as reader is not very involved. The novel is a 'lovingly detailed representation of her invented world'; pre and post Apocalyptic Flood 'when the battle for the Earth's soul is joined between the few scattered survivors, benevolent and malign'.[6] But should the characters be eaten by the spliced mutant creatures, especially the dangerous liobams, she would feel no loss. Shilling describes the quasi-religious tone. '[It] strikes the mild, hortatory and occasionally bathetic note of mainstream Anglicanism: "Much hard work still lies before us, but fear not, my Friends: for we shall move forward undaunted. I am glad we have all remembered our sunhats."'[7]

This has to be ironic, and so attributing a sudden religious conversion to Atwood who has always declared herself agnostic, would be an error. The wry tone of the novel simultaneously emphasises an ecological warning and undercuts the sometimes rather silly sermonising of the cult.

Philip Hensher views the novel as an ambitious task, the product of a 'marvellously confident and intricate imagination',[8] which finally falls apart. He enjoys the 'seething' variety of religious cults and groups which Atwood imagines, and the full and richly defined post-apocalyptic world. Cults/gangs include: the Known Fruits, the Petrobaptists, Lion Isaiahists, Wolf Isaiahists and a number of pleebrat gangs, including the brown Tex-Mexes.

Rosemary Goring thinks it is 'marginally less bleak'[9] than *Oryx and Crake*, but an unsatisfactory tonal mix. While detailing the unpleasant brutalised lives of her women in their back stories, Atwood moves uncomfortably between irony and jollity:

> [She] maintains an almost sprightly tone, using flashes of dry wit to punctuate what might be otherwise unremitting gloom. The intention might be good, but it creates a tension that undermines her material, emasculating the fear her setting should evoke.[10]

She finds the novel more suited to Young Adult fiction, too long, with not enough artistry. Joan Frank is similarly unimpressed, declaring a dislike for post-apocalyptic work, and Philip Marchand sees the usual Atwood focus on attacking snobberies and sanctimony with satire as evidence of her origins in 'Protestant Ontario'. He balances the pros and cons of the novel, tonally, in terms of message and readability and finds the whole thing dreary, a little over-religious, filled with quotations from scripture. It ends 'with a nod toward the virtue of forgiveness which is also without embarrassment and without irony'. So that there is a 'struggle between irony and eloquence, human vanity and human heroism'.[11]

Coleen Grissom, on the other hand, finds it 'consciousness-raising' and highly enjoyable, reminding her about feeling less guilty over eating meat.[12] Ellen Akins enjoys the language, the ironic names, such as the company 'Happicuppa', and the novel's division into saints days. She sees it as a product of Atwood's 'humor and sheer goofiness'.[13] As part of showcasing the novel or perhaps bringing it more into public view, emphasising its performativity, there was the auctioning of the right to be a character both in it and in its predecessor *Oryx and Crake*. Atwood donated the naming rights to characters to charity auctions. Journalist Rebecca Eckler paid $7,000 at a benefit for the magazine *The Walrus* and later noted that she was not actually killed off in the novel.[14]

Dystopia and science fiction

This world grows, as in all good dystopias, from a satirical view of our own. There is cosmetic surgery, dubious food sourcing, drug running, religious cults, brutality and the treatment of women as sex workers and sex slaves. In this near future, criminals are punished in public at Painball, the interestingly named derivation of Paintball and *Fight Club*. Hensher is amused by the language, though less so by the unlikelihood of all the wandering characters finally meeting again in a clearing. He notes:

> Like all dystopias, this is a satire on present-day life ... I enjoyed Atwood's Painball, and rather wanted her to have more fun with it. The strip clubs, oppressive labour of the female proletariat coupled with pampered and plastic-surgery-addicted wives have been distinctive Atwood-dystopia territory since *The Handmaid's Tale* at least, and it gains an added dimension from the biologically manipulative fantasy which she started to explore in *Oryx and Crake*.[15]

Other reviewers are also not pleased by the plots. Robert Charles Wilson sees:

> some clumsy plotting undermines the story. A plague that eliminates much of the human species coincidentally spares an extraordinary number of the book's main characters, who run across one another in the wasteland with startling regularity. This is perfectly appropriate to a fable or a fairy tale.[16]

However, he likes the familiar sci-fi 'depopulated world'. With its 'futuristic stage sets ... *The Year of the Flood* often reads like a novel of substance gene-spliced with a back issue of *MAD* magazine',[17] though it is not necessarily its mix of the fantastic and the realistic which confuses and irritates. There is space for a critique of a society in which women play secondary roles, can be mutilated, murdered, sold or enslaved, as is Ren's friend Amanda, a streetwise girl who briefly joins the Gardeners and the brothel/club 'Scales and Tails'.

Darryl Whetter is unimpressed, finding the characters unlovable and the novel dull, and thinks that Atwood 'fails to galvanize

its unquestionably relevant environmental material'.[18] Margaret
Atwood talks about survival skills, and not just the literary kind.
John Barber, writing in the *Globe and Mail*,[19] sees Atwood as twitch-
ing with intelligence and traces the origins of her concern about
survival to the influence of a book given to her by the poet Al Purdy.
He reviews areas of interest which will most probably be the reasons for the book's survival – an ironic treatment of post-apocalyptic
survival, a dire warning about the lack of sustainability, the terror
of police states, brothels. *The Year of the Flood* invites reading for its
social engagement: 'the author-as-activist is busy spreading hope in
the same straightforward spirit as her silly/holy Gardeners'.[20] He
alerts us to the website which links to environmental causes and so
can draw readers in further.

Jane Ciabattari finds it a credible view of the future – Atwood
'reminds us, scientists are capable of terrible, Earth-changing
errors'.[21] Melanie Kirkpatrick is equally dour and sees in the novel:
'a future made grim by greed and the wanton destruction of the
environment', there is 'a shot at the patriarchy' and confusing flashbacks in a 'not-so-peaceable kingdom. Her vision is more Revelations
than Genesis, and as Apocalypse stories go, it's as dull as it gets.'[22]
Perhaps it is the worthiness of the text which people find dull.

Caroline Moore points out the mixture of writing and tone, seeing it as on the one hand 'a straight-forward, gripping survival yarn
of vulnerable humans in a vivid wilderness, where the prowling
beasts are man-made monsters',[23] leading us through them and
Toby's flashbacks to 'a decadent, science-led, self-destructive society
controlled by corporate businesses, in which environmentalism has
developed into a cultish religion'.[24] Though she sees the emphasis
on corporate ills as hardly new, she finds it at times chaotic and
overall remarkably tightly knit, a view we see infusing Gillian
Beer's review.

Taking up Atwood's insistence that neither this work nor *Oryx
and Crake* are science fiction, Ursula Le Guin finds it more difficult
to critique and celebrate the novel as a realistic piece – which she
argues it clearly isn't. She finds herself limited without using the
fine-tuned vocabulary and approach of science fiction. While references to swine flu and the Black Plague indicate knowledge of
devastating sickness, Le Guin is unsure that the novel is credible in
its portrayal of the Waterless Flood, arguing that 'failure to describe
the nature of the illness and the days of its worst virulence leaves
the epidemic an abstraction, novelistically weightless'.[25] This could

be a result of Atwood's claim that it is based in the seeds of current events, and its intertextuality is a postmodern feature. However, Le Guin felt she was being tested on the earlier novel. She finds the Gardeners 'memorable', and presented with 'irony and affection'. This setting in Year 2025 is no improvement on the dystopian world of 1984 in Orwell's novel, and in fact many of the murderous corporations which Atwood warns against are governing our world in 2009, argues Le Guin. 'Irrational hope' dominates the loyalties which spring up among the characters. The powerless women through whose eyes it is seen remind her of other horrifying spectacles in art, such as those portrayed by Goya (1746–1828), the Spanish painter. But she takes issue with Atwood's denial that the novel is science fiction and argues that as a reviewer, Le Guin is somewhat hamstrung by this denial, unable to use the discourse of science fiction criticism to recognise much of its mixture of satire and prediction, 'a work of unusual cautionary imagination and satirical invention'.

An earlier review compares the text to the painter of scenes of hell by Hieronymus Bosch (c. 1450–1416), and the novel *A Clockwork Orange* (1962) by Anthony Burgess (1917–93), another brutal dystopia in which aesthetic tastes are not an indication of humanity. Michiko Kukatani calls it 'a cautionary tale about a pandemic'.[26] For Kakutani, *Oryx and Crake* was 'lumpy' and, strangely, she sees this and *The Handmaid's Tale* as 'hobbled by didactic asides and a preachy, moralistic tone', while the current novel is 'loosened up', which is not a reading agreed on by many other reviewers.

Another great critic, Fredric Jameson in the *London Review of Books*, takes up the task of exploring the effects and characteristics of dystopian fictions.[27] He finds the cliffhanger of *Oryx and Crake* 'somewhat spoiled' by Atwood continuing into this world unnecessarily. He speculates that while the world of *Oryx and Crake* was male, populated by Jimmy (Snowman) and Glen (Crake), the world of *The Year of the Flood* is more female and their stories need telling too, perhaps. Jameson places the new novel with Atwood's other great sociological novels, particularly *Surfacing*, and sees the influence of the Canadian quality of the novel where the moral descent is 'into Americanism', or into consumerism and artifice. Here, Atwood moves beyond those elements of Americanism and the world is horribly artificial: 'Its colours have a loathsome pastel quality, like drugstores; its bunny suits and fluffy fabrics reflect the bad taste of infantile mass production; the bloody physical violence is that of cartoons rather than Hitler.'[28]

The only aesthetic pleasure is 'a syrupy nausea that repeats on you' and in such a cloying destructive context before the Waterless Flood, 'the end of the world has some of the cleansing, bracing effect of sand and waste landscape, of the seashore'.[29] Jameson finds Adam One's closing, tentatively hopeful words most positive. Hannes Bergthaller links the novel with *Oryx and Crake* and sees its development of the biotechnology and eco-criticism in the earlier novel as a fundamental indictment of flaws in human nature, out of alignment with the needs and being of the planet. The only hope is that people will change. The novel explores an 'ecological crisis as arising from flaws in humanity's biological make-up; sustainability is thus a question of housebreaking the human animal, that is, of aligning human behaviour to the requirements of the planetary *oikos*'.[30] In order to survive, 'anthropo-technologies' offer some hope and Bergthaller suggests in this light that 'Atwood's novels arrive at a qualified humanism informed by evolutionary biology and disenchanted with human nature.'

Bernardine Evaristo is not so pleased with the novel, seeing the horror and the hope as a little simplistic, and states that Atwood descends into being some kind of prophet. The story seems simplistic, 'old-fashioned' because of its hippy commune lifestyle set against the evil corporations and abuse. However, when Toby and Ren emerge, they are energetic.[31] So, too, are the Crakers, gentle genetically modified humans of whom we first learned in *Oryx and Crake*, 'Mutant, naked humans emerge from the deluge, freakishly youthful: "Resurfaced. Airbrushed." The men have huge, bright-blue erections that "wag from side to side like the tails of happy dogs". Novelist as prophet? Let's hope not.'[32]

Another sceptical voice is Jane Shilling. Her review mainly takes us through the novel and, like Le Guin's, feels an opportunity has been lost by avoiding the science fiction nature of the piece. In the end, though, she is relatively untouched:

> As an artefact, her novel is a remarkable feat of the imagination, as well as a salutary warning. As a record of the best qualities of the human spirit, it is curiously untouching. One is sufficiently engaged to want to finish the book, but if it ended with everyone eaten alive by liobams, one would hardly care.[33]

Gillian Beer's review probably provides the most insightful, all-round interpretation of the novel because she appreciates the rather bizarre comic elements, the eco-hymns and community spirit of

God's Gardeners as a way of vehicling the sombre message and providing a form of hope which is qualified, slightly sceptical, as are her views on Toby, who became a member of the group, despite her misgivings. Where others see a confused structure, Beer sees something more structured but organic, flexible but knit, perhaps we could argue like human groups more in harmony with the natural world.

For her, 'The Gardeners are at once exhilarating, absurd and truth-telling. They have invented their own rituals and saints, as other revolutionaries have done: Witness the French revolutionary calendar and the Positivist saints' days.'[34] Various characters are given saints' names, and Adam One, the evolutionist, is himself a mix, held in some balance, 'a former scientist, one who believes in their mission as makers of God's ark against destruction'. Our entry into their world, their 'often bossy and comic company' is probably balanced and managed because it is enabled by the more sceptical, tough Toby and 'The Gardeners themselves are down-to-earth and enraptured at once, and Atwood invents a wonderful means by which we share their being even as we smile at their wackier behaviour.'[35]

She sees the hymns as structuring the novel:

> [They are] moving, humorous, compelling and perfectly rhymed. The rhyming means much. It knits up disorder; it discovers kinships; it solaces; it reveals. It persists to the end. These are songs to be sung, together. They are also anomalies, since the Gardeners distrust writing.[36]

Beer captures the contradictions which are held in tension in this novel, and which are perhaps overlooked by critics who either celebrate the godliness or deride the wackiness of the text.

Feminist view: women's lives

The novel focuses on the women's stories rather than the men's, which dominated the first novel in the trilogy, and the caring and everyday tones of the two women, Ren and Toby. Nisi Shawl points out that Ren, like Oryx, also a sex worker, is a much more prosaic character:

> Her first person account skims the surface of her job's unpleasant aspects, and she plays down the rapes and tortures other survivors

inflict on her. Yet the mere fact that she tells her own story gives her a grounding Oryx lacked.[37]

Toby works with willow bark, maggots and honey to cure her world and other people. Le Guin sees the book as more of 'a lament' than an affirmation, and finds the men unredeemably violent, while the women 'are real people, but heartbreaking ones'.[38]

One would expect Jeannette Winterson to have a more feminist take on the Strange New World. She enjoys the spliced liobam 'engineered by a lunatic fringe religious group that's tired of waiting for the prophecy of the lion lying down with the lamb to come true'.[39] She sees it as representative of the brutality couched in fluffiness which dominates the world before the Waterless Flood. The liobam will rip your throat out while looking beautiful with its long curly golden hair: 'The metaphor for the world of lethal paternalism created by CorpSeCorp.'[40]

Book tour and reception

Atwood manages her own carbon footprint by bringing her reading of the novel to the UK and Europe by travelling by ship, not on an airplane, using local choirs and actors to play the part of Adam One, the head Gardener and leader, and Toby and Ren, survivors so far of the Waterless Flood. Some of the mixed reviews could be based on seeing the road show, which had a charm of its own, and something of the feel of a school Christmas play. The road show, at Manchester Cathedral, is described in *The Independent* by Arifa Akbar as: 'a cross between a funky church choir – her hymns were sung by the city's lesbian and gay singers – and an enthralling storytelling session for grown-ups'.[41] Atwood herself is seen as sprightly and bird-like. Nicola Barr reviews one of the tour performances in London, portraying Atwood as 'serene and queenly',[42] sitting to one side and occasionally interjecting while actors play the parts with plummy voices, not quite the same experience as I had in Ely Cathedral, which had a Fenland local village quality. This reviewer sees 'lost, demented' singers and a 'bemused' audience responding to the odd choir and the chanting and clapping. Here, Barr speculates about Atwood's fans, wondering 'when Atwood tipped from endearingly eccentric to exasperatingly barking'.[43]

Critics continue to take a variety of approaches developed from those in the earlier novels. They look at Atwood's language, the feminism, the science fiction, and the irony. Unusually, they also comment on the way in which the book has been presented as a form of road show, which might well underline the homely warnings or undermine the novel's quality. We might wonder how the third novel in the trilogy will develop the themes and the world Atwood has created.

12

Conclusion

On entering the St Lawrence Market in Toronto, you meet a small stand offering examples of ecologically sound goods and views. The advertisement fronting it portrays Margaret Atwood, watering can in hand, exhorting us to act in a sustainable fashion. A TV programme casually switched on gives her talking about the future of the planet and the plight of the polar bear, or talking, reading and being interviewed at the World Book night in March, London, 2011. She is culturally active and creatively prolific, at the height of her powers, and seemingly everywhere.

Atwood is such a versatile writer that both the variety and volume of her work constantly surprise. It is difficult to speculate what she will turn to explore next, although returning to her main themes and concerns provides insights. Atwood has produced outstanding work in all her favourite genres. She is writing critically, and in *The Tent* (2006), her short stories push further the flash fiction format of earlier work, while developing parody, the ways people construct fictions of self and the world, identity and gender roles. Her poetry continually develops. *The Door* (2007) offers insights into periods of her own life, into relationships, versions of reality, responses to events and world movements. It develops the reflective, lyrical achievements of earlier work. There is no let-up here. We can expect a new novel, the third in the trilogy beginning with *Oryx and Crake* (2003). But she is also likely to support her books being translated into films or operas, and to embark on worldwide tours reading and talking about her critical essays, or latterly, more often, her writing origins.

Ongoing writing and scholarship

Major themes in Atwood criticism over the years have included Coral Ann Howells' exploration of how she has furthered women's writing, challenging masculine forms of genre fictions, and cultural myths.

In 2010, Howells reviewed Ellen McWilliams' book on Atwood in *Contemporary Women's Writing*, replaying here the themes of 'historical reconstruction', feminism, and female versions of genre fictions, all themes she herself has focused on over the years as a major critic of Atwood's work.[1] In 2010, another consistent critic of Atwood's, Reingard M. Nischik, wrote on her reconfigurations of genre fictions in *Engendering Gender: The Works of Margaret Atwood*,[2] which considers ways in which Atwood intervenes on largely masculine-informed genres such as science fiction, crime and thrillers, highlighting gendered concerns. It also gives us new information on and a critical stance towards those perhaps less mainstream elements of her work, her cartoons, flash fictions and film scripts.

There is an immense critical industry on Atwood's work, that has developed since her first publications and prizes. Howells finds Atwood influential in the development and recognition of Canadian literature and in maintaining a focus on ecology, sustainability and survival. Howells, Eleanor Rao and Jane Brooks Bouson deal with Atwood's versions of feminism and revisioning of opportunities available for women who escape constraining narratives. Sherrill Grace sees polarities as structuring devices, motifs and ways of exploring and identifying representations of the self.

Judith McCombs collected hundreds of reviews and essay abstracts, and produced her own study focusing on Atwood's interest in ways in which people create a sense of self, identity, in the face of social imperatives and narratives which hem them in, a theme taken up by several critics who show how Atwood deals with the constraints of internalised narratives upon women's development of self. These narratives include the Rapunzel fairytale, a metaphor for the Canadian woman, trapped in a tower awaiting a man to release her into a socially defined, limited version, or the Red Shoes tale, a favourite of Sharon Wilson, where women must choose between relationships or being an artist. Wilson's work on fairytale and myth is very scholarly, tracing Atwood's feminist variants in traditional sources.

Jane Brooks Bouson tracks Atwood's feminist approaches and explorations of the Gothic, recognising playful ironies and the exposure of social and cultural contradictions enabled by the literary Gothic. Frank Davey and George Woodcock critique Atwood's treatment of Canadian themes in a context of Canadian narrowness, while Diana Brydon is unusual in looking at Atwood's rare postcolonialism, mainly in *Bodily Harm* (1981). These issues are connected in Sharon Wilson's *Myths and Fairy Tales in Contemporary Women's Fiction: From Atwood to Morrison,*[3] which takes an unusually postcolonial perspective, mainly looking at Atwood, Doris Lessing and Toni Morrison's use and revisions of fairytales and myths. It explores intertexts, meanings and re-written versions. For Wilson, myths and fairytales indicate ways in which characters transform from individualism and alienation to broader, often hybrid or postcolonial, community, responsibility and engagement. In a most unusual and cohesive fashion, this relates Atwood's Gothic tales and fairytales to the readings of her postcolonialism, celebration of diversity as a form of survival, and her community consciousness, linking people to their communities and to nature.

Interestingly, criticism which recognises Atwood's developing ecological themes and her concern with survival, sustainability and diversification from *Surfacing* (1972), through the speculative/science fiction-influenced *The Handmaid's Tale* (1985), *Oryx and Crake* and *The Year of the Flood* (2009), fails to see these works argue similar points to postcolonial criticism, which emphasises the importance of celebrating difference and taking care to avoid misreadings of different cultures and events.

Coral Ann Howells' *Cambridge Companion to Margaret Atwood* (2006) set the trend for critical work appearing later in an established writer's career, which sums up trends in her work. Something of a hiatus in book-length Atwood criticism led to the most recent books by Reingard Nischik, and Ellen McWilliams, both in 2009. Heidi McPherson's (2010) *The Cambridge Introduction to Margaret Atwood* could be seen as a companion piece to this text. It concentrates on developing McPherson's own discussions about the variety of Atwood's work, rather than summarising and synthesising works of critics and critical trends throughout the years, and provides some useful information, insights and new ways through her established works. Importantly, it shows a lively interest in Atwood's ingenuity, energy and originality. 'Each Atwood text is a treat, whether it spans only a few lines, or offers up an intricate puzzle in the form of a multilayered novel.'[4] Gina Wisker's *Atwood's Handmaid's Tale* (2009) offers a close look at main themes and issues with which critics engage in Atwood's work, from the dystopian ecological, to the feminist and concerns with the constructedness of narrative and of the self, in an in-depth exploration of the most popular of Atwood's novels.

Margaret Atwood's works are studied all over the world and so there are now a number of critical texts at the level of student guides, which enable student readers to engage with the work in an informed manner. Some of these are explanatory notes, some online.

The Thomas Fisher rare book library at the University of Toronto seems to have new acquisitions on every visit. Atwood's poetry, novels, short stories, literary criticism and essays have been translated into more than 20 languages and published in over 25 countries. There is a rich wealth of PhD theses in Finnish, for example, see Johanna Lahikanen's 'You look delicious: food and eating in Margaret Atwood's novels'[5] for an extensive list.

As discussions of the fictions indicate, Atwood is a feminist author who decries the limitations of that label. She constantly deals with gendered relations, and explores, reinvents and replays myths and fictional patternings with which we report versions of our lives and which people have used to construct narratives by which to live, direct or constrain themselves through different periods of history. Some of these myths and narratives concern the lure of the Far North, or Canadian voyages seeking adventure and achievement, which are dangerous, fatal even, but never release their hold on the imagination. Other conditions in which we seem trapped are romantic fictions, including those explored in *Lady Oracle* (1976), *The Edible Woman* (1969) and elements of the novels or meta-narratives about courage, finding closure to problems, and surviving deadly mistakes, punitive constraints and regimes, as in *The Handmaid's Tale*, *Oryx and Crake* and *The Year of the Flood*. Many of Atwood's characters rebel against being cast as romantic heroines, gendered victims of the social narratives in which they are confined by society, by others or by their own collusion, victims of their bodies. Myths are exposed and sometimes rewritten, using the Gothic, starting with *Lady Oracle* and the romantic Gothics of Joan Foster. This peaks with the imprisoning Gothic fictions of *The Robber Bride* (1993) and Zenia's predatory manipulation of three women who needed her insinuation and destructive behaviour in order to develop their versions of self. Like other Atwood female characters, they also needed to break from a deadly narrative hold of popular fiction and myths about how women should be: nurturing, maternal victims. Atwood's short stories in her middle period consistently attacked popular cultural versions of women's roles, using various Gothic, often grotesque, ironic and amusing scenarios to puncture pomposity and constraining narratives of life. 'Hairball', an early story, explores the underbelly of romance, manipulation and rejection of others, and self-questioning and self-affirmation through a bizarre act. Atwood problematises and undercuts rather than preaches. She offers enacted speculations about motives, values, the stories we tell ourselves about families, relationships, power games and reasons for living.

One constant theme, developed in *Lady Oracle* and throughout her work, is the stories we tell ourselves, the ways in which we produce and accept new constructions and live by them, unaware of their constraining power. Atwood focuses on the fictionalising role of narratives, those with power over the language and versions of events. In this respect, she often produces strong narrative voices, from one woman seeking her own identity through tracking into the wilderness to rediscover her past and the body of her father in *Surfacing*, to Offred in *The Handmaid's Tale*, hindered by the danger of any form of expression yet somehow getting her voice out. In *Alias Grace* (1996), Grace's murderous history is both embellished and occluded in the trickeries of her tale-telling and the uncertain grasp of the truth, available in public, journalistic, balladic, documentary or psychotherapeutic versions of tales.

The Blind Assassin (2000) also deals with versions of fictions, since the narrator hides her own and the history of her sister, which she claims to be recounting, overwhelming us with descriptive, realistic detail, evidence and stories within stories. Atwood deals with ways in which people are constructed as outsiders, manipulated, ignored or harmed. Artist Elaine Risley suffers spiteful girlish tricks at the hands of her friends in *Cat's Eye* (1988).

However, the postcolonial and postcolonial Others are generally underplayed in her work. In the short stories, a few Otherised beings emerge, and *Bodily Harm* is set in a postcolonial context: the Caribbean. But Atwood deals constantly with social structures, beliefs and regimes which select insiders and outsiders, and so provides insights into what it means to be disempowered and marginalised, and how some can rewrite their own stories and develop self-affirmation, resilience and self-worth as a result. This is one description of her most popular novel: *The Handmaid's Tale*.

The Handmaid's Tale brought Atwood to a very wide readership. It breaks new ground in its exploration of the power politics of gender and religion, and the duplicitous nature of discourse, focusing on a post-holocaust future in which women's reproductive value is everything, and a fundamentalist regime reigns over thought, language, sexuality and behaviour. The novel has been studied by thousands of students at 'A' level, during degree courses or in adult education classes. It touches on eternally sensitive areas about identity, power, image, freedom and social construction, the issues which fuel such great dystopian science fiction as *Nineteen Eighty-Four* and *Brave New World*, both of which have been significant influences on its development. Touching on, manipulating and developing the genres of popular fictions have been a great development in Atwood's work. Science fiction re-appeared in the embedded tale of the 'Peach women of Aa'A' in *The Blind Assassin* and in the novels *Oryx and Crake* and *The Year of the Flood*. They grew from Atwood's concern with the environment, an ecological focus which emerged first in *Surfacing* and in some of her tales of the Canadian North. Those include work by literary Canadians in *Survival* (1970) and, latterly, in *Strange Things: The Malevolent North* (1996), also in both *Moral Disorder* (2006), her story sequence about a family history very similar to her own, and flash fiction, *The Tent*. Atwood's focus on sustainable development is probably now the most topical of her concerns and could well produce further work. In this respect, *Oryx and Crake* was ahead of its time. It indicts a fatally frivolous playing around with humankind and life itself, which leads to terrible consequences. Such tendencies to overlook, use up and play dangerous games with existence, whether genetic, social, psychological, technological, chemical or territorial have been criticised in a range of disaster movies, from *The Day After Tomorrow* (2004, directed by Roland Emmerich) to the topical Al Gore film, *An Inconvenient Truth* (2006, directed by Davis Guggenheim).

Staging and filming Atwood

Atwood is no stranger to staging her work. Between 1985 and1993, the Company of Sirens, a group of Toronto-based women theatre practitioners, created and performed *Penelope*, derived from the *Circe/Mud* poem sequence.

In 1981, several Canadian film producers produced an adaptation of *Surfacing*. In 1990, a US/German collaboration adapted *The Handmaid's Tale* into a film. The Women's Network (Canada) commissioned a series of six of Atwood's short stories for television in 2003, and in 2007, Canada's CBC TV presented a version of *The Robber Bride*. These four ventures translated her fiction to the screen.

Canadian theatre artists have also turned Atwood's work out on stage. David Carley's script of *The Edible Woman* was performed in 2002 at the Canadian Stage Company, Toronto, and in 1999 Clare Coulter dramatised selections from *Good Bones* in a one-woman show at the Tarragon Theatre's Extra Space in Toronto.[6]

An opera of *The Handmaid's Tale* was produced by Danish composer and producer Poul Ruders, of which Canada's *The National Post* reviewer Tamara Bernstein wrote:

> The opera gives us something no novel can: the force of communal experience. It's one thing to read a novel, quite another to experience Atwood's vision with thousands of others. You could feel the cathartic power in the opening-night ovations for all ... But when Atwood herself came onstage, the audience released the greatest roar I've ever heard from a Toronto audience. Don't miss this show.[7]

Shannon Hengen says that Bernstein attributes the opera's success partly to the 'the timeliness of the issues raised in *The Handmaid's Tale*: the defiance and reluctant heroism of the female lead, the haunting by its Puritan theocratic origins of a nation – the US – attempting to "reinvent itself"'. Important current themes along with elaborate public presentation of them seem to give Atwood's work a new immediacy, indeed a new public.

Hengen also tells us that in the United States, musicians in New York's Syracuse University performed and recorded some of Atwood's poetry in songs commissioned by young female US composers.[8] The dramatic, operatic quality of Atwood texts seems to contribute to their success in this medium.

In 2004, the opera version of *The Handmaid's Tale* was produced by the Canadian Opera Company at Toronto's Hummingbird Centre, with a seating capacity of 3,200.[9]

Next steps

In 2008, a local Toronto film company filmed *The Robber Bride* and released it on TV in Canada. To take a favourite ecological image, this will be but the tip of an iceberg. Also, in 2008, Atwood announced via a television hook-up between Toronto and Vancouver that she had accepted her first chamber opera commission based on the life and work of Pauline Johnson, a writer and Canadian artist, in whom

Atwood has long been interested. 'Pauline' will be set in Vancouver, British Columbia, in March 1913, in the last year of Johnson's life, will star Judith Forst, with music by Christos Hatzis, and will be produced by the City Opera of Vancouver.

Atwood is clear about the imaginative and more practical functions of literature:

> Literature is an uttering, or outering, of the human imagination. It lets the shadowy forms of thought and feeling – heaven, hell, monsters, angels and all – out into the light, where we can take a good look at them and perhaps come to a better understanding of who we are and what we want, and what the limits to those wants may be. Understanding the imagination is no longer a pastime, but a necessity; because increasingly, if we can imagine it, we'll be able to do it.[10]

Margaret Atwood is technologically ahead of many writers half her age. To cut down ecological damage caused by travel she visited the UK and elsewhere travelling by ship in 2009. To aid with book signing she invented the 'long pen' which signs remotely and in 2010 she embraced the social networking capabilities of Twitter. She has invited graphic contributors to her new e-book *In Other Worlds: Science Fiction and the Human Imagination*.

Keeping up to date with Atwood's work and plans is now possible through seeing her Twitter contributions, e.g. on twitter.com/margaretatwood, where she also can be contacted directly, and by staying in touch with her website at: http://www.owtoad.com/.[11] Atwood is a commentator on our times, a highly gifted creative and critical writer in fiction and prose, and someone who ensures that the origins of her work and its impact are meticulously collated and managed. Researching Atwood's work causes us to think not only about what she writes and how she does so, but also about the relationship of the writer to her own sources of inspiration and origins. Atwood also makes us think about writing's relationship to engagement and environmental activism, as well as the power of the literary genres to represent, dissect and engage in a dialogue with historical, individual, cultural and social constructions of reality.

Notes

Introduction

1. Atwood in interview with Lucy White, *Varsity*, 21 January 1983.
2. Earl G. Ingersoll (ed.) *Margaret Atwood: Conversations* (Willowdale, ON: Firefly Books, 1990), p. 163.
3. Michael Ondaatje, *Canadian Forum* (1972).
4. Jeremy Brooks, *The Sunday Times*, 27 May 1973.
5. Margaret Atwood, 'Introduction', in *The Edible Woman* (Toronto: McClelland & Stewart, 1969), p. 8.
6. Faye Hammill, *Canadian Literature* (Edinburgh: Edinburgh University Press, 2007).
7. W. H. New, *A History of Canadian Literature* (London: Macmillan, 1989).
8. Diana Brydon and Helen Tiffin, *Decolonising Fictions* (Sydney: Dangaroo Press, 1993), p. 63.
9. Gina Wisker, *Margaret Atwood's Alias Grace* (London: Continuum, 2000), p. 11.
10. David Guterson, *Snow Falling on Cedars* (New York: Harcourt Brace, 1994).
11. Catherine Pepinster, 'The writer's tale: how a story chose an author and wowed the critics; Canada's top author tells Catherine Pepinster about her new book's spiritual inspiration', *The Independent*, 20 September, 1996, p. 9.
12. Coral Ann Howells, *Margaret Atwood* (Basingstoke: Palgrave Macmillan, 2005), p. 62.
13. Ibid., p. 62.
14. Barbara Hill Rigney, *Madness and Sexual Politics in the Feminist Novel: Studies in Bronte, Woolf, Lessing and Atwood* (Madison, WI: University of Wisconsin Press, 1978), pp. 91–127.
15. Nathalie Cooke, *Margaret Atwood: A Critical Companion* (Westport, CT: Greenwood Press, 2004).
16. Joan Smith, 'Atwood's delicious, vicious heroines', *San Francisco Examiner*, 21 February, 1994, p. d6.
17. Hilde Staels, *Atwood's Novels: A Study of Narrative Discourse* (Tübingen: Gulde, 1995), p. 5.
18. Ibid., p. 5.
19. Ibid., p. 6.
20. Sherrill Grace, *Violent Duality: A Study of Margaret Atwood* (Montreal: Véhicule Press, 1994).
21. Ibid., p. 130.
22. Ibid., p. 134.
23. Sharon Rose Wilson, *Margaret Atwood's Fairy-Tale Sexual Politics* (Jackson, MO: University Press of Mississippi, 1993).

24. Sharon Rose Wilson, 'Mythological intertexts in Margaret Atwood's works', in R. M. Nischik (ed.), *Margaret Atwood: Works and Impact* (Rochester, NY: Camden House, 2000), p. 215.
25. Howells, *Margaret Atwood*, p. 63.
26. Ibid., p. 65.
27. Ibid., p. 65.
28. Ibid., p. 65.
29. Colin Nicholson (ed.), *Margaret Atwood: Writing and Subjectivity: New Critical Essays* (Basingstoke: Palgrave Macmillan, 1994).
30. Jane Brooks Bouson, *Brutal Choreographies: Oppositional Strategies and Narrative Design in the Novels of Margaret Atwood* (Amherst, MA: University of Massachusetts Press, 1993).
31. Gina Wisker, *Alias Grace*, Gina Wisker, *Atwood's Handmaid's Tale* (London: Continuum, 2010); Pilar Cuder, *Beginners' Guide* (London: Hodder, 2003).
32. Margaret Atwood, '*The Handmaid's Tale*: before and after', papers, MS collection 200 (University of Toronto, November 1986), box 96, folder 11.

1 The Quest for Identity

1. Margaret Atwood, 'Progressive insanities of a pioneer', in John Thieme (ed.) *The Arnold Anthology of Post-colonial Literatures in English* (London: Edward Arnold, 1996), pp. 356–7.
2. Judith McCombs, 'Atwood's fictive portraits of the artist: from victim to surfacer, from oracle to birth', *Women's Studies*, 12(1) (1986): 72.
3. Ibid., p. 69.
4. Ibid., p. 72.
5. Ibid., p. 73.
6. Ibid., p. 73.
7. Ibid., p. 73.
8. George Woodcock, 'Margaret Atwood: poet as novelist: power, politics, *The Circle Game, The Edible Woman, The Journal of Susanna Moodie, The Animals in That Country, Survival* and *Surfacing*', in Judith McCombs (ed.), *Critical Essays on Margaret Atwood* (Boston: GK Hall and Co., 1988); Gloria Onley, 'Power politics in Bluebeard's castle', *Canadian Literature*, 60 (1974): 21–42; Robin Matthews, *Canadian Literature: Surrender or Revolution*, ed. Gail Dexter (Toronto: Steel Rail, 1978).
9. McCombs 'Atwood's fictive portraits', p. 74.
10. Ibid., p. 74.
11. Frank Davey, 'Atwood walking backwards', *Open Letter, a Journal*, second series, 5 (1973): 83.
12. Jerome K. Rosenberg, 'Margaret Atwood', in Obe Lecke (ed.) *Twayne's World Author Series: Canadian Literature* (Boston: Twayne Publishers, 1984), pp. 139–43.
13. Colin Nicholson (ed.) *Margaret Atwood: Writing and Subjectivity: New Critical Essays* (Basingstoke: Palgrave Macmillan, 1994), p. 4.
14. Ibid., pp. 4–5.
15. Ibid., p. 5.

16. Sherrill Grace, *Violent Duality: A Study of Margaret Atwood* (Montreal: Véhicule Press, 1994), p. 4.
17. Margaret Atwood, 'Introduction', in *Survival: A Thematic Guide to Canadian Literature* (Toronto: Anansi, 1972).
18. Fraser Sullivan, 'The Predator', in Margaret Atwood, *Survival*.
19. Coral Ann Howells, *Margaret Atwood* (Basingstoke: Palgrave Macmillan, 1996); Roberta Rubenstein, '*Surfacing*: Margaret Atwood's journey to the interior', *Modern Fiction Studies*, 22 (1976): 3; Carol Christ, 'Margaret Atwood: the surfacing of matriarchal religion in Atwood', *papers*, 153. 2, Thomas Fisher Rare Book Library, Toronto; Marie-Françoise Guedon, 'Surfacing: Amerindian themes and shamanism', in Grace and Weir, 1981, pp. 91–111; and Kathryn Van Spanckeren (ed.), *Margaret Atwood: Vision and Forms* (Carbondale, IL: Southern Illinois University Press, 1988).
20. Diana Brydon, 'Caribbean revolution and literary convention', *Canadian Literature*, 95 (Winter 1981): 181–5.
21. Peter Martin, Review, *Canadian Reader*, 14(1) (1973): 3.
22. Ibid., p. 3.
23. Frank Davey's *Margaret Atwood: A Feminist Poetics* (Vancouver: Talon, 1984), p. 165; George Woodcock's 'Recent Canadian novels, major publishers', *Queens Quarterly*, 89(4) (Winter 1981): 744–8; Paul Goetsch's (2000) 'Margaret Atwood, a Canadian nationalist', in Reingard M. Nischik (ed.), *Margaret Atwood: Works and Impact* (New York: Camden House, 2000).
24. Alice M. Palumbo, 'On the border: Margaret Atwood's novels', in Nischik, *Margaret Atwood: Works and Impact*.
25. Ibid. p. 75.
26. *Sg*, p. 191.
27. McCombs, 'Atwood's fictive portraits', p. 32.
28. Ibid., p. 32.
29. *Sg*, p. 191.
30. Susan Wood Glicksohn, 'The Martian point of view', *Extrapolation*, 15(2) (May 1974): 161–73.
31. Susan Fromberg Schaeffer, 'Is it time that separates us?', *Centennial Review*, 18 (Fall 1974): 319–37.
32. Karen F. Stein, 'Reflections on a jagged mirror: some metaphors of madness', *Aoha*, 6(2) (Spring 1975): 2–11.
33. Catherine N. Davidson, 'Chopin and Atwood: woman drowning, woman surfacing', *Kate Chopin Newsletter*, 1(3) (Winter 1975): 6–10.
34. Rubenstein, '*Surfacing*', pp. 387–99.
35. Josie P. Campbell, 'The woman as hero in Margaret Atwood's *Surfacing*', in Judith McCombs (ed.) *Critical Essays on Margaret Atwood* (Boston: Hall, 1978), p. 168.
36. Marge Piercy, 'Margaret Atwood: beyond victimhood,' *American Poetry Review*, 2(6) (November–December 1973): 44.
37. Margaret Laurence, 'Review of *Surfacing*', *Quarry*, 22(2) (Spring 1973): 62–4.
38. Gloria Onley, 'Power politics in Bluebeard's castle', *Canadian Literature*, 60 (1974): 21–42.
39. Ibid., pp. 21–42.

40. Josie P. Campbell, 'The woman as hero in Margaret Atwood's *Surfacing*', *Mosaic* (Spring 1978): 17.
41. Hilde Staels, *Atwood's Novels: A Study of Narrative Discourse* (Tübingen: Gulde, 1995), p. 5.
42. Jane Brooks Bouson, *Brutal Choreographies: Oppositional Strategies and Narrative Design in the Novels of Margaret Atwood* (Amherst, MA: University of Massachusetts Press, 1993), p. 40.
43. Ibid., p. 54.
44. Ibid., p. 61.
45. Carol Christ, 'Margaret Atwood'.
46. Ibid., p. 4.
47. Ibid., p. 4.
48. Piercy.
49. Francine du Plessix Gray, 'Nature as the nunnery', *The New York Times Book Review*, 17 July 1977, pp. 3, 29.
50. Barbara Hill Rigney, *Madness and Sexual Politics in the Feminist Novel: Studies in Bronte, Woolf, Lessing and Atwood* (Madison, WI: University of Wisconsin Press, 1978), pp. 91–127.
51. Davey, 'Atwood walking backwards', p. 83.
52. Sherrill Grace, *Violent Duality: A Study of Margaret Atwood* (Montreal: Véhicule Press, 1994).
53. Cathy N. Davidson and Arnold E. Davidson (eds), *The Art of Margaret Atwood: Essays in Criticism* (Toronto: Anansi, 1981).
54. Annis Pratt, *Archetypal Patterns in Women's Fiction* (Bloomington, IN: Indiana University Press, 1981).
55. *Sg*, p. 154.
56. Davidson and Davidson, *Art of Margaret Atwood*, p. 94.
57. *Sg*, p. 168.
58. *Sg*, p. 60.
59. Staels, *Atwood's Novels*, p. 68.
60. Christina Newman, 'Critical essays on Margaret Atwood: in search of a native tongue', *Maclean's*, September 1972: 43.
61. Laurence, 'Review of *Surfacing*', p. 62.
62. Joan Larkin (1973) 'Soul survivor', *Ms*, 1, 11, May, pp. 33–5.
63. *Sg*, p. 33.
64. Piercy, pp. 331–9.
65. Ibid., pp. 331–9.
66. David Ward, '*Surfacing*: separation, transition, incorporation', in Colin Nicholson (ed.), *Margaret Atwood: Writing and Subjectivity: New Critical Essays* (Toronto: Macmillan, 1994), p. 95.
67. Ibid., p. 95.
68. Ibid., p. 95.
69. Ibid., p. 95.
70. Staels, *Atwood's Novels*, pp. 55–6.
71. Ibid., p. 68.
72. Ward, *Surfacing*, p. 124.
73. Ibid., pp. 124–5.
74. *Sg*, p. 44.
75. *Sg*, p. 44.

76. Staels, *Atwood's Novels*, p. 40.
77. Ibid., p. 45.
78. R.D. Laing, *The Politics of Experience and The Bird of Paradise* (Harmondsworth: Penguin, 1967).
79. Larkin, 'Soul survivor', p.33.
80. Nicholson, *Margaret Atwood*, p. 6.
81. *Sg*, p. 162.
82. *Sg*, p. 181.
83. Fromberg Schaeffer, 'Is it time that separates us?', pp. 319–37.
84. Rosemary Sweetapple, 'Margaret Atwood: Victims and Survivors', *South Review*, 9, (1976), p. 50.
85. Keith Garebian, '*Surfacing*: Apocalyptic Ghost Story', *Mosaic*, 3 (1976): 1–9.
86. Margaret Atwood, in Graeme Gibson, 'Margaret Atwood', in *Eleven Canadian Novelists* (Toronto: Anansi, 1973), p. 29.
87. Ward, *Surfacing*, p. 188.
88. Piercy, pp. 331–9.
89. Ibid., pp. 331–9.
90. Campbell, 'The woman as hero in Margaret Atwood's *Surfacing*', *Mosaic* (Spring, 1978): 17–28.
91. George Woodcock, 'Notes on the recent Atwood', *Ariel* 4 (July 1973): 22–8.
92. Du Plessix Gray, 'Nature as the nunnery'.
93. Sherrill Grace, *Violent Duality: A Study of Margaret Atwood* (Montreal: Vehicule, 1980). p. 80.
94. Du Plessix Gray, 'Nature as the nunnery', p. 62.
95. Laurence (1973) 'Review of *Surfacing*', p. 62.

2 Constraining the Feminine

1. Margaret Atwood, 'Margaret in marketing land', ms, Atwood papers, Thomas Fisher Rare Book Library, Box 90, File 37.
2. Ibid.
3. Janice Radway, *Rereading the Romance: Women, Patriarchy and Popular Literature* (Chapel Hill, NC: University of North Carolina Press, 1991).
4. Lynne Pearce and Jackie Stacey (eds), *Romance Revisited* (New York: New York University Press, 1995).
5. Gina Wisker, *It's My Party: Reading Twentieth Century Women's Writing* (London: Pluto Press, 1994).
6. Jane Brooks Bouson, *Brutal Choreographies: Oppositional Strategies and Narrative Design in the Novels of Margaret Atwood* (Amherst, MA: the University of Massachusetts Press, 1993).
7. Ibid., p. 17.
8. Ibid., p. 23.
9. Coral Ann Howells, *Margaret Atwood* (Basingstoke: Palgrave Macmillan, 1996), p. 20.
10. Ibid., p. 20.
11. George Woodcock, 'Margaret Atwood: poet as novelist: power, politics, *The Circle Game, The Edible Woman, The Journal of Susanna Moodie, The*

Animals in That Country, Survival and *Surfacing'*, in Judith McCombs (ed.), *Critical Essays on Margaret Atwood* (Boston: GK Hall and Co, 1988), p. 93.
12. Marge Piercy, 'Margaret Atwood: beyond victimhood', in Judith McCombs (ed.), *Critical Essays on Margaret Atwood* (Boston: GK Hall and Co., 1988), p. 83.
13. Howells, *Margaret Atwood*, p. 21.
14. Ibid., p. 21.
15. Sherrill Grace, *Violent Duality: A Study of Margaret Atwood* (Montreal: Véhicule Press, 1980), p. 20.
16. Ibid., p. 91.
17. Catherine McLay, , 'The divided self: theme and pattern in Margaret Atwood's *Surfacing'*, *Journal of Canadian Fiction*, 4(1) (1975): 82.
18. *EW*, p. 3.
19. McLay, p. 138.
20. Grace, *Violent Duality*, p. 91.
21. *EW*, p. 102.
22. Grace, *Violent Duality*, p. 91.
23. Ibid., p. 23.
24. Sharon Wilson, *Margaret Atwood's Fairy-Tale Sexual Politics* (Jackson, MO: University Press of Mississippi, 1993), p. 83.
25. Ibid., p. 83.
26. McLay (1981), p. 136.
27. Ibid., p. 138.
28. Ibid., p. 138.
29. Hilde Staels, *Atwood's Novels: A Study of Narrative Discourse* (Tübingen: Gulde, 1995), p. 34.
30. Woodcock, 'Margaret Atwood: poet as novelist', p. 93.
31. Ibid., p. 93.
32. *EW*, p. 108.
33. *EW*, p. 105.
34. Woodcock, 'Margaret Atwood: poet as novelist', p. 93.
35. Devendra Varma, 'Gothic shadows in the early novels of Margaret Atwood', *Anglo-American Studies*, 6(1) (April 1986): 31-43.
36. Sharon Wilson, *Margaret Atwood's Fairy-Tale Sexual Politics* (Jackson, MO: University Press of Mississippi, 1993), p. 6.
37. Robert Lecke, 'Janus through the looking glass: Atwood's first three novels', in Cathy N. Davidson and Arnold E. Davidson (eds), *The Art of Margaret Atwood: Essays in Criticism* (Toronto: Anansi, 1981).
38. Alan Dane, *The Edible Woman* (Toronto: McClelland and Stewart, 1973).
39. Linda Sandler, Interview with Margaret Atwood, *Malahat Review*, 41 (January 1977): 16.
40. Staels, *Atwood's Novels*, p. 34.
41. Lecke, 'Janus', p. 186.
42. Judith McCombs, 'Atwood's fictive portraits of the artist: from victim to surfacer, from oracle to birth', *Women's Studies*, 12(1) (1986): 76.
43. Ibid., p. 77.
44. Frank Davey, 'Alternative stories', in Frank Davey, *Margaret Atwood: A Feminist Poetics* (Vancouver: Talon, 1984).

45. Barbara Godard, 'Tales within tales: Margaret Atwood's folk narrative in Canadian literature', 109 (Summer 1986): 57.
46. David McFadden, 'Review', *Quill & Quire*, January (1984): 24.
47. Godard, 'Tales within tales', p. 57.
48. Grace, *Violent Duality*, p. 112.
49. Ibid., p. 124.
50. Wilson, *Margaret Atwood's Fairy-Tale Sexual Politics*, p. 121.
51. Ibid., p. 69.
52. Brooks Bouson, *Brutal Choreographies*, p. 75.
53. Ibid., p. 75.
54. Ibid., p. 75.
55. McCombs, 'Atwood's fictive portraits', p. 77.
56. Ibid., p. 77.
57. Alice M. Palumbo, 'On the border: Margaret Atwood's novels', in Reingard M. Nischik (ed.), *Margaret Atwood: Works and Impact* (Rochester, NY: Camden House, 2000), p. 77.
58. Ibid., p. 77.
59. Catherine Sheldock-Ross, 'Banished to this other place: Atwood's *Lady Oracle*', *English Studies on Canada*, 6(4) (Winter 1980).
60. Susan J. Rosowksi, 'Margaret Atwood's *Lady Oracle*: Fantasy and the modern Gothic novel', in Judith McCombs, *Critical Essays on Margaret Atwood* (Boston: GK Hall and Co., 1988), pp. 197–8.
61. Ibid., p. 197.
62. Ibid., p. 197.
63. Palumbo, 'On the border', p. 76.
64. Varma, 'Gothic shadows', pp. 31–43.
65. Ibid., p. 31.
66. Ibid., p. 32.
67. *LO*, p. 33.
68. *LO*, p. 33.
69. *LO*, p. 34.

3   Explorations, Bones and Murder

1. Judith McCombs (ed.), *Critical Essays on Margaret Atwood* (Boston: GK Hall and Co., 1988), p. 83.
2. *DG*, p. 1.
3. Lee Biscoe Thompson, 'Minuets and madness: Margaret Atwood's *Dancing Girls*', in Cathy N. Davidson and Arnold E. Davidson (eds), *The Art of Margaret Atwood: Essays in Criticism* (Toronto: Anansi), p. 113.
4. Ibid., p. 118.
5. Ibid.
6. Charlotte Sturgess, 'Margaret Atwood's short fiction', in Reingard M. Nischik, *Margaret Atwood: Works and Impact* (Rochester, NY: Camden House, 2000).
7. Thomas Fisher rare books library box 80.1, collection 20, p. 3.
8. Thompson, 'Minuets and madness', p. 110.

9. *DG*, p. 111.
10. *DG*, p. 111.
11. Sturgess, 'Margaret Atwood's short fiction', p. 36.
12. Barbara Godard, 'Tales within tales', *Canadian Literature*, Summer (1986): 57–84.
13. Carole H. Carpenter, 'The ethnicity factor in Anglo-Canadian folkloristics', in Edith Fowke and Carole H. Carpenter (eds), *Explorations in Canadian Folklore* (Toronto: McClelland and Stewart Ltd, 1985), p. 59.
14. Ibid., p. 59.
15. Godard, 'Tales within Tales', p. 58.
16. Ibid., p. 58.
17. Sharon Wilson, 'Bluebeard's forbidden room: gender images in Margaret Atwood's visual and literary art' (1986), p. 385.
18. Sturgess, 'Margaret Atwood's short fiction', p. 91.
19. *BE*, p. 61.
20. Sturgess, 'Margaret Atwood's short fiction', p. 91.
21. Ibid., p. 92.
22. *BE*, pp. 101–2.
23. Coral Ann Howells, *Margaret Atwood* (Basingstoke: Palgrave Macmillan, 1996), pp. 2–3.
24. Sturgess, 'Margaret Atwood's short fiction', p. 94.
25. Reingard M. Nischik, '*Murder in the Dark*: Margaret Atwood's inverse poetics of intertextual minuteness', in Sharon R. Wilson (ed.), *Margaret Atwood's Textual Assassinations* (Columbus, OH: Ohio State University Press, 2003), pp. 5–6.
26. Ibid., pp. 13–14.
27. Sharon Wilson (ed.), 'Fiction flashes: genre and intertexts in *Good Bones*', in *Margaret Atwood's Textual Assassinations* (Columbus, OH: Ohio State University Press, 2003), pp. 20–1.
28. *GBSM*, pp. 50–6; *MD*, pp. 37–40 and Wilson, 'Fiction flashes', pp. 20–1.
29. Wilson, 'Fiction flashes', pp. 22–3.
30. Ibid., pp. 25–6.
31. *GB*, p. 26.
32. Ibid., p. 43.
33. Ibid., p. 43.
34. Ibid., p. 46.
35. Wilson, 'Fiction flashes', p. 26.
36. Sherrill Grace, 'Atwood's postmodern fairytale', in *Canadian Forum* (March 1994), p. 86.
37. Ibid., p. 86.
38. *GB*, p. 53.
39. Ibid., p. 55.
40. Ibid., p. 58.

4 Violence, Trauma and History

1. Coral Ann Howells, *Margaret Atwood* (Basingstoke: Palgrave Macmillan, 1996), p. 68.

2. Jane Brooks Bouson, *Brutal Choreographies: Oppositional Strategies and Narrative Design in the Novels of Margaret Atwood* (Amherst, MA: The University of Massachusetts Press, 1993).
3. Molly Hite, 'Tongueless in Toronto', *The Women's Review of Books*, 18(6) (March 2001): 1.
4. Sharon M. Wilson, *Margaret Atwood's Fairytale Sexual Politics* (Jackson, MO: University Press of Mississippi, 1993), p. 112.
5. Diana Brydon, 'Caribbean revolution and literary convention', *Canadian Literature*, 95 (1981): 181–5.
6. Judith McCombs, 'Country, politics and gender in Canadian Studies: a report from twenty years of Atwood criticism', *Canadian Issues*, 10(5) (1988): 39.
7. George Woodcock, 'Victor – or victim', *Canadian Literature*, 86 (Autumn 1980): 138.
8. Sherrill Grace, *Violent Duality: A Study of Margaret Atwood* (Montreal: Véhicule Press, 1980).
9. Marylou Antonnelli, 'Atwood over the hurdle', *Edmonton Sun*, 28 October 1979, p. S6.
10. Dave Billington, 'A novel of bleak brilliance', *Edmonton Sun*, 28 October 1979, p. S6.
11. Carol Corbel, 'Surfacing from a damaging decade', *Quill and Quire*, 45:12 (October 1979): 31.
12. Paul Delaney, 'Grim, nasty loves', *Vancouver Province Magazine*, 30 September 1979, p. 16.
13. Robert Fulford, 'Life before man', *Canadian Reader*, 20:9 (1979): 1–2.
14. Marion McCormick, 'Dinosaur bones', *Gazette (Montréal)*, 29 September 1979, p. 53.
15. Sam Solecki, 'Excess of ideas', *Canadian Forum*, 59 (November 1979): 28–9.
16. Unnamed reviewer, 'Dinosaurs in the wasteland', *Windsor Sun*, 20 October 1979, p. 59.
17. Adele Wiseman, 'Readers can rejoice: Atwood's on form', *Toronto Star*, 29 September 1979, p. F7.
18. Interview with Margaret Atwood, *Atlantis*, 5:2 (Spring 1980): 202–11.
19. Brooks Bouson, *Brutal Choreographies*, p. 88.
20. Bruce King, 'More than novelists', *CRNLE Reviews Journal*, 2 (1980): 3–5.
21. Valerie Miner, 'Complex Canadian novel of three painful lives', 'This World' section, *San Francisco Sunday Examiner and Chronicle*, 16 March 1980, p. 38.
22. Human, Margaret Atwood in interview, *Books, Bookmen*, 25:7 (April 1980), pp. 40–1.
23. Janice Kulyk Keefer, 'Hope against hopelessness: Margaret Atwood's *Life Before Man*', in Colin Nicholson (ed.), *Writing and Subjectivity* (New York: St. Martin's Press, 1994), p. 155.
24. Ibid., p. 155.
25. Wilson, *Fairytale Sexual Politics*, p. 112.
26. Kulyk Keefer 'Hope against hopelessness', pp. 155–6.
27. Valerie Miner, 'Complex Canadian novel', p. 38.
28. Blake Morrison, 'Love among the fossils', *The Observer*, 16 March 1980, p. 39.

29. Peter Oecoott, 'Three human flies caught in a web', *Newsweek*, 95:7 (18 February, 1980): p. 108.
30. Brooks Bouson (1993), p. 87.
31. Ibid., p. 88.
32. Ibid., p. 88.
33. Ibid., p. 108.
34. Rosellen Brown, 'Anatomy of melancholia', *Saturday Review*, 7:32 (February 1980), pp. 33–5.
35. Marilyn French, 'Spouses and lovers', *New York Times Book Review*, 3 February 1980, pp. 1, 26.
36. Unnamed reviewer, *The Kirkus Review*, 47:23 (1 December, 1979): 1385–6.
37. Victoria Glendinning, 'Survival of the fittest', *Washington Post Books*, 27 January, 1980, p. 4.
38. Kulyk Keefer, 'Hope against hopelessness', pp. 157–8.
39. Ibid., pp. 1556.
40. Sherrill Grace, *Violent Duality*, p. 37.
41. Kulyk Keefer, 'Hope against hopelessness', p. 167.
42. Frank Davey, *Margaret Atwood: A Feminist Poetics* (Vancouver: Talon, 1984), p. 165.
43. Kulyk Keefer, 'Hope against hopelessness', p. 170.
44. Helen Hoy, 'Letters in Canada, 1981: fiction 2', *University of Toronto Quarterly*, 51:4 (Summer 1981): 328–9.
45. Peter Kemp, *Times Literary Supplement*, 11 June 1981, p. 643.
46. John Mellor, 'Sweet Canadian', *The London Magazine*, 22:3 (June 1981) 61–5.
47. Martin Seymour Smith, 'Women often with Men', *The Financial Times*, 19 June 1982, p. 12.
48. George Woodcock, 'Recent Canadian novels, major publishers', *Queens Quarterly*, 89:4 (Winter 1981): 744–8.
49. Michael F. N. Dixon, Review in *The Fiddlehead*, 132 (April 1981): 87–9.
50. Margaret Dyment, in *Quarry*, 31:2 (Spring 1981): 71–6.
51. Sal Enesin, 'Recent fiction', *Illustrated London News*, 270 (August 1981): 59.
52. Margaret Forster, 'Survivors', *Books and Bookmen*, 322 (July 1981): 17.
53. Kate Fullbrook, Review, *British Book News* (November 1981): 705.
54. Sharon Wilson, 'A note on Margaret Atwood's visual art in *Bodily Harm*', in *Margaret Atwood's Fairy-Tale Sexual Politics* (Jackson, MO: University of Mississippi Press, 1993), pp. 115–16.
55. *BH*, p. 262.
56. Jennifer R. Waelti-Walters, *Fairy Tales and the Female Imagination* (Montreal: Eden Press, 1982).
57. Roberta Rubenstein, *Boundaries of the Self: Culture, Gender, Fiction* (Urbana, IL: University of Illinois, 1987).
58. Lorna Irvine, *Subversion* (Toronto: ECW Press, 1986), pp. 37–53.
59. Mary K. Kirtz, 'The thematic imperative: didactic characterization in *Bodily Harm*', in Beatrice Mendez-Egle (ed.), *Margaret Atwood: Reflection and Reality* (Texas: Pan American University, 1987).
60. Brooks Bouson, *Brutal Choreographies*, p. 112.

61. Ibid., p. 114.
62. Ibid., p. 115.
63. Ibid., p. 115.
64. Alice M. Palumbo, 'On the border: Margaret Atwood's novels', in Reingard M. Nischik (ed.), *Margaret Atwood: Works and Impact* (Rochester, NY: Camden House, 1999), p. 79.
65. *BH*, p. 27.
66. Stanley S. Atherton, 'Travel pieces: tropical traumas: images of the Caribbean, recent Canadian fiction', *Canadian Literature,* 95 (Winter 1982): 8–14.
67. Blaire Clark, 'Tale of two colonies', *Canadian Literature,* 95 (Winter 1981): 110–12.
68. Anatolia Broyard, 'And Toronto too', *New York Times,* 6 March 1981, p. 21.
69. Roselyn Brown, 'Critical condition', *New York Times,* 12 (22 March 1981): 56.
70. Unnamed reviewer, Review, *The Westerly,* 27:1 (March 1981): 98–100.
71. Diana Brydon, 'Caribbean revolution and literary convention', *Canadian Literature,* 95 (Winter 1981): 181–5.
72. Ibid., p. 184.
73. Diana Brydon, 'Atwood's postcolonial imagination: Reading *Bodily Harm*', in Lorraine M. York (ed.), *Various Atwoods: Essays on the Later Poems, Short Fiction and Novels* (Toronto: Anansi, 1995).
74. Ibid., p. 97.
75. Helen Tiffin, 'Voice and form', in Russell McDougall and Gillian Whitlock (eds), *Australian/Canadian Literatures in English* (Melbourne: Methuen Australia, 1987), pp. 119–32.
76. Marlene Nourbese Philip, *Frontiers, **Selected Essays and Writings on Racism and Culture 1984–1992*** (Stratford: Mercury Press, 1993), p. 278.
77. Brydon, 'Atwood's postcolonial imagination', pp. 97–8.
78. bell hooks, *Black Looks, Race and Representation* (Boston: South End Press, 1992), p. 174.
79. Tiffin, 'Voice and form', pp. 119–32.
80. Brydon, 'Atwood's postcolonial imagination', p. 112.
81. Gayatri Chakravorty Spivak, 'Criticism, feminism and the institution: interview with Elizabeth Grosz', in Sarah Hazy (ed.), *The Post-Colonial Critic: Interviews, Strategies, Dialogues* (London: Routledge, 1990), p. 9.
82. *BH*, p. 301.

5 The Oppressive Future

1. Margaret Atwood, An interview with Margaret Atwood on her novel *The Handmaid's Tale* (1998). Available online at: http://www.randomhouse.com/resources/bookgroup/handmaidstale_bgc.html#interview (accessed 3 January 2008).
2. Ibid.

3. Margaret Atwood, '"Aliens have taken the place of angels": Margaret Atwood on why we need science fiction', the *Guardian*, Friday, 17 June 2005. Available at: http://www.guardian.co.uk/film/2005/jun/17/ sciencefictionfantasyandhorror.margaretatwood.
4. Ellen Coughlin, 'Margaret Atwood', *Books and Arts*, 7 March 1980, p. 6.
5. Ken Adachi, 'Atwood's futuristic fiction', *The Sunday Star*, 29 September 1985, p. G11.
6. Mary McCarthy, Review, *Book Review*, 9 February 1986. Available at: http://partners.nytimes.com/books/00/03/26/specials/mccarthy-atwood.html (accessed 3 January 2008).
7. Ibid.
8. Ibid.
9. Lorna Sage, 'Projections from a messy present', *Times Literary Supplement*, 21 March 1986, p. 307.
10. Ibid., p. 307.
11. Ibid., p. 307.
12. Kate Fullbrook, *Free Women: Ethics and Aesthetics in Twentieth-Century Women's Fiction* (Hemel Hempstead: Harvester Wheatsheaf, 1990).
13. Cathy N. Davidson, 'A feminist 1984: Margaret Atwood talks about her exciting new novel', *Ms*, 14 February 1986, p. 24.
14. Jane Brooks Bouson, *Brutal Choreographies: Oppositional Strategies and Narrative Design in the Novels of Margaret Atwood* (Amherst, MA: The University of Massachusetts Press, 1993), p. 135.
15. Ibid., p. 146.
16. Mervyn Rothstein, quoting Atwood in 'No balm in Gilead for Margaret Atwood', the *New York Times*, 17 February 1986. Available at: http://partners.nytimes.com/books/00/09/03/specials/atwood-gilead.html, (accessed 3 January 2008).
17. Anne K. Kaler, '*A sister, dipped in blood*: satiric inversion of the formation techniques of women religious in Margaret Atwood's novel *The Handmaid's Tale*', *Christianity and Literature*, 38:2 (Winter 1989): 43–62.
18. Cotton Mather, quoted in Mark Evans, 'Versions of history: *The Handmaid's Tale* and its dedicatees', in Colin Nicholson (ed.), *Margaret Atwood: Writing and Subjectivity* (New York: St Martin's Press, 1994), p. 177.
19. Ibid., p. 182.
20. Kaler, '*A sister, dipped in blood*'.
21. Genesis, in Sharon Wilson, *Margaret Atwood's Fairy Tale Sexual Politics* (Jackson, MO: University of Mississippi Press, 1993), p. 274.
22. Ibid., p. 274.
23. Ibid., p. 274.
24. John Updike, Review, *The New Yorker*, 12 May 1986, p. 118.
25. Ibid., p. 121.
26. Ibid., p. 121.
27. Coral Ann Howells, 'Transgressing genre: a generic approach to Margaret Atwood's Novels: *The Handmaid's Tale* and *Dystopia*', in R.M. Nischik (ed.), *Margaret Atwood: Works and Impact* (Rochester, NY: Camden House, 2000), p. 142.
28. Ibid., p. 143.

29. Marta Dvorak, 'Margaret Atwood's humour', in Coral Ann Howells (ed.), *The Cambridge Companion to Margaret Atwood* (Cambridge: Cambridge University Press, 2006), p. 123.
30. Alice Palumbo, 'On the border: Margaret Atwood's novels', in Reingard M. Nischik (ed.), *Margaret Atwood: Works and Impact* (Rochester, NY: Camden House, 2000), p. 81.
31. Reingard M. Nischik, *Engendering Genre: The Works of Margaret Atwood* (Ottawa: University of Ottawa Press, 2009).
32. Sheldon Teitelbaum, 'The Handmaid's Tale', *Cinefantastique*, 20:4 (1990): 16–25, 57–8, 61.
33. Mary K. Kirtz, 'Teaching literature through film: an interdisciplinary approach to *Surfacing* and *The Handmaid's Tale*', in Sharon R. Wilson, Thomas B. Friedman and Shannon Hengen (eds), *Approaches to Teaching Atwood's The Handmaid's Tale and Other Works* (New York: MLA, 1996), pp. 140–5.

6 Feminist Gothic

1. Philip Howard, 'Back on her home ground', *The Times*, 26 January 1989.
2. Atwood, quoted in Mark Glassman, 'Atwood's eye,' *The Metropolis*, 13 October 1988, p. 652.
3. Alberto Manguel, Bookcase, *Saturday Night*, November 1988.
4. Ibid.
5. Ken Adachi, Review, *The Saturday Magazine*, 1 October 1988.
6. Claire Tomalin, 'What little girls are made of', *The Observer*, Sunday 29 January 1989, p. 49.
7. Sharon Wilson, *Margaret Atwood's Fairytale Sexual Politics* (Jackson, MO: University Press of Mississippi, 1993), p. 295.
8. Jane Brooks Bouson, *Brutal Choreographies: Oppositional Strategies and Narrative Design in the Novels of Margaret Atwood* (Amherst, MA: The University of Massachusetts Press, 1993), p. 164.
9. Ibid., p. 166.
10. Tomalin, 'What little girls are made of', p. 49.
11. Glassman, 'Atwood's eye', p. 652.
12. Brooks Bouson, *Brutal Choreographies*, p. 160.
13. Judith McCombs, 'The creating self and feminism in *Cat's Eye*', in *Canadian Literature*, 129 (1991), pp. 9–22.
14. Ibid., p. 9.
15. Wilson, *Margaret Atwood's Fairytale Sexual Politics*, p. 295.
16. Anita Brookner, 'Unable to climb out of the abyss', *The Spectator*, 28 January 1989, p. 32.
17. Carole Angier, '"The Genesis of Cruelty": Review of *Cat's Eye*, by Margaret Atwood', *New Statesman & Society*, 2(34) (1989): 37.
18. Brooks Bouson, *Brutal Choreographies*, p. 177.
19. Brookner, 'Unable to climb out of the abyss', p. 32.
20. Angier, 'Review of *Cat's Eye*', p. 37.

21. Douglas Rice, 'Physics and psyche in *Cat's Eye*', *English Review – Oxford*, 9(4) (April 1999), p. 1.
22. Ibid., p. 1.
23. Peter Kemp, 'Childhood through alien's eyes', *The Sunday Times Books Review*, 29 January 1989, p. 7.
24. Ibid., p. 7.
25. *CE*, p. 20.
26. McCombs, 'The creating self and feminism in *Cat's Eye*', p. 9.
27. Ibid., p. 9.
28. Reingard M. Nischik (ed.), *Margaret Atwood: Works and Impact* (Rochester, NY: Camden House, 2000), p. 183.
29. Tomalin, 'What little girls are made of', p. 49.
30. Brookner, 'Unable to climb out of the abyss', p. 32.
31. Beverly Pagam, Book reviews, *Ms London*, 13 March 1989, p. 109.
32. *CE*, p. 300.
33. Wilson, *Margaret Atwood's Fairytale Sexual Politics*, p. 295.
34. Ibid., p. 295.
35. *CE*, p. 403.
36. *CE*, p. 405.
37. *CE*, p. 398.
38. Brooks Bouson, *Brutal Choreographies*, p. 180.
39. Earl Ingersoll (ed.) *Margaret Atwood: Conversations* (New York: Ontario Review Press, 1990).
40. Stephanie McKinnon, 'In search of evil women', *The Lansing State Journal* (1994).
41. Margaret Atwood, *LA Village Review*, 4–10 February 1994, pp. 28–9.
42. McKenzie, *The Saturday Review* (1993).
43. Gabriele Annan, 'Donna Giovanna', *The New York Review of Books*, 40(21) 16 December 1993.
44. Maureen Nicholson, 'Unpopular gals', *The Vancouver Review* (Spring 1994), p. 22.
45. Ibid., p. 22.
46. Marina Warner, 'Atwood dips into Plath depths', *The Globe and Mail*, Saturday, 2 October 1994.
47. Ibid.
48. Mark Lawson, 'Canadian Gothic', *The Independent Magazine*, 2 October 1993, p. 33.
49. Salman Rushdie, Review, *The Independent on Sunday*, 17 October 1993.
50. Harry Ritchie, quoting Atwood in 'Come into the Garden', *Sunday Times Review*, 10 October 1993, p. 69.
51. Peter Kemp, 'Bewitched, bothered and bewildered', *The Sunday Times*, 17 October 1993, p. 6.
52. Ibid., p. 6.
53. Francis King, 'Ruthless charm of a monster', *London Evening Standard*, 14 October 1993, p. 44.
54. Ibid., p. 44.
55. Anthony Thorncroft, 'Miraculous yes, but hardly edible', *Financial Times*, 17 October 1993.

56. Sherrill Grace, 'Atwood's postmodern fairytale', *Canadian Forum* (March 1994), pp. 44–5.
57. Ibid., p. 45.
58. Ibid., p. 45.
59. Ibid., p. 45.
60. Shannon Hengen, 'Atwood's novel may be a potboiler of a modern tale', Review, *Sudbury Star*, 6 February 1994.
61. Ibid.
62. Alice Palumbo, Review, *Paragraph*, 15(3–4) (Winter 1993–Spring 1994), pp. 40–1.
63. Fiedler, in ibid., p. 40.
64. Ibid., p. 40.
65. *RB*, p. 114.
66. Sandra Mackenzie, Review, *The Vancouver*, 16 October 1993, p. K652.
67. Ibid., p. K652.
68. Val Ross, Review, *Globe and Mail Toronto*, 7 October 1993, p. C1.
69. Ibid., p. C2.
70. Christopher Gully, 'In a class of her own', *Good Times* (April 1994), p. 10.
71. Judith Timson, Review, *Maclean's*, 4 October 1993, p. 55.
72. Ibid., p. 33.
73. *RB*, p. 392
74. *RB*, p. 35
75. *RB*, p. 35.
76. Palumbo, Review, pp. 82–3.
77. Howells (1996), pp. 163–4.
78. Coral Ann Howells, 'The Robber Bride or, who is a true Canadian', in Sharon R. Wilson (ed.), *Margaret Atwood Textual Assassinations* (Columbus, OH: State University Press, 2003), p. 89.
79. Ibid., p. 89.
80. Ibid., p. 89.
81. Sandra Martin, 'Playing with razor blades', *Quill and Quire*, 25 August 1993, p. 94.
82. Ibid., p. 94.
83. *RB*, p. 111.

7   No Nearer the Truth

1. Hilary Mantel, 'Murder & memory', 1996. Available online at: http://nybooks.com/articles/article-preview?article_id=1316 (Dec 5, 2001).
2. Frank Davey, Class and power in Margaret Atwood's suburbs and edge cities', *Etudes canadiennes*, 32: 97–108. Available at: http://cat.inist.fr/?aModele=afficheN&cpsidt=18385881 (accessed 25 July 2011).
3. Rosario Arias, 'How can I be all of these different things at once?: Fiction and history in *Alias Grace* by Margaret Atwood' (2000). Available at: http://www.eng.helsinki.fi/main/news/ESSE5-2000/rosario.arias.htm (accessed 24 January 2008).

4. Linda Hutcheon, *Historiographic Metafiction: Parody and the Intertextuality of History* (Baltimore, MD: Johns Hopkins University Press, 1989).
5. Lindsay Duguid, 'If truth be told', the *Guardian*, 3 October 1996, p. 14.
6. Peter Kemp, 'A gorgeous patchwork of art', *Sunday Times*, 8 September 1996, p. 11.
7. Francine Prose, 'Death and the maid', *New York Times*, 29 December 1996. Available at: http://www.nytimes.com/books/00/09/03specials/atwood-alias.html (accessed 10 March 2008).
8. Ibid.
9. Ibid.
10. Catherine Pepinster, 'The writer's tale: how a story chose an author and wowed the critics; Canada's top author tells Catherine Pepinster about her new book's spiritual inspiration', *The Independent*, 20 September 1996, p. 9.
11. Carole Angier, 'Books: In the prison of male fantasy: Margaret Atwood's new novel is a Gothic tale of sex and class', *The Independent*, 14 September 1996, p. 5.
12. Ibid.
13. Christopher Lehmann-Haupt, 'Did she or didn't she? A tale of two murders', *The New York Times Review of Books*, 12 December 1996, p. 3. Available at: http://query.nytimes.com/gst/fullpage.html?res=9506EEDA1F3FF931A25751C1A960958260 (accessed 8 January 2008).
14. Duguid, 'If truth be told', p. 14.
15. Ibid., p. 14.
16. David Wiley, 'Atwood at a glance, interview' (1996). Available at: http://womenwriters.about.com/library/blatwood.htm (accessed 14 April 2001).
17. Lehmann-Haupt, 'Did she or didn't she?'
18. Kemp, 'A gorgeous patchwork of art', p. 11.
19. Maureen Freely, Books: 'What is Grace's guilty secret? And will she ever come out from under that quilt?', *The Observer*, 22 September 1996, p. 18.
20. Ibid., p. 18.
21. Arias, 'How can I be all of these different things at once?', p. 1.
22. Margaret Rogerson, 'Reading the patchworks in *Alias Grace*', *Journal of Commonwealth Literature*, 33:1 (1998): 21.
23. Arias, 'How can I be all of these different things at once?', p. 1.
24. Kemp, 'A gorgeous patchwork of art', p. 11.
25. Mantel, 'Murder & memory', p. 18.
26. Earl Ingersoll, 'Engendering meta-fictions: textuality and closure in *Alias Grace*', *American Review of Canadian Studies* (Autumn 2001): 385–401.
27. Hutcheon, *Historiographic Metafiction*.
28. Jennifer Murray, 'Historical figures and paradoxical patterns: the quilting metaphor', *Studies in Canadian Literature*, 26(1) (2001). Available at: http://74.125.127.132/scholar?q=cache:K1OMZ7OQ35cJ:scholar.google.com/+JENNIFER+MURRAY++(Historical+Figures+and+Paradoxical+Patterns:The+Quilting+Metaphor+in+Margaret+Atwood%E2%80%99s+Alias+Grace+&hl=en&as_sdt=0,5 (accessed 25 July 2011).
29. Ibid.
30. Ibid., p. 2, online version.

31. *AG*, p. 162.
32. Murray, 'Historical figures;' p. 11, online version.
33. Ibid., p. 16.
34. *AG*, p. 459.
35. Ingersoll, 'Engendering meta-fictions', p. 13.
36. Ibid., p. 13.
37. Rogerson, 'Reading the patchworks in *Alias Grace*', p. 17.
38. Lehmann-Haupt, 'Did she or didn't she?'
39. Ibid.
40. Tom LeClair, 'Quilty verdict' (1996). Available at: http://www.past. thenation.com/issue/961209/1209lect.htm (accessed 5 December 2001).
41. Nicholas A. Basbanes, 'Margaret Atwood Lizzie Borden's tale,' *George Jr Magazine* (1997). Available at: http://womenswriters.about.com/ library/blatwood.htm (accessed 5 December 2001).
42. Arias, 'How can I be all of these different things at once?'
43. Alison Moore, 'Margaret Atwood's latest novel pieces together a compelling collision between science and mysticism', *Tucson Weekly*, 16–22 January 1997. Available at: http://www.tucsonweekly.com/ tw/01-16-97/review3.htm (accessed 8 January 2008).
44. The Charles R. Bronfman lecture in Canadian Studies at the University of Ottawa, November 1996. Atwood's lecture, 'In search of *Alias Grace*: on writing Canadian historical fiction', p. 17, ms, Thomas Fisher Rare Book Library, Atwood archives.
45. Ibid., p. 18.
46. Ibid., p. 32.
47. Wiley, 'Atwood at a glance, interview', p. 25.
48. Bronfman lecture, p. 39.

8 Rewriting History and Myth

1. *BA*, p. 1.
2. Sharon Wilson, 'Fairy tales, myths, and magic photographs in Atwood's *The Blind Assassin*', in Sarah Appleton (ed.), *Once Upon a Time: Myth, Fairy Tales and Legends in Margaret Atwood's Writing* (Newcastle: Cambridge Scholars Publishing, 2008), p. 74.
3. Ibid., p. 74.
4. Barbara Mujica, Review, Americas (January 2001). Available at: http:// www.articlearchives.com/trends-events/historical-events-world-war-ii/764034-1.html.
5. Roberta Rubenstein, *Home Matters: Longing and Belonging, Nostalgia and Mourning in Women's Fiction* (New York: Palgrave, 2001).
6. Lorna Sage, Review, *THES*, 29 September 2000.
7. Thomas Mallon, 'Wheels within wheels', *The New York Times*, 3 September 2000.
8. Molly Hite, 'Tongueless in Toronto', *The Women's Review of Books*, 18(6) (March 2001): 1.
9. *BA*, p. 29.

10. Hite, 'Tongueless in Toronto', p. 1.
11. *BA*, p. 518.
12. Elaine Showalter, 'Virgin suicide', *The New Statesman*, 129: 4506 (2 October 2000), p. 53. Available at: http://www.newstatesman.com/200010020045.
13. Earl Ingersoll, 'Waiting for the end: closure in Margaret Atwood's *The Blind Assassin*', (Critical Essay) in *Studies in the Novel*, 35:4 (Winter 2003), p. 543. Full Text: 2003, University of North Texas.
14. Wendy Roy, 'The body of/as evidence: Margaret Atwood, *The Blind Assassin*, and the feminist literary mystery', in John Moss and Tobi Kozakwich (eds), *Margaret Atwood: The Open Eye* (Ottawa: University of Ottawa Press, 2006), p. 358.
15. Wilson, 'Fairy tales, myths, and magic photographs in Atwood's *The Blind Assassin*', p. 74.
16. David Punter, *The Gothic* (Oxford: Blackwell, 2003), pp. 97–8.
17. Wilson, 'Fairy tales, myths, and magic photographs', p. 500.
18. Ibid., p. 379.
19. Jane Brooks Bouson, 'A commemoration of wounds endured and resented': Margaret Atwood's *The Blind Assassin* as feminist memoir', (Critical Essay) *CRITIQUE: Studies in Contemporary Fiction*, 44:3 (Spring 2003), p. 251, Heldref Publications.
20. Helena Hytinnen, 'The dead are in the hands of the living: memory haunting storytelling in Margaret Atwood's *The Blind Assassin*', in John Moss and Tobi Kozakwich (eds), *Margaret Atwood: The Open Eye* (Ottawa: University of Ottawa Press, 2006), p. 373.
21. Ibid., p. 374.
22. Sharon Wilson, 'Margaret Atwood and popular culture: *The Blind Assassin* and other novels', *Journal of American & Comparative Cultures* (Fall–Winter 2002): 270.
23. Showalter, 'Virgin suicide', p. 53.
24. Mallon, 'Wheels within wheels', p. 17.
25. Karen F. Stein, 'A left-handed story: *The Blind Assassin*', in S. Wilson (ed.), *Textual Assassinations* (Columbus, OH: Ohio State University Press, 2003) , p. 138.
26. Ibid., p. 147.
27. Hytinnen, 'The dead are in the hands of the living', p. 381.
28. Ellen McWilliams, *Margaret Atwood and the Female Bildungsroman* (Farnham: Ashgate Press, 2009), p. 1.
29. Ibid., p. 116.
30. Ibid., p. 116.
31. Ibid., p. 117.
32. Catherine Taylor, '*The Penelopiad*, by Margaret Atwood; 'Weight', by Jeanette Winterson, What kind of a hero chases after fruit?', *Independent on Sunday*, 27 November, 2005.
33. *P*, p. 10.
34. Taylor (2005).
35. Simon Goldhill, *New Statesman*, 31 October 2005.
36. Rebecca Ascher-Walsh, *Entertainment Weekly*, 28 October 2005.
37. Sam Leith, *The Spectator*, 22 October 2005.

38. *The Penelopiad: The Play,* p. v.
39. Coral Ann Howells, *The Cambridge Companion to Margaret Atwood* (Cambridge: Cambridge University Press, 2006), p. 57.
40. Ibid., p. 61.
41. Ibid., p. 68.
42. Shannon Hengen, in Sarah A. Appleton (ed.), *Once Upon a Time: Myth, Fairy Tales and Legends in Margaret Atwood's Writings* (Newcastle: Cambridge Scholars Publishing, 2008), pp. 48–54.
43. *P*, p. 3.
44. Howells, *Cambridge Companion,* p. 65.
45. Ibid., p. 68.
46. Hengen, *Once Upon a Time.*
47. Ibid.
48. Elizabeth Hand, *The Washington Post,* 25 December 2005.

9 Writers, Readers, Constructions of the Real and the Future

1. Coral Ann Howells, *The Cambridge Companion to Margaret Atwood* (Cambridge: Cambridge University Press, 2006), p. 162.
2. *O&C,* p. 46.
3. Howells, *Cambridge Companion,* p. 162.
4. Earl Ingersoll (ed.), *Margaret Atwood: Conversations* (Willowdale, ON: Firefly Books, 1990), p. 193.
5. Ibid., p. 193.
6. Tara Pepper, 'Pigs with six kidneys', *Newsweek International,* 14 July 2003, p. 49.
7. Lisa Appignanesi, the *Independent,* Saturday, 26 April 2003. Available at: http://www.independent.co.uk/arts-entertainment/books/reviews/oryx-and-crake-by-margaret-atwood-595662.html.
8. Natasha Walter, the *Guardian,* 10 May 2003. Available at: http://www.guardian.co.uk/books/2003/may/10/bookerprize2003.bookerprize.
9. Margaret Atwood, 'Writing *Oryx and Crake*', Thomas Fisher Rare Book Library, University of Toronto, archive coll. 335, box 108, folder 11: 12, p. 6.
10. *O&C,* pp. 7–8.
11. Appignanesi, the *Independent.*
12. Margaret Atwood, 'Aliens have taken the place of angels', Margaret Atwood, *The Guardian,* Friday, 17 June 2005.
13. Ibid.
14. Ibid.
15. Ibid.
16. Ibid.
17. Ibid.
18. Walter, the *Guardian,* 10 May 2003.
19. Jane Brooks Bouson, '"It's game over forever": Atwood's satiric vision of a bioengineered posthuman future in *Oryx and Crake*', *Journal of Commonwealth Literature,* 3(9) (2004): 139–42.

20. *North of Caution: A Journey through the Conservation Economy on the Northwest Coast of British Columbia* (Canada: Ecotrust, 2001).
21. Janine M. Benyus, *Biomimicry: Innovation Inspired by Nature* (New York: Morrow, 1997).
22. Coral Ann Howells, 'Margaret Atwood's dystopian visions', in Coral Ann Howells, *The Cambridge Companion to Margaret Atwood* (Cambridge: Cambridge University Press, 2006), p. 163.
23. Ibid., p. 163, quoting Bill McKibbens, *Enough: Staying Human in an Engineered Age* (New York: Times Books, 2003), p. 108.
24. Daniel Mendelsohn, 'After the fall', *New York Times*, 3 July 2003, p. 44.
25. Ibid., p. 44.
26. Ibid., p. 44.
27. Ibid., p. 44.
28. Ibid., p. 44.
29. Shuli Barzilai, 'Unfabulating a fableo: Or two readings of "Thylacine Ragout"', *Critique – Studies in Contemporary Fiction*, 50(1) (2008): 87–110.
30. Brooks Bouson, '"It's game over forever", pp. 139–56.
31. Mendelsohn, 'After the fall', pp. 45–6.
32. Howells, *Cambridge Companion*, p. 172.
33. Brooks Bouson, '"It's game over forever", p. 143.
34. Eleonora Rao, 'Home and nation in Margaret Atwood's later fiction', in Coral Ann Howells (ed.), *The Cambridge Companion to Margaret Atwood* (Cambridge: Cambridge University Press, 2006), p. 108.
35. Ibid., p. 108.
36. Sarah A. Appleton (ed.), *Once Upon a Time: Myth, Fairy Tales and Legends in Margaret Atwood's Writings* (Newcastle: Cambridge Scholars Publishing, 2008), p. 11.
37. Rao, 'Home and nation', p. 110.
38. Ibid., p. 260.
39. Ibid., p. 110.
40. Margaret Atwood, p. 78, quoted by Coral Ann Howells, 'Margaret Atwood's dystopian visions: *The Handmaid's Tale* and *Oryx and Crake*', in Coral Ann Howells (ed.), *The Cambridge Companion to Margaret Atwood* (Cambridge: Cambridge University Press, 2006), p. 172.
41. Appleton, *Once Upon a Time*, p. 11.
42. Ingersoll, *Margaret Atwood: Conversations*, p. 193.
43. Howells, *Cambridge Companion*, p. 164.
44. Ibid., p. 164.
45. Ibid., p. 164.
46. Ibid., p. 164.
47. Appleton, *Once Upon a Time*, p. 15.
48. Ibid., p. 21.
49. Carol Osborne, 'Mythmaking in Margaret Atwood's *Oryx and Crake*', in J. Brooks Bouson, *Margaret Atwood: The Robber Bride, the Blind Assassin, Oryx and Crake* (New York: Continuum, 2011), p. 28.
50. Howells, *Cambridge Companion*, p. 170.
51. Margaret Atwood, *Negotiating with the Dead: A Writer on Writing* (Cambridge: Cambridge University Press, 2002), p. 159.

52. Osborne, *Mythmaking*, p. 42.
53. Eleanor Case and Maggie McDonald, 'Interviewing Margaret Atwood', in Fiona Tolan (ed.), *Margaret Atwood, Feminism and Fiction* (Amsterdam: Rodopi, 2007), p. 40.
54. Margaret Atwood, p. 433, quoted in Howells, *Cambridge Companion*, p. 173.
55. Osborne, *Mythmaking*, p. 43.
56. Ibid., p. 35.

10 Re-Telling Old Tales

1. Book review, *Publishers Weekly*, 253(29) (2006): 32.
2. A. S. Byatt, Book review, *The Washington Post*'s Book World, 'Times of Her Life', Sunday, 15 October 2006.
3. Ibid.
4. Ibid.
5. Book review, *The Boston Globe*, 15 October 2006.
6. Ibid.
7. *MD*, p. 1.
8. *MD*, p. 2.
9. *MD*, p. 5.
10. R. Nischik, *Engendering Gender: The Works of Margaret Atwood* (Ottawa: University of Ottawa Press, 2010), p. 83.
11. *MD*, p. 7.
12. Joyce Carol Oates, Book review, *New York Book Review*, 53(17) (2 November 2006).
13. Ibid.
14. Nischik, *Engendering Gender*, p. 83.
15. Kasia Boddy, Book review, *The Observer*, 17 September 2006. Available at: http://books.guardian.co.uk/reviews/generalfiction/0,1874066,00.html (accessed 7 December 2007).
16. Ibid.
17. *MD*, p. 122.
18. Oates, Book review.
19. *MD*, p. 17.
20. Nischik, *Engendering Gender*, p. 85.
21. Nancy Schiefer, Review, 'A rich layering of truths', Special in *The London Free Press* (2006), p. 160.
22. Ibid., p. 160.
23. *The Booklist*, Starred Review, 15 October 2006.
24. Schiefer, Review, p. 160.
25. Ellen McWilliams, *Margaret Atwood and the Female Bildungsroman* (Farnham: Ashgate, 2009), p. 127.
26. Ibid., p. 128.
27. Ibid., p. 131.
28. Anita Sethi, 'Inside looking out', *The Observer*, 12 March 2006.
29. Ibid.

30. Ibid.
31. Ibid.
32. Kate Washington, Review, 'Atwood's musings beckon readers into her eclectic work', *San Francisco Chronicle*, 22 January 2006, p. M – 3. Available at: http://www.sfgate.com/cgibin/article.cgi?f=/c/a/2006/01/22/RVG4OGLSBH1.DTL&type=books#ixzz0wOjYzKSp.
33. Hermione Lee, 'Beware the sponge that ate Florida', the *Guardian*, 25 February 2006.
34. *TT*, p. 88.
35. Nischik, *Engendering Gender*, p. 50.
36. Ibid., p. 50.
37. *The Times*, 'Three novels I won't write soon', Saturday, 18 December 2004. Available at: http://entertainment.timesonline.co.uk/tol/arts_and_entertainment/books/article403298.ece?token=null&offset=0 (accessed 7 December 2007).
38. Shuli Barzilai, 'Unfabulating a fable, or two readings of "Thylacine Ragout"', in Sarah Appleton (ed.) *Once Upon a Time: Myth, Fairy Tales and Legends in Margaret Atwood's Writings* (Newcastle: Cambridge Scholars Publishing, 2008), p. 48.
39. The Tent by Margaret Atwood and marsupials, 21 October 2010. Available at: http://emeire.wordpress.com/2010/10/21/the-tent-by-margaret-atwood-and-marsupials/.
40. Ibid.
41. Heather Birrell, Review, January 2006, Available at: http://www.quillandquire.com/reviews/review.cfm?review_id=5010.
42. Julia Keller, Book review, *Chicago Literary Tribune Magazine*, 30 October 2005, p. 14.
43. Ibid., p. 18.
44. *TT*, p. 5.
45. *TT*, p. 19.
46. *TT*, p. 47.
47. *TT*, p. 51.
48. *TT*, p. 58.
49. *TT*, p. 63.
50. *TT*, p. 63.
51. *TT*, p. 139.
52. *TT*, p. 142.

11   The End of the World?

1. Margaret Atwood the Canadian novelist talks to Sinclair McKay about books and bees, *Telegraph* New. Available at: http://www.telegraph.co.uk/culture/books/6061404/Margaret-Atwood.html.
2. Gillian Beer (2009) 'Facing a poisoned future', *Globe and Mail*, 11 September 2009.
3. Robert Allen Papinchak, '*The Year of the Flood*: Margaret Atwood returns to a post-apocalyptic future', *The Seattle Times*, 4 October 2009. Available

at: http://seattletimes.nwsource.com/html/books/2009977746_br04at
wood.html (accessed 20 October 2009).

4. Beer, 'Facing a poisoned future'.
5. Joan Frank, *San Francisco Chronicle*, 27 September 2009, p. F-1. Available at: http://www.sfgate.com/cgi-bin/article.cgi?f=/c/a/2009/09/27/RV8F195PCP.DTL (accessed 20 October 2009).
6. Jane Shilling, Review, *The Telegraph*, 7 September 2009. Available at: http://www.telegraph.co.uk/culture/books/bookreviews/6133557/The-Year-of-the-Flood-by-Margaret-Atwood-review.html (accessed 20 October 2009).
7. Ibid.
8. Philip Hensher, Review, *The Observer*, 6 September 2009. Available at: http://www.guardian.co.uk/books/2009/sep/06/year-of-the-flood-atwood http://reviewcanada.ca/reviews/2009/10/01/a-dystopia-sketched-in-crayon/.
9. Rosemary Goring, 'Margaret Atwood faces a bleak future in *The Year of the Flood*', *Herald Scotland*, 3 August 2009. Available at: http://www.heraldscotland.com/arts-ents/fiction-reviews/margaret-atwood-faces-a-bleak-future-in-the-year-of-the-flood-1.825503 (accessed 20 October 2009).
10. Philip Marchand, 'Eloquence and irony do battle in *The Year of the Flood*', *Weekend Post*, 1 September 2009. Available at: http://network.nationalpost.com/np/blogs/afterword/archive/2009/09/12/philip-marchand-eloquence-and-irony-do-battle-in-margaret-atwood-s-the-year-of-the-flood.aspx (accessed 20 October 2009).
11. Ibid.
12. Coleen Grissom, Review, *San Antonio Express*, 20 September 2009. Available at: http://www.mysanantonio.com/entertainment/books/Review_The_Year_of_the_Flood.html (accessed 20 October 2009).
13. Ellen Akins, Special to the *Star Tribune*, 27 September 2009. Available at: http://www.startribune.com/entertainment/books/61256562.html (accessed 20 October 2009).
14. Rebecca Eckler, 'Margaret Atwood didn't kill me', *Maclean's*, 23 September 2009.
15. Hensher, Review.
16. Robert Charles Wilson 'A dystopia sketched in crayon', *The Literary Review of Canada*, 1 October 2009. Available at: http://reviewcanada.ca/reviews/2009/10/01/a-dystopia-sketched-in-crayon/ (accessed 20 October 2009).
17. Ibid.
18. Darryl Whetter, 'Atwood's pen returns to apocalyptic theme', *The Chronicle Herald*, 13 September 2009. Available at: http://42blips.dailyradar.com/story/the_year_of_the_flood_by_margaret_atwood_book_review/ (accessed 20 October 2009).
19. John Barber, 'Atwood: "Have I ever eaten maggots? Perhaps ..."', *Globe and Mail*, 11 September 2009. Available at: http://www.theglobeandmail.com/news/arts/atwood-have-i-ever-eaten-maggots-perhaps/article1284530/ (accessed 20 October 2009).
20. Ibid.

21. Jane Ciabattari, 'Disease and dystopia in Atwood's "Flood"', *NPR*, 10 September 2009. Available at: http://www.npr.org/ (accessed 20 October 2009).
22. Melanie Kirkpatrick, 'Drowning in dreariness', *The Wall Street Journal*, 18 September 2009, p. A21. Available at: http://online.wsj.com/article/SB10001424052970204518504574419111637864676.html (accessed 20 October 2009).
23. Caroline Moore *The Telegraph*, 10 September 2009.
24. Ibid.
25. Ursula K. Le Guin, 'Margaret Atwood doesn't think she writes science fiction. Ursula K Le Guin would like to disagree', *The Guardian*, 29 August 2009, Features and Review Section, p. 5. Available at: http://www.guardian.co.uk/books/2009/aug/29/margaret-atwood-year-of-flood (accessed 20 October 2009).
26. Michiko Kakutani, 'From Margaret Atwood, a cautionary tale about a pandemic', *New York Times*, 10 January 2009. Available at: http://www.nytimes.com/2009/09/15/books/15kaku.html (accessed 20 October 2009).
27. Fredric Jameson, 'Then you are them', *London Review of Books*, 10 September 2009. Available at: http://www.lrb.co.uk/v31/n17/fredric-jameson/then-you-are-them (accessed 20 October 2009).
28. Ibid.
29. Ibid.
30. Hannes Bergthaller, 'Housebreaking the human animal: humanism and the problem of sustainability in Margaret Atwood's *Oryx and Crake* and *The Year of the Flood*', *English Studies*, 91(8) (2010): 728.
31. Bernadine Evaristo, Review, *Financial Times*, 5 September 2009. Available at: http://www.ft.com/cms/s/2/7a12aeca-98e5-11de-aa1b-00144feabdc0.html (accessed 20 October 2009).
32. Ibid.
33. Jane Shilling, the *Telegraph*, 7 September 2009, no title.
34. Beer, 'Facing a poisoned future.'
35. Ibid.
36. Ibid.
37. Nisi Shawl, 'The capsizing ark', *MS Magazine*, 2 August 2009. Available at: http://www.msmagazine.com/summer2009/year_of_the_flood.asp (accessed 20 October 2009).
38. Le Guin, 'Margaret Atwood doesn't think she writes science fiction.'
39. Jeanette Winterson, Review, *New York Times*, 20 September 2009, p. BR1. Available at: http://www.nytimes.com/2009/09/20/books/review/Winterson-t.html (accessed 20 October 2009).
40. Ibid.
41. Arifa Akbar, 'Margaret Atwood: "People should live joyfully"', by The Big Interview, *The Independent*, 4 September 2009. Available at: http://www.independent.co.uk/arts-entertainment/books/features/margaret-atwood-people-should-live-joyfully-1781166.html (accessed 20 October 2009).
42. Nicola Barr 'Atwood live in London – with friends', *The Observer*, 6 September 2009. Available at: http://www.guardian.co.uk/books/2009/sep/06/year-of-the-flood-atwood (accessed 20 October 2009).
43. Ibid.

12 Conclusion

1. Coral Anne Howells, Review of Ellen McWilliams' 'Margaret Atwood and the female Bildungsroman', *Contemporary Women's Writing*, 4(2) (2010): 153–4.
2. Reingard Nischik, *Engendering Gender: The Works of Margaret Atwood* (Ottawa: University of Ottawa Press, 2010).
3. Sharon Wilson, *Myths and Fairy Tales in Contemporary Women's Fiction: From Atwood to Morrison* (Basingstoke: Palgrave, 2009).
4. Heidi McPherson, *The Cambridge Introduction to Margaret Atwood* (Cambridge: Cambridge University Press, 2010).
5. Johanna Lahikanen, 'You look delicious: food and eating in Margaret Atwood's novels', PhD thesis, Turku, Finland, 2007.
6. Shannon Hengen, in Sarah A. Appleton (ed.) *Once Upon a Time: Myth, Fairy Tales and Legends in Margaret Atwood's Writings* (Newcastle: Cambridge Scholars Publishing, 2008), p. 48.
7. Tamara Bernstein, 'Handmaid opera perfectly tailored', *National Post*, 27 September 2004, AL3.
8. Hengen, p. 48.
9. Ibid.
10. Gina Wisker, *Atwood's Handmaid's Tale* (London: Continuum, 2010).
11. See http://www.suite101.com/content/margaret-atwood-uses-twitter-to-seek-for-contributors-to-new-book-a339944#ixzz1GUEQW0mv.

Appendix: The Works of Margaret Atwood

Books

Kaleidoscopes Baroque: A Poem, Bloomfield Hills, MI: Cranbrook Academy of Art, 1965.

Talisman for Children, Bloomfield Hills, MI: Cranbrook Academy of Art, 1965.

The Edible Woman, Toronto: McClelland & Stewart, 1969.

Surfacing, Toronto: McClelland & Stewart, 1972.

Lady Oracle, Toronto: McClelland & Stewart, 1976.

Day of the Rebels: 1815–1840, Toronto: Natural Science of Canada Limited, 1977.

Up in the Tree: Toronto: McClelland & Stewart, 1978.

Life Before Man, Toronto: McClelland & Stewart, 1979.

Anna's Pet, Toronto: Lorimer, 1980.

Bodily Harm, Toronto: McClelland & Stewart, 1981.

Encounters with the Element Man, Concord, NH: William B. Ewert, 1982.

Murder in the Dark, Toronto: Coach House Press, 1983.

Unearthing Suite, Toronto: Grand Union Press, 1983.

The Handmaid's Tale, Toronto: Fawcett Crest, 1985.

Cat's Eye, Toronto: McClelland & Stewart, 1988.

The Robber Bride, New York: Nan A. Talese, 1993.

Strange Things: The Malevolent North, Oxford: Clarendon Press, 1995.

Princess Prunella and the Purple Peanut, Bath: Barefoot Books, 1995.

Alias Grace, Toronto: McClelland & Stewart, 1996.

The Blind Assassin, Toronto: McClelland & Stewart, 2000.

Oryx and Crake, New York: Nan A. Talese, 2003.

The Penelopiad, Edinburgh: Canongate, 2005.

Moral Disorder, New York: Nan A. Talese, 2006.

The Year of the Flood (God's Gardeners), Toronto: McClelland & Stewart, 2009.

Short stories

Dancing Girls, and Other Stories, Toronto: McClelland & Stewart, 1977.

Bluebeard's Egg and Other Stories, Toronto: McClelland & Stewart, 1983.

Wilderness Tips, and Other Stories, Toronto: McClelland & Stewart, 1991.

Good Bones, Toronto: Coach House Press, 1992.

Good Bones and Simple Murders, New York: Nan A. Talese, 1994.

The Tent, London: Bloomsbury, 2006.

Poetry

Double Persephone, Toronto: Hawkshead Press, 1961.
The Circle Game, Bloomfield Hills, MI: Cranbrook Academy of Art, 1964.
Expeditions, Bloomfield Hills, MI: Cranbrook Academy of Art, 1966.
Speeches for Doctor Frankenstein, Bloomfield Hills, MI: Cranbrook Academy of Art, 1966.
The Animals in That Country, Toronto: Open University Press, 1968.
The Journals of Susanna Moodie, Toronto: Oxford University Press, 1970.
Procedures for Underground, Toronto: Oxford University Press, 1970.
Power Politics, Toronto: Anansi, 1971.
You Are Happy, Toronto: Oxford University Press, 1974.
Selected Poems, Toronto: Oxford University Press, 1976.
Two-Headed Poems, Toronto: Oxford University Press, 1978.
True Stories, Toronto: Oxford University Press, 1981.
Interlunar, Toronto: Oxford University Press, 1984.
Selected Poems II. Poems Selected & New, 1976–1986, Toronto: Oxford University Press, 1986.
Morning in the Burned House, Toronto: McClelland & Stewart, 1995.
Eating Fire: Selected Poetry, 1965–1995, London: Virago Press Limited, 1998.

Essays

Survival: A Thematic Guide to Canadian Literature, Toronto: Anansi, 1972.
Second Words: Selected Critical Prose, Toronto: Anansi, 1982.
Negotiating with the Dead: A Writer on Writing, Cambridge: Cambridge University Press, 2002.

Select Bibliography

Books

Becker, Susanne (1999) *Gothic Forms of Feminine Fictions*, Manchester: Manchester University Press.

Brooks Bouson, Jane (1993) *Brutal Choreographies: Oppositional Strategies and Narrative Design in the Novels of Margaret Atwood*, Amherst, MA: The University of Massachusetts Press.

Brydon, Diana and Tiffin, Helen (1993) *Decolonising Fictions*, Sydney: Dangaroo.

Burwell, Jennifer (1997) *Notes on Nowhere: Feminist Utopian Logic and Social Transformation*, Minneapolis: University of Minnesota Press.

Cooke, Nathalie (1998) *Margaret Atwood: A Biography*, Toronto: ECW Press.

Cooke, Nathalie (2004) *Margaret Atwood: A Critical Companion*, Westport, CT: Greenwood Press.

Davey, Frank (1984) *Margaret Atwood: A Feminist Poetics*, Vancouver: Talon.

Davidson, Cathy N. and Davidson, Arnold E. (eds) (1981) *The Art of Margaret Atwood: Essays in Criticism*, Toronto: Anansi.

Deer, Glenn (1994) *Postmodern Canadian Fiction and the Rhetoric of Authority*, Montreal: McGill-Queen's University Press.

Dvorak, Marta (2006) 'Margaret Atwood's Humour', in Coral Ann Howells (ed.), *The Cambridge Companion to Margaret Atwood*, Cambridge: Cambridge University Press.

Foucault, Michel (1978) *The History of Sexuality*, Vol. 1, Toronto: Random House.

Freibert, Lucy M. (1988) 'Control and creativity: the politics of risk in Margaret Atwood's *The Handmaid's Tale*', in Judith McCombs (ed.) *Critical Essays on Margaret Atwood*, Boston: G. K. Hall, pp. 280–91.

Frye, Northrop (1971) *Bush Garden: Essays on the Canadian Imagination*, Toronto: Stoddart.

Fullbrook, Kate (1990) *Free Women: Ethics and Aesthetics in Twentieth-Century Women's Fiction*, Hemel Hempstead: Harvester Wheatsheaf.

Grace, Sherrill (1980) *Violent Duality: A Study of Margaret Atwood*, Montreal: Véhicule Press.

Guterson, David (1995) *Snow Falling on Cedars*, New York: Vintage.

Hammill, Faye (2007) *Canadian Literature*, Edinburgh: Edinburgh University Press.

Heiland, Donna (2004) *Gothic and Gender: An Introduction*, Oxford: Blackwell.

Hill Rigney, Barbara (1978) *Madness and Sexual Politics in the Feminist Novel: Studies in Bronte, Woolf, Lessing and Atwood*, Madison, WI: University of Wisconsin Press, pp. 91–127.

hooks, bell (1992) *Black Looks, Race and Representation*, Boston: South End Press.

Howells, Coral Ann (1996) *Margaret Atwood*, Basingstoke: Palgrave Macmillan.

Howells, Coral Ann (2000) 'Transgressing genre: a generic approach to Margaret Atwood's novel *Cat's Eye*', in R.M. Nischik (ed.), *Margaret Atwood: Works and Impact*, Rochester, NY: Camden House, pp. 148, 139–56.

Howells, Coral Ann (ed.) (2006) *The Cambridge Companion to Margaret Atwood*, Cambridge: Cambridge University Press.

Hutcheon, Linda (1983) 'From poetic to narrative structures: the novels of Margaret Atwood', in Sherrill Grace and L. Weir (eds), *Margaret Atwood: Language, Text, and System*, Vancouver: University of British Columbia, pp. 17–31.

Hutcheon, Linda (1994) *Irony's Edge: The Theory and Politics of Irony*, London and New York: Routledge.

Ingersoll, Earl (ed.) (1990) *Margaret Atwood: Conversations*, New York: Ontario Review Press.

Keefer, Janice Kulyk (1994) 'Hope against hopelessness: Margaret Atwood's *Life Before Man*', in C. Nicholson (ed.), *Writing and Subjectivity*, New York: St. Martin's Press, p. 155.

Kirtz, Mary K. (1987) 'The thematic imperative: didactic characterization in *Bodily Harm*', in Beatrice Mendez-Egle (ed.), *Margaret Atwood: Reflection and Reality*, Edinburg, TX: Pan American University.

Laing, R.D. (1967) *The Politics of Experience and The Bird of Paradise*, Harmondsworth: Penguin.

Lecke, Robert (1981) 'Janus through the looking glass: Atwood's first three novels' in Cathy N. Davidson and Arnold E. Davidson (eds), *The Art of Margaret Atwood: Essays in Criticism*, Toronto: Anansi.

Lee, Hermione (2006) 'Beware the sponge that ate Florida', the *Guardian*, 25 February.

McCombs, Judith (ed.) (1988) *Critical Essays on Margaret Atwood*, Boston: GK Hall and Co.

McCombs, Judith and Falmer, Carole (1991) *Margaret Atwood: A Reference Guide*, Boston: GK Hall.

McLay, Catherine (1981) 'The dark voyage: *The Edible Woman* as romance', in Cathy N. Davidson and Arnold E. Davidson (eds), *The Art of Margaret Atwood: Essays in Criticism*, Toronto: Anansi, pp. 123–38.

Nicholson, Colin (ed.) (1994) *Margaret Atwood: Writing and Subjectivity: New Critical Essays*, New York: St Martin's Press.

Nischik, Reingard M. (ed.) (2000) *Margaret Atwood: Works and Impact*, Rochester, NY: Camden House.

Nischik, Reingard M. (2003) 'Murder in the dark: Margaret Atwood's inverse poetics of intertextual minuteness', in Sharon M. Wilson, *Margaret Atwood's Textual Assassinations*, Columbus, OH: Ohio State University Press.

Palumbo, Alice (2000) 'On the border: Margaret Atwood's novels', in R.M. Nischik (ed.), *Margaret Atwood: Works and Impact*, Rochester, NY: Camden House, pp. 73–87.

Philip, Marlene Nourbese (1993) *Frontiers: Selected Essays and Writings on Racism and Culture, 1984–1992*, Stratford: Mercury Press.

Pratt, Annis (1981) *Archetypal Patterns in Women's Fiction*, Bloomington, IN: Indiana University Press.

Radway, Janice (1991) *Rereading the Romance: Women, Patriarchy and Popular Literature*, Chapel Hill, NC: University of North Carolina Press.

Rao, Eleonora (1993) *Strategies for Identity: The Fiction of Margaret Atwood*, New York: P. Lang.

Rao, Eleonora (2006) 'Home and nation in Margaret Atwood's later fiction', in Coral Ann Howells, *The Cambridge Companion to Margaret Atwood*, Cambridge, Cambridge University Press, pp. 7–8.

Richardson, Colin (1994) *Margaret Atwood: Writing and Subjectivity: New Critical Essays*, Basingstoke: Palgrave Macmillan.

Rosowksi, Susan J. (1988) 'Margaret Atwood's *Lady Oracle*: fantasy and the modern Gothic novel', in J. McCombs, *Critical Essays on Margaret Atwood*, Boston: GK Hall and Co., pp. 197–8.

Rubenstein, Roberta (1987) *Boundaries of the Self: Culture, Gender, Fiction*, Urbana, IL: University of Illinois.

Rubenstein, Roberta (2001) *Home Matters: Longing and Belonging, Nostalgia and Mourning in Women's Fiction*, New York: Palgrave.

Staels, Hilde (1995) *Atwood's Novels: A Study of Narrative Discourse*, Tübingen: Gulde.

Sturgess, Charlotte (2000) 'Margaret Atwood's short fiction', in R.M. Nischik (ed.), *Margaret Atwood: Works and Impact*, Rochester, NY: Camden House.

Sullivan, Fraser (n.d.) Thomas Fisher Rare Books Library, Toronto, Canada, Box 53, *Survival* Two, p. 9.

Waelti-Waters, Jennifer R. (1982) *Fairy Tales and the Female Imagination*, Montreal: Eden Press.

Wilson, Sharon Rose (1993) *Margaret Atwood's Fairy-Tale Sexual Politics*, Jackson, MO: University Press of Mississippi.

Wisker, Gina (2000) *Postcolonial and African American Women's Writing*, Basingstoke: Palgrave Macmillan.

Wisker, Gina (2002) *Margaret Atwood's Alias Grace: A Reader's Guide*, London: Continuum.

Wisker, Gina (2006) *Key Concepts in Postcolonial Literature*, Basingstoke: Palgrave Macmillan.

Wisker, Gina (2010) *Atwood's The Handmaid's Tale*, London: Continuum.

Essays

Atherton, Stanley S. (1982) 'Travel pieces: tropical traumas: images of the Caribbean, recent Canadian fiction', *Canadian Literature*, 95, Winter, pp. 8–14.

Brooks Bouson, Jane (2003) 'A commemoration of wounds endured and resented: Margaret Atwood's *The Blind Assassin* as feminist memoir', (Critical Essay) *CRITIQUE: Studies in Contemporary Fiction*, 44(3): 251.

Brown, Russell M. (1980) 'Atwood's sacred wells', *Essays on Canadian Writing*, 17(Spring): 5043.

Brydon, Diana (1981) 'Caribbean revolution and literary convention', *Canadian Literature*, 95(Winter): 181–5.

Brydon, Diana (1995) 'Atwood's postcolonial imagination: reading *Bodily Harm*', in Lorraine M. York (ed.), *Various Atwood's Essays on the Later Poems, Short Fiction and Novels*, Toronto: Anansi.

Campbell, Josie P. (1978) 'The woman as hero in Margaret Atwood's *Surfacing*', *Mosaic*, Spring: 17–28.

Carpenter, Carole H. (1985) 'The ethnicity factor in Anglo-Canadian folk-loristics', in Edith Fowke and Carole H. Carpenter (eds), *Explorations in Canadian Folklore*, Toronto: McClelland and Stewart.

Chesley, S. (1971) Review, *Varsity* (University of Toronto magazine), 26 March.

Christ, Carol (1976) 'Margaret Atwood: the surfacing of women's spiritual quest and vision', *Signs*, 23(2): 316–30.

Christ, Carol (1980) 'Margaret Atwood: the surfacing of matriarchal religion in Atwood', *papers* 153.2, Thomas Fisher Rare Book Library, Toronto, Canada.

Clark, Blaire (1981) 'Tale of two colonies', *Canadian Literature*, 95(Winter): 110–12.

Corbel, Carol (1979) 'Surfacing from a damaging decade', *Quill and Quire*, 45(12): 31.

Dahlie, Hallvard (1979) Review, *Dalhousie Review*, 59(3); 561–3.

Dane, Alan (1973) *The Edible Woman*, New Canadian Library no. 93, Toronto: McClelland and Stewart.

Davey, Frank (1973) 'Atwood WALKING BACKWARDS', *Open Letter, A Journal*, second series, 5.

Davey, Frank (1977) 'Atwood's Gorgon touch', *Studies in Canadian Literature*, 2(2): 146–63.

Davey, Frank (1984) 'Alternative stories', paper read at the Association Canadian and Quebec Literature, Guelph, 5 June.

Davidson, Cathy N. (1975) 'Chopin and Atwood: woman drowning, woman surfacing', *Kate Chopin Newsletter*, 1(3): 6–10.

Davidson, Cathy N. (1981) 'Prospects and respect in *Life Before Man*', pp. 205–21.

Dyment, Margaret (1981) 'Review', *Quarry*, 31(2), Spring, pp. 71–76.

Evans, Mark (1994) 'Versions of history: *The Handmaid's Tale* and its dedicatees', in Colin Nicholson (ed.) *Margaret Atwood: Writing and Subjectivity*, New York: St Martin's Press.

Fromberg Schaeffer, Susan (1974) 'Is it time that separates us?', *Centennial Review* 18, Fall.

Frye, Northrop (1971) *Bush Garden: Essays on the Canadian Imagination*, Toronto: Stoddart.

Fulford, Robert (1979) 'Life before man', *Canadian Reader*, 20(9): 1–2.

Fullbrook, Kate (1990) *Free Women: Ethics and Aesthetics in Twentieth-Century Women's Fiction*, Hemel Hempstead: Harvester Wheatsheaf.

Garebian, Keith (1976) '*Surfacing*: apocalyptic ghost story', *Mosaic*, 3: 1–9.

Gibson, Graeme (1973) 'Margaret Atwood', in *Eleven Canadian Novelists*, Toronto: Anansi.

226   *Select Bibliography*

Godard, Barbara (1986) 'Tales within tales: Margaret Atwood's folk narrative', *Canadian Literature*, 109(Summer): 57–84.

Goodwin, Ken (1990) 'Revolution as bodily functions: Thea Astley and Margaret Atwood', *Antipodes*, 4(2): 109–15.

Grace, Sherrill (1980) *Violent Duality: A Study of Margaret Atwood*, Montreal: Véhicule Press.

Grace, Sherrill and Weir, Lorraine (eds) (1983) *Margaret Atwood: Language, Text, and System*. Vancouver: University of British Columbia Press.

Hammill, Faye (1981) '"Forest and fairy stuff": Margaret Atwood's *Wilderness Tips*', *49th Parallel: An Interdisciplinary Journal of North American Studies*, Department of American and Canadian Studies, University of Birmingham.

Hammill, Faye (1999) 'Margaret Atwood, Carol Shields, and "that Moodie bitch,"' *American Review of Canadian Studies*, 29(1): 67–92.

Hammill, Faye (2007) *Canadian Literature*, Edinburgh: Edinburgh University Press.

Hill Rigney, Barbara (1978) *Madness and Sexual Politics in the Feminist Novel: Studies in Bronte, Woolf, Lessing and Atwood*, Madison, WI: University of Wisconsin Press.

Howells, Coral Ann (2000) 'Transgressing genre: a generic approach to Margaret Atwood's Novels, *Cat's Eye*', in R.M. Nischik (ed.), *Margaret Atwood: Works and Impact*, Rochester, NY, Camden House.

Howells, Coral Ann (2003) '*The Robber Bride* or, who is a true Canadian?' in Sharon R. Wilson (ed.), *Margaret Atwood Textual Assassinations*, Columbus, OH: Ohio State University Press.

Hoy, Helen (1981) 'Letters in Canada, 1981: fiction 2', *University of Toronto Quarterly*, 51(4): 328–9.

Hutcheon Linda (1994) *Irony's Edge: The Theory and Politics of Irony*, London and New York: Routledge.

Ingersoll Earl (2003) 'Waiting for the end: closure in Margaret Atwood's *The Blind Assassin*', (Critical Essay) in *Studies in the Novel*, 35(4): 543, University of North Texas.

Irvine, Lorna (1986) *Subversion*, Toronto: ECW Press.

Kaler, Anne, K. (1989) '"A sister, dipped in blood": satiric inversion of the formation techniques of women religious in Margaret Atwood's novel *The Handmaid's Tale*', *Christianity and Literature*, 38(2): 43–62.

Larkin, Joan (1973) 'Soul survivor', *Ms*, 1(11): 33–5.

Laurence, Margaret (1973) 'Review of *Surfacing*', *Quarry*, 22(2): 62–4.

LeBihan, Jill (1991) '*The Handmaid's Tale, Cat's Eye* and *Interlunar*: Margaret Atwood's feminist(?) futures(?)', in Coral Ann Howells *et al.* (eds), *Narrative Strategies in Canadian Literature: Feminism and Postcolonialism*, Milton Keynes: Open UP, pp. 93–107.

Lurie, Alison (1973) 'Wise women: review of Lessing's *The Summer before the Dark* and *The Black Prince*', *The New York Review of Books*, 20(10): 2.

Mahoney, Elisabeth (1996) 'Writing so to speak: the feminist dystopia', in Sarah Sceats and Gail Cunningham (eds), *Image and Power: Women in Fiction in the Twentieth Century*, London and New York: Longman, pp. 29–40.

Martin, Sandra (1993) 'Playing with razor blades', *Quill and Quire*, 25 August, p. 94.

McCombs, Judith (1986) 'Atwood's fictive portraits of the artist: from victim to surfacer, from oracle to birth', *Women's Studies*, 12(1): 69–88.

McCombs, Judith (1988) 'Country, politics and gender', in *Canadian Studies: A Report from Twenty Years of Atwood Criticism, Canadian Issues*, 10(5): 31.

McFadden, David (1984) Review, *Quill and Quire*, January, p. 24.

Mount Holyoake (1985) *Mount Holyoake Alumnae Quarterly*.

Newman, Christina (1972) 'Critical essays on Margaret Atwood: in search of a native tongue', *Maclean's*, September, pp. 43–75.

Nicholson, Colin (ed.) (1994) *Margaret Atwood: Writing and Subjectivity: New Critical Essays*, Toronto: Macmillan.

Ondaatje, Michael (1972) *Canadian Forum*.

Onley, Gloria (1974) 'Power politics in Bluebeard's castle', *Canadian Literature*, 60: 21–42.

Pearce, Lynne and Stacey, Jackie (eds) (1995) *Romance Revisited*, New York: New York University Press.

Piercy, Marge (1973) cited in Judith Plaskow's 'On Carol Christ on Margaret Atwood: some theological reflections', *Signs* 2(2): 331–9.

Piercy, Marge (1988) 'Margaret Atwood: beyond victimhood', in Judith McCombs (ed.), *Critical Essays on Margaret Atwood*, Boston: GK Hall and Co.

Pratt, Annis (1981) *Archetypal Patterns in Women's Fiction*, Bloomington, IN: Indiana University Press.

Radway, Janice (1991) *Rereading the Romance: Women, Patriarchy and Popular Literature*, Chapel Hill, NC: University of North Carolina Press.

Rao, Eleonora (2006) 'Home and nation in Margaret Atwood's later fiction', in Coral Ann Howells, *The Cambridge Companion to Margaret Atwood*, Cambridge: Cambridge University Press, pp. 100–14.

Rice, Douglas (1999) 'Physics and psyche in *Cat's Eye*', *English Review – Oxford*, 9(4): 1.

Rogerson, Margaret (1998) 'Reading the patchworks in *Alias Grace*', *Journal of Commonwealth Literature*, 33(1): 21.

Rosenberg, Jerome K. (1984) 'Margaret Atwood', in Obe Lecke (ed.), *Twayne's World*, Author Series Canadian Literature, Boston: Twayne Publishers.

Rosenthal, Caroline (1996) 'Canonizing Atwood: her impact on teaching in the US, Canada, and Europe', in Reinegard M. Nischik (ed.), *Margaret Atwood. Works and Impact*, Rochester, NY: Camden House.

Ross, Malcolm (1973) Frank Davey, quoted in a review of *Survival*, *Dalhousie Review*, 53: 160.

Rubenstein, Roberta (1976) '*Surfacing*: Margaret Atwood's journey to the interior', *Modern Fiction Studies*, 22(3).

Rubenstein, Roberta (1987) *Boundaries of the Self: Culture, Gender, Fiction*, Urbana, IL: University of Illinois.

Sage, Lorna (1986) 'Projections from a messy present', *Times Literary Supplement*, 21 March, p. 307.

Scott, D.C. (1926) 'At the Cedars', in *The Poems of Duncan Campbell Scott*, Toronto: McClelland and Stewart.

Sheldock, Catherine (1980) 'Banished to this other place: Atwood's *Lady Oracle*', *English Studies on Canada*, Vol. VI, Winter, No. 4.

Solecki, Sam (1979) 'Excess of ideas', *Canadian Forum*, 59, November, pp. 28–9.

Spivak, Gayatry Chakavorty (1990) 'Criticism, feminism and the institution: interview with Elizabeth Grosz', in Sarah Hazy (ed.), *The Post-Colonial Critic: Interviews, Strategies, Dialogues*, London: Routledge, pp. 1–16.

Stein, Karen F. (1975) 'Reflections on a jagged mirror: some metaphors of madness', *Aoha*, 6(2): 2–11.

Stein, Karen, F. (2003) 'A left-handed story: *The Blind Assassin*', in S. Wilson (ed.), *Textual Assassinations*, Columbus, OH: Ohio State University Press, p. 138.

Steine, George (1971) *In Bluebeard's Castle: Notes Towards the Redefinition of Culture*, New Haven, CT: Yale University Press.

Sturgess, Charlotte (2000) 'Margaret Atwood's short fiction', in Reingard M. Nischik (ed.), *Margaret Atwood: Works and Impact*, Rochester, NY: Camden House.

Sweetapple, Rosemary (1976) 'Margaret Atwood: victims and survivors', *South Review*, 9: 50.

Thompson, Lee Biscoe (1981) 'Minuets and madness: Margaret Atwood's *Dancing Girls*', in Cathy Davidson and Arnold E. Davidson (eds), *The Art of Margaret Atwood: Essays in Criticism*, Toronto: Anansi.

Tiffin, Helen (1987) 'Voice and form', in Russell McDougall and Gillian Whitlock (eds), *Australian/Canadian Literatures in English*, Melbourne: Methuen Australia, pp. 119–32.

Ward, David (1994) '*Surfacing*: separation, transition, incorporation', in Colin Nicholson (ed.), *Margaret Atwood: Writing and Subjectivity: New Critical Essays*, Toronto: Macmillan.

Wight, Austin (ed.) (1961) 'Charlotte Bronte's new Gothic', in *Victorian Literature: Modern Essays in Criticism*, Oxford: Oxford University Press, p. 84.

Wilson, Sharon Rose (1989) 'Fairy-tale cannibalism in *The Edible Woman*', in Mary Anne Schofield (ed.), *Cooking by the Book: Food in Literature and Culture*, Bowling Green, OH: Bowling Green State University Popular Press, pp. 78–88.

Wilson, Sharon Rose (1990) 'A note on Margaret Atwood's visual art and *Bodily Harm*', *Antipodes*, 4(2): 115–16.

Wilson, Sharon Rose (2000) 'Mythological interests in Margaret Atwood's works', in R.M. Nischik (ed.), *Margaret Atwood: Works and Impact*, Rochester, NY: Camden House.

Wilson, Sharon Rose (2002) 'Margaret Atwood and popular culture: *The Blind Assassin* and other novels', *Journal of American & Comparative Cultures*, Fall–Winter.

Wilson, Sharon Rose (2003) 'Fiction flashes: genre and interests in *Good Bones*', in Sharon R. Wilson (ed.), *Margaret Atwood's Textual Assassinations*, Columbus, OH: Ohio State University Press, pp. 20–1.

Wood, Glicksohn, Susan (1974) *Extrapolation*, 15(2): 161–73.

Woodcock, George (1973) 'Notes on the recent Atwood', *Ariel* 4: 22, 28.

Woodcock, George (1980) 'Victor – or victim', *Canadian Literature*, 86, Autumn, p. 138.

Woodcock, George (1988) 'Margaret Atwood: poet as novelist: power, politics, *The Circle Game, The Edible Woman, The Journal of Susanna Moodie, The Animals in That Country, Survival* and *Surfacing'*, in Judith McCombs (ed.), *Critical Essays on Margaret Atwood*, Boston: GK Hall and Co.

Woodcock, George (1982) 'Recent Canadian novels, major publishers', *Queens Quarterly*, 89(4): 744–8.

Index